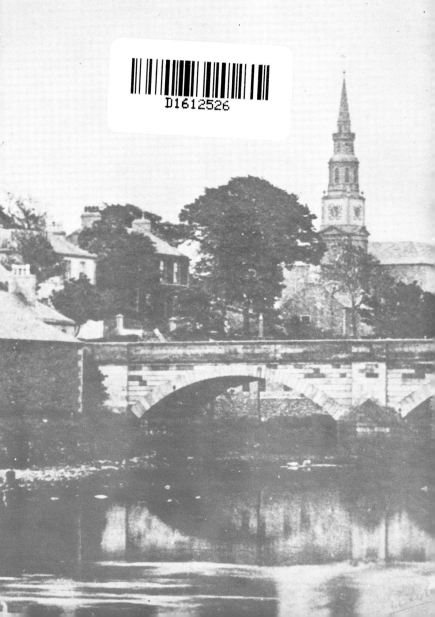

JOHN GALT 1779-1979

JOHN GALT 1779-1979

EDITED BY

CHRISTOPHER A. WHATLEY

THE RAMSAY HEAD PRESS EDINBURGH

ISBN 0 902859 52 8

First published in 1979 by
The Ramsay Head Press
36 North Castle Street
Edinburgh EH2 3BN

Printed in Scotland by
Macdonald Printers (Edinburgh) Limited
Loanhead, Midlothian

Contents

Illustrations

The endpaper illustrations, reproduced by permission of Irvine Development Corporation, show (*front*) Irvine Bridge and Trinity Church before the spire was added in 1861, and (*back*) the new Shopping Centre, and, behind, the church as it is today.

ACKNOWLEDGEMENTS

In compiling this book to commemorate the Bi-centenary of the birth of John Galt I am indebted for help and encouragement to Douglas Gifford, Alistair Weir, Graham Cummings and the Cunninghame History Society. My thanks are also due to Ian Donnachie, Sheena Andrews, Alex Welford and friends on Skye. I have also been assisted by Sam Gaw, Irvine Burns Club, Provost Mathew Brown and Councillor Jack Carson.

I am indebted to the staffs of the Carnegie Library, Ayr, the National Library of Scotland, the Scottish Record Office and the National Galleries of Scotland for their prompt and courteous help.

This volume could not have been produced without financial assistance from Cunninghame District Council, the Scottish Arts Council, the Clement Wilson Foundation, Irvine Development Corporation and the Cunninghame History Society.

C. A. W.

Map of Irvine and north Ayrshire, from 1775, just before Galt's birth. On it can be seen many of the names which Galt was to use later, such as Garnock, Annick, Eglintoune (Eglesham), Dunlop (Delap) and Irvine (Irville) itself.

INTRODUCTION

When, on the 2nd of May 1779, the tiny John Galt entered the world, few can have forecast that this son of an Irvine ship-master would, two centuries later, be the object of growing public and scholarly interest. Although much of the work published during his lifetime was accorded a great deal of critical acclaim, for long periods after his death in April 1839 his literary productions remained unread, unappreciated and often unavailable because they were not republished. Scottish literature of the late eighteenth and early nineteenth century has normally been represented by Robert Burns, who also belonged to Ayrshire and who died when Galt was seventeen years old, and Sir Walter Scott, whom he outlived by seven years. However in the last two decades in particular there has been something of a revival of interest in Galt and his achievement, with many of his better known works, such as *Annals of the Parish* and *The Provost* being reprinted, while stories like *The Member* and *Ringan Gilhaize,* which have been virtually un-noticed for one hundred and fifty years, are receiving deserved attention. This volume, which coincides with the bi-centenary of the birth of the writer, is an attempt to place the name of John Galt even more firmly amongst the ranks of Scotland's literary successes and to try to convince the public, teachers, students and academics that Galt's writings are both a unique and inseparable part of the Scots literary tradition.

There are many aspects of Galt's life which make it difficult for us to take Galt's writing seriously. He does not present the normal picture of the artist, working alone with the sole aim of communing with the creative muses. Having spent the first ten years of his life in the Ayrshire seaport of Irvine, he was then taken by his family to Greenock, which too was an important seaport, where his father had become the owner of a West Indiaman. In Greenock his schooling was strictly practical and designed to prepare him for a com-mercial career; mathematics, geography and penmanship were the major components of the syllabus. Not surprisingly his

9

first job, which he got when he was sixteen, was in Greenock Customs House, where there were further opportunities to develop penmanship. Soon afterwards he moved to the firm of James Miller and Company, where he remained for eight years. He was not merely a pen-pushing clerk, however. Galt was actively involved in the local Literary and Debating Society, a subscription member of the Greenock Public Library, a self-confessed "voracious reader," a keen walker, a member of the Loyal Greenock Volunteers, but perhaps most importantly for his development as a writer he continued to write poetry (he claimed that he had written his first poem when he was six) which appeared in the *Greenock Advertiser* and even the *Scots Magazine*.

In May 1804, after concluding that Greenock did not offer sufficient scope for furthering his career, he moved to London. While it appears that he was busy enough visiting art galleries and attending theatrical performances and dinners, he could not obtain the sort of business opening for which he was searching. Between 1805 and 1808 he was involved with two business ventures as a partner, but as was to happen all too often during his lifetime, they resulted in failure. The following months were spent gathering material for a book he wanted to write on the life of Cardinal Wolsey and attempting to begin a new career as a lawyer. Both schemes were abandoned as a nervous illness became markedly worse and he embarked on a new and important stage in his life— he went on a tour of the Mediterranean countries, and in August 1809 met Lord Byron who suspected Galt's sanity and thought none too highly, at that stage, of Galt's poems, one of which he described as "damned nonsense." Later a curious mutual respect developed between the two men, and in Byron's *Journal* for 1813 there is a reference to Galt's strong sense, in spite of his "eccentricities." The expedition, which ended with his return to Britain in September 1811, was a success for Galt the writer. At the beginning of 1812 he published his *Voyages and Travels in the Years 1809, 1810 and 1811,* which was an account of his travels and his impressions of the countries he had visited. It was a type of publication which Galt was to fall back on frequently during his lifetime, not least because it provided a useful form of income. Professor Ian Gordon has shown that under the nom-de-plume "the Rev. T. Clark" Galt had in the years 1819 and 1820 written a number of books for general and even juvenile readers, such as *A Tour of Europe, A Tour of Asia,* and a *New General School Atlas.* In the early 1830s he contributed a number of articles to *Fraser's Magazine* which were largely based on his Canadian experiences. He seemed to have a penchant for the nom-de-plume, and used a wide variety of names—such as Cabot, Nantucket, Agricola and even Domenichino.

In spite of the tenuous literary success which he achieved with *Voyages and Travels* and soon afterwards with *The Life and Administration of Cardinal Wolsey,* Galt returned to commercial life, this time in the employment of the Glasgow firm of Kirkman Finlay and Company who wanted him to open a branch of their operations in Gibraltar. Want of money and a poor response to five plays he had written may have combined to force this decision upon him. On the other hand he later claimed that he had always "held literature to be a secondary pursuit" and perhaps he genuinely felt that his contribution to the commercial world could be the greater one. The venture ended in failure, not, it should be said because of any weaknesses on Galt's part, but because the Duke of Wellington's victory over the French in Spain removed the raison d'être for Finlay's blockade beating scheme.

Galt, now thirty-three, returned home and in April he married Elizabeth Tilloch whose father provided him with an income of around £300 per annum. The next decade was to be the most productive of Galt's life, because although his greatest works were not written until the period between 1820 and 1823, he did in the years prior to that begin to write in the novel form (*The Majolo,* published in 1816, for example) and indeed in 1813 he produced the first draft of *The Pastor,* which was rewritten in 1820, to appear in 1821 under the now famous title of *Annals of the Parish.* His writing technique was further assisted by his becoming a hack writer, pouring out articles and occasional pieces for the periodicals. In 1818 he became involved in yet another commercial venture which, almost predictably, came to an end. In the following year he was employed by the directors of the Edinburgh and Glasgow Union Canal Company to promote their bill (which would have allowed them to raise more money for the scheme) through the difficult and corrupt lobbying process which then characterised much of the activity of the British Parliament. The experience was to provide him with some of the material for his novel *The Member,* published in 1832, which in an intensely amusing and perceptive way, points to some of the worst excesses of the pre-reformed Parliament.

In 1819 however Galt's literary star began to burn a little more brightly—he began to submit work to *Blackwood's Magazine*—and early in 1820 the publisher William Blackwood accepted Galt's scheme for a regular series of connected articles which would be called *The Ayrshire Legatees.* It was a great success and sales of the magazine soared. Galt was accepted by the reading public, encouraged by his publisher and for three years he produced work of the highest quality. In 1821 *Annals of the Parish* appeared, and was in its second edition in the spring of 1822. Also in that year came *Sir Andrew Wylie, The Provost, The Entail* and *The Steam-Boat,* and by the end of 1823 *The Gathering of the West, Ringan Gilhaize* and *The Spaewife* had all been completed.

Galt's star however quickly burned itself out and only occasionally did his pen again match the feats of this triumphant period. Never again did he manage to kindle such a flurry of creativity—other works which are worthy of note appeared with long periods of flatness between them— *The Last of the Lairds* in 1826, *The Life of Lord Byron* in 1830, and *The Member* in 1832. Of these only the first and last were novels, and in the former Galt's plot virtually collapsed half-way through the work.

In no sense was Galt the man of commerce nearing the end of his career in 1823 at the age of forty-four. In 1820 he had become agent for a group of Canadian settlers who wanted compensation for damage done during the hostilities which had broken out between America and Britain in 1812. The business had been carried on during his period of literary triumph—but even during those years Galt's business brain had been active and he had devised a scheme for raising money in Canada by the sale of Crown Lands. He had hoped that the sums raised could be used to satisfy the claimants, but despite frequent appeals on their behalf he was unsuccessful. He was however appointed secretary of the Canada Company which was formed in July 1824 with the aim of developing the lands and then selling them at a profit. For the next five years, with the exception of a brief interlude in 1825-1826 which he used to produce *The Last of the Lairds,* Galt was to be immersed in his Canadian venture where he was in charge of the Canada Company's land improvement scheme in Ontario and during which he staked yet another claim to temporal immortality by founding the town of Guelph in 1827. For some of his time there he was immensely happy and successful, playing the rôle of coloniser and entrepreneur, and being rewarded with a salary of around £1600 per annum, a small estate and other trappings of the good life of the Briton overseas in the earlier part of the nineteenth century.

The episode had an ending which by now was clearly the trademark of John Galt, businessman. During 1828 the Company's stock had fallen dramatically and Galt was recalled to London, to be met by a pack of panicking creditors, one of whom instituted legal proceedings to recover a comparatively small sum of money. From July until November 1829 home for John Galt was the debtors' prison in Southwark.

There he produced several pieces for his former publisher William Blackwood, and after his release drew on his Canadian experiences to produce a minor novel about an emigrant Scot in Canada, Laurie Todd. For a short time he edited a London newspaper, *The Courier,* but later returned to an earlier idea of his, a biography of Lord Byron, which was published in 1830. His *Life of Lord Byron* produced sales, controversy (Byron was at this time a topical and even shocking subject of conversation) as well as some respect for a writer who largely ignored the more colourful aspects of the rapidly growing Byronic legend. The next three years were busy ones of Galt—he wrote numerous articles for the periodicals, mainly *Fraser's Magazine,* in 1831 another novel based on his Canadian adventure was published, *Bogle Corbet or the Emigrant,* and in 1832 two of his most underrated works, *The Member* and *The Radical* appeared. *The Member* can certainly lay claim to be on a par with the political novels and descriptions which appeared later in the century, from the pens of Disraeli and Dickens.

In October Galt was struck down by a stroke—and the ensuing months were intensely frustrating for him—although he did continue to dictate respectable if not inspired material including his two-volume *Autobiography,* which incidentally is an indispensable source for the reader anxious to follow the Galt story in detail. It was followed in 1834 by his *Literary Life,* which concentrates more on the life of John Galt the writer.

In 1834 the circle of his life began to close. In August he returned to Greenock, but found it very different from the town he had left thirty years earlier. Formerly one of the most prolific writers in the land, Galt now presented a slow and sad face to the world. Thomas Carlyle, who saw him at this time, commented on his having the "air of a sedate Greenock Burgher" who must have looked rather odd, having no eyelashes, which gave Carlyle "a sort of wae interest for him." He died on the 11th of April 1839, aged fifty-nine.

Galt's writing, which is the main concern of this collection of essays, was rarely, until recently, the subject of enthusiastic critical and public acclaim. And there is no doubt that amongst his vast collection of literary outpourings there was much that is turgid and very ordinary. His volume of five blank-verse plays, *The Tragedies,* published in 1812, was the subject of much hostile criticism, and Walter Scott declared that they were the worst he had ever seen.

Even his best work however has sometimes been ignored and certainly underrated, and even though some novels and short stories have for long periods been out of print and virtually inaccessible to potential readers, this does not fully explain why he has not been accorded a proper placing within the Scottish literary tradition. It is true that Scott and Burns did dominate the period in which he wrote and that Galt's subject matter, ostensibly the smaller concerns of the parochial Scot, later became the feeding ground for the Kailyard "tradition," the worst excesses of which it may be thought can be traced back to Galt. A more convincing argument for Galt's relative obscurity lies in his continued use of the Scots vernacular and the faithful presentation of the Ayrshire dialect. Both Susan Ferrier and Sir Walter Scott considered Galt's language to be "vulgar." How far this can be ascribed to east coast snobbishness which developed amongst literary men in Edinburgh during the eighteenth century is not clear, but certainly this criticism of Galt was widespread. Indeed

14

Henry Mackenzie, the author of *The Man of Feeling,* was unable to understand the language of Galt's characters. For the twentieth-century reader (especially those who have been educated north of the border) whose early taste of language teaching was MacIvor's *First Aid in English,* followed in the secondary school by a large helping of Shakespeare, Dickens and Charles Lamb, and topped up with tawse enforced strictures about the merits of speaking "correctly," Galt's use of "couldna," "mysel," and "lang" would be offensive while his use of words like "clishmaclaver" and "langnebbit" must make him well-nigh incomprehensible. Fortunately the modern Scot is in some areas being allowed to consider the study of his own linguistic history on a par with that of medieval English, and that, allied to the general awareness that there is a Scottish cultural past (and present) is helping to bring the work of John Galt very much to the forefront of Scottish literary studies.

This volume builds on that increasing interest and explores a number of features of Galt's work which have either received little attention or which it has been felt deserve re-interpretation. Professor Ian Gordon has undoubtedly done more than anyone else in the last decade to stimulate interest in John Galt's life and writings. His essay, a short critical biography, draws on his wide knowledge of his subject, points to the vital connection between Galt and his major publisher, William Blackwood, and underlines the debt which Irvine owes to her most eminent (yet often forgotten) son.

Galt claimed that it was not his purpose to write mere novels, but that his writing had a greater purpose, that of producing "theoretical history." Whether or not he succeeded is a different matter, and certainly most would agree that Galt's better productions are important milestones in the development of the novel. He was certainly very much a man of his time, using as his subject matter the changes in society which were being produced by the new industrial order. He lived too in the age of the Romantic literary creation, of Byron, Coleridge, Shelley, Southey and Wordsworth, with whose work he seems to have been familiar. Eighteenth-century Scotland produced one of the country's finest periods in terms of her intellectual development and Anand C. Chitnis demonstrates how the Scottish philosophers too had their influence on Galt's attitudes and work, particularly where his view of history was concerned.

Annals of the Parish is probably Galt's best known work, read not only for its literary merit but also because of its value as an accurate picture of changing life in Scotland during the reign of George III. My own article tests *Annals* against recent interpretations of Scottish history in the period, and explores the possibility that Galt's conviction of the validity of "theoretical history" may have led him to distort some of the facts and personages in order to achieve his philosophic end.

There is however much more to *Annals of the Parish* than historical realism and Kenneth G. Simpson in a detailed examination of the book shows clearly that in the Reverend Micah Balwhidder Galt has created a complex and self-revealing character, suggesting that despite Galt's pleas that *Annals* should not be considered as a novel, his acute psychological penetration in this case places him in the very first ranks of creative writers.

Published in the same year as *Annals* was *The Ayrshire Legatees,* another book which draws heavily on Ayrshire names, associations and language. It has been viewed as a work which contrasts the small world of Garnock with that of the London metropolis, but in his essay Ian Campbell explains that within the apparently simple technique which Galt uses here, a collection of letters written from "abroad" upon which the assembled family comment, there is a series of plots running through the story which hold our attention while allowing the writer to make his social observations.

The Covenanting era is one of those periods of Scottish debate and where accuracy about events, personalities and motives is rarely in evidence. Galt's immediate inspiration for writing a book about the subject, *Ringan Gilhaize,* appears to have been Sir Walter Scott's publication of *Old Mortality,* where the Presbyterian Church and its adherents were felt by Galt to have been treated with "too much levity." There has been something of a resurgence of interest in this neglected work which contrasts very favourably with Walter Scott's treatment of the subject. Professor John MacQueen relates *Ringan Gilhaize* to Galt's other work, his Calvinist beliefs and to his view of history, which required that

JOHN GALT
Portrait by Charles Grey. Reproduced by permission of
the Scottish National Portrait Gallery

JOHN GALT

Pencil drawing by Alfred, Count d'Orsay. Reproduced
by permission of the Scottish National Portrait Gallery

society develop in a series of phases, with the Covenanting phase having to be experienced before further improvement of society takes place. Patricia J. Wilson explores the text in more detail and demonstrates that there is a wealth of technical skill and psychological penetration in the novel which transcend the possibility that Galt was merely using the work to express his own Presbyterian sympathies—a matter of some controversy which is discussed in the text.

A book which owes little to Scotland for its inspiration is *The Member,* published during the period leading up to the 1832 Reform Bill. Professor John Ward argues that while Galt's unreformed parliamentary seat of Frailtown is somewhat exaggerated, having only six electors (even the notorious Old Sarum had eleven) the view of corrupted British politics seen through the eyes of the "hero" Archibald Jobbry is one of the most illuminating and amusing literary accounts of the period. If *Annals of the Parish* is to be recommended reading for students of the industrial revolution and social history in later eighteenth-century Scotland, *The Member* must be essential reading for those interested in the remarkable political habits and morality of the early nineteenth century.

Galt's reputation may well be higher in Canada than in Scotland and the naming of the town of Galt (now Cambridge) after him serves as a permanent reminder of his activities there. It is apt that a Canadian and one of the most prominent Galt commentators has written on what many consider to have been Galt's finest achievement, *The Entail.* Keith M. Costain certainly argues that this is Galt's masterpiece and indeed it was a work which impressed Lord Byron, Sir Walter Scott and the Earl of Blessington, who read it three times. Galt had a remarkable number of leading industrialists, politicians and landowners amongst his followers—a list of subscribers for his *Literary Life* included the cotton kings of Glasgow, the Finlays, the Duke of Wellington, Viscount Castlereagh and the Marquess of Londonderry. Costain shows that in *The Entail* Galt is not merely a master of the comic, but includes elements of the best Romantic writing and the tragedy of the human condition.

It has been suggested earlier that Galt's use of the Scots dialect of Ayrshire and the West of Scotland has contributed to his relative lack of popularity. Galt himself was quite unrepentant about criticisms like that of Sir Walter Scott, that he "out-Scottifies the Scotch dialect." What others considered a fault Galt argued was a positive merit and he thought that the peculiarities of the language had a beauty of their own which enhanced the realism of his Scottish based novels. J. Derrick McClure examines *Annals* and *The Provost* in detail and shows that the mingling of the "best" English with the various registers of the Scots adds immensely to the depth of the two novels, and that Galt's careful application of the different linguistic modulations enhances the irony and even self-betrayal of the two main characters, Provost Pawkie and Micah Balwhidder. It is to be hoped that McClure's invaluable approach is applied to Galt's other works in the future.

William R. Aitken has, in a brief but essential bibliography, brought the list of recent editions of Galt and Galt criticism up to date. That five of his novels have been republished within the last ten years is ample testimony to the author's growing resurgence in popularity.

This collection of essays makes another contribution to this. It is to be hoped that in this year of the bi-centenary of his birth, John Galt will be even better recognised as a writer of the first rank in the Scottish lists. He wrote about the concerns which seem to be part and parcel of the Scottish way of life; the minister, the town councillor, hyper-active and self-destroying religious sentiments, unjustifiable self-esteem, a pathetic hankering after a lost way of life (if indeed it ever existed) and an inability to come to terms with the city. His language was Scots, but not sentimental, his characters are real, and recognisably so, and his lesson, which his disastrous commercial life must have taught him so harshly, is that to take ourselves too seriously is to risk becoming caricatures of those models after which we seek.

CHRISTOPHER A. WHATLEY

JOHN GALT

IAN A. GORDON

1.

John Galt was born in Irvine on 2nd May 1779, the son of a substantial ship-master. When Galt was ten years old his father became the owner of a West Indiaman and moved the family to Greenock. Young Galt, a day-dreaming bookish boy, was firmly directed by his sea-going merchant father towards the world of commerce. He was educated by private tutors, for two years at a school in Irvine, and from the age of ten to sixteen in Greenock. When his schooling came to an end, he had learned enough Latin to tackle Horace; but the main bias had been towards mathematics, geography, penmanship, French and English. It was essentially a commercial education.

After spending a few months in the Greenock Custom House to improve his penmanship, Galt at the age of seventeen became a junior clerk with a firm of Greenock merchants. He remained with the firm till in 1804 he left for London at the age of twenty-five. Galt was to write all this up in his *Autobiography* of 1833. He described himself as at that time an active young man, a "voracious reader," subscription member of the Greenock Public Library, an ardent theatre-goer in Greenock and Glasgow, founder of a Literary and Debating Society, a keenly patriotic volunteer "sharp-shooter," an assiduous participant in extensive walking tours. Well satisfied with himself and the world of commerce, he nursed literary ambitions. He and his club entertained the new poet James Hogg in 1804 (and Hogg was to record later his admiration for the literary company of the town). In this period Galt wrote a considerable amount of verse and made appearances in print in the *Greenock Advertiser* and Constable's *Scots Magazine*.

Growing restless "at the narrowness of my prospects," he set out for London in May 1804. At the end of the year he had printed in volume form "a sort of Gothic epic" *The Battle of Largs.* It had a chilly reception. His first attempts to enter the business world were equally unsuccessful and he spent an "idle six months" reading and frequenting the theatres and the art galleries. With money advanced from his father he formed two successive business partnerships. Each ended in failure and in 1808 Galt found himself at a loose end. He tried various outlets for his "restless disposition," collected documentary material for a life of Cardinal Wolsey, decided to be a lawyer and entered Lincoln's Inn, then abandoning his legal ambitions set off for the Continent. He was there from mid-1809 till September 1811; travelling extensively in Mediterranean countries, particularly Spain, Greece and Asia Minor, meeting Lord Byron and travelling part of the way with him. He returned to England full of plans to utilise these recent experiences for both commercial and literary projects.

It says much for Galt's characteristic self-assurance that he put his commercial plans immediately before the Foreign Office. The officials were unimpressed. His literary plans were more successful. He gathered together the travel letters he had been writing during the previous three years and in January 1812 published at his own expense in two handsome volumes his *Voyages and Travels in the Years 1809, 1810 and 1811.* It was well received and "paid the expenses of my travels." Encouraged by this success, Galt threw himself into other literary ventures. By the end of the year he had published a little book on economics, a large collection of blank-verse *Tragedies* written in periods of *longeur* during his travels and (returning to his research notes of 1808) *The Life and Administration of Cardinal Wolsey.* Galt's confidence was such that he presented inscribed copies of the latter work to Sir Walter Scott and the Duke of Sussex.

Satisfied with his literary success, Galt turned once again to commerce. A Glasgow firm appointed him their agent in Gibraltar. He remained there till the Spring of 1813. The venture, like so many of Galt's commercial schemes, turned out a failure. What Galt did not know at the time was that the experience contained in it the seeds of his greatest success. Before he set out on the agency, he had been invited by the firm to visit Glasgow, and while he was in the west of Scotland he took the opportunity to revisit "every place I could recollect, with which in my boyhood I had been familiar." The ambitious—and ultimately frustrated—man of business did not know till later that he had been quietly gathering the material for what was to be his best-loved book, *Annals of the Parish.*

He returned to London and by April he was married. His wife, Elizabeth Tilloch, was the daughter of Dr Alexander Tilloch, editor-proprietor of *The Star* and the *Philosophical Magazine,* to which Galt was already a contributor. Dr Tilloch settled on his daughter £300 a year but Galt's need to supplement this income—and his obvious inability to succeed in the commercial world—turned him once more to his pen. The fluent hand he had learned in the Greenock Custom House was to prove invaluable. In 1813 there appeared a second volume of his travels, *Letters from the Levant.* It sold well. In the summer of the same year 1813 he completed a novel which he entitled *The Pastor,* a village minister's recollections in Scots prose. Constable in Edinburgh rejected it. "I was informed," Galt wrote later, "that Scottish novels would not succeed (*Waverley* was not then published); and in consequence I threw the manuscript aside." Galt, undeterred, continued to write what would bring him income, contributing articles and acting as play-editor for the London publisher Colburn.

A temporary secretaryship to a London-Scottish charity, the Royal Caledonian Asylum, provided a supplement useful to a man who now had a young family. It also provided him with what Galt always enjoyed—contact with the great world. He organised for his society a grand dinner, the Duke of York in the chair, and invited Sir Walter Scott to "provide a song for the Dinner." Scott pleaded other duties, and Galt promptly had printed off a broadsheet "triumphal Glee by Mr Galt" which was "sung after drinking the health of the Prince Regent."

Galt had always been interested in the theatre. He had haunted those of Greenock and Glasgow. On one of his early walking tours he had seen Mrs Siddons play Lady Macbeth in Durham. When he first came to London his interest expanded from the theatre to the world of art. These first six months of apparent idleness in 1804 were given over to an unconscious self-education in the fine arts. He continued visiting the galleries; he attended the Royal Academy shows at the old rooms in Somerset House; he got to know artists and visited their studios. An early admirer of Wilkie (who had arrived in London from Scotland shortly after Galt), he wrote him an enthusiastic letter on his Royal Academy successes. He became a friend of Benjamin West, the American painter who had succeded Sir Joshua Reynolds as President of the Royal Academy, and set himself to write his life.

The Life and Studies of Benjamin West appeared in 1816, the first volume of a two-volume study. A second edition was called for the following year and the *Monthly Review* exhorted Galt to "continue with every allowable degree of rapidity." The second volume, however, did not appear till 1820, but when it was completed the life of West was Galt's major work, solid, documented, based on first-hand knowledge of the man and his work, equipped with an admirable catalogue. It has never been supplanted.

Galt remained short of money for his style of life and his growing responsibilities. He turned to whatever was at hand. He threw his travel experiences into the form of a novel *The Majolo,* 1816. It was (deservedly) a failure. He wrote articles for Sir Richard Phillip's *Monthly Magazine* and up till 1820 wrote for the same entrepreneur under several assumed names a series of elementary school textbooks. He was rescued from this situation by a group of Glasgow business-men who were interested in the passage through Parliament of a series of private bills. Galt became a parliamentary lobbyist, and was later to write that they paid him "a carriage and all expenses and handsomely."

Galt turned forty in the middle of 1819. Half of his adult life was over. After a great deal of restless wandering, he had achieved a modest success; material comfort; a settled marriage; three little boys; business failure on his own account but a reputation as an honourable and effective agent on behalf of others; dozens of friends and acquaintances, some in high places; an adequate income so long as he kept on the treadmill that had produced thousands of pages of competent writing in pamphlets, books, periodicals and textbooks, none of them likely to survive. It was less than he would once have settled for, but it was not unagreeable.

Meantime, he remained dependent on his ability to continue writing copiously and fast. He did not dream that literary fame was just round the corner. How could he know —how could anyone know—that it was to come from a rejected manuscript that he had thrown aside?

2.

William Blackwood, already in the early years of the nineteenth century an established Edinburgh bookseller, decided to found his own periodical. He called the journal *Blackwood's Edinburgh Magazine.* It first appeared in April 1817 and (arguably the most important literary journal ever to be produced) has continued to appear every month since. Galt, in London, at first saw in the new journal no more than an expansion of his market. He began in the middle of 1819 sending articles to Blackwood and was pleased to have them published and paid for. Considering that he was at the time engaged on the second volume of his *Benjamin West,* it is no surprise that four out of the first half-dozen printed between October 1819 and March 1820 were on art topics.

Blackwood was impressed by his new contributor. Galt, on his side, saw in *Blackwood's Magazine* the possibility of writing something different—and something Scottish. He knew he was capable of more than general journalism for the periodicals, and in March 1820 he put up to Blackwood the outline plan for *The Ayrshire Legatees.* Blackwood thought the plan "an exceedingly good one," offering to publish a section each month in the magazine and "the whole separately" later. This was encouragement Galt had never had in his life and he responded with speed. *The Ayrshire Legatees* ran in the magazine from June 1820 till February 1821. It was an instantaneous success both for the author and for the magazine, which reported later that the work has "increased our sale prodigiously." It appeared each month without an author's name, Galt perhaps unconsciously vying with Sir Walter Scott's ill-concealed anonymity. Certainly, "everyone" knew who was Blackwood's new author.

Writing for the London papers, Galt had shown himself to be a competent journalist. Accepted by the leading Scottish periodical, he had become a novelist. The writing of *The*

Ayrshire Legatees released him from the tyranny of hack-writing. More important, it freed his imagination and his creative powers. By dipping into the memories of his Irvine boyhood, he recreated a small eighteenth century Scottish town, peopled with characters richly alive. The plot is simple enough. Dr Pringle, the incumbent of the parish church of "Garnock" (which is Irvine) journeys with his son and daughter to London to collect a considerable legacy. The country visitors recount their experiences and adventures in a series of letters which, back in Garnock, are read aloud and commented on sometimes with deflationary bluntness. Galt's ear for the language of his birthplace is infallible. West country Scots, for the first time, rose to the status of an assured medium for literary prose, and *The Ayrshire Legatees* became both for Galt and for the Scottish novel a significant breakthrough.

Galt's immediate reaction to his success was ill-judged. He had an old romantic novel, already rejected by Constable, lying around in sheets printed at his own expense. A canny Scot, he could not bear to see anything wasted and he persuaded Blackwood to issue it. *The Earthquake* (1820) was a failure. Fortunately it did not matter. Part of Galt's past, it was speedily and (by Blackwood) thankfully forgotten in the ensuing months of creative activity. *The Ayrshire Legatees* had opened up a floodgate.

The first of the new novels to reach print was *The Steam-boat,* which ran through eight numbers of *Blackwood's Magazine* in 1821. The central character, Mr Duffle ("Cloth-Merchant in the Salt-Market of Glasgow"), expanded Galt's growing gallery of West Coast originals. In the early episodes, his function was that of auditor (his fellow-travellers recounting detached short stories, economically salvaged by Galt from earlier writing). As the book developed, with Mr Duffle taking the steamboat to London, his personality flowered, characters from *The Ayrshire Legatees* reappeared, complete with off-stage voices from Garnock. Blackwood thought it all so "capital" that he went to the unheard-of length of sending Galt an advance of ten guineas to ensure that Mr Duffle and the Pringles could be portrayed attending George IV's Coronation! The appearance of *The Steam-boat* in 1822 in book form revealed the fragmented and episodic nature of the whole. But, read in the original format, it is heart-warming comedy and excellent magazine writing.

While *The Steam-boat* was appearing in the magazine, Galt had offered to Blackwood his old and rejected *Pastor* manuscript of 1813 and was going over it for a final revision. It appeared in book form in May 1821, Blackwood (not Galt) having provided the ultimate form of the title *Annals of the Parish; or the Chronicle of Dalmailing.* "I shall be very much mistaken," Blackwood wrote, "if it is not popular." William Blackwood's publisher's nose for a good book was remarkable. From 1821 to the present day, the *Annals* has continued to be Galt's best-loved novel.

Galt in the *Annals* dug deep into the memories of his Ayrshire boyhood. He later recounted that he wanted "to write a book that would be for Scotland what The Vicar of Wakefield is for England." The elderly narrator, the Rev. Micah Balwhidder, recounts in chronicle form the events of a small country parish in the half-century after 1760. From one point of view, it is a study of the impact of social and economic change during that half-century, done with such detailed realism that the book has sometimes read not as fiction but as primary documentation. Christopher North called it "not a book but a fact." G. M. Trevelyan used it to illustrate his English Social History. It would be a pity if the *Annals* were to be thought of as mere social documentation. It is imaginative recreation of a high order and the product of considerable art.

Annals of the Parish established Galt's reputation as a novelist. His portrait of the life of a village, a microcosm of the great world recorded in Scots by the humane but shrewd Micah Balwhidder, has continued to appeal to readers. Perhaps the most remarkable part of its success lay in the book's reception both north and south of the border. The London weekly *John Bull* (no enthusiast for dialect writing) announced that the *Annals* "bears strong marks of genius and talent, and we recommend it strongly to our readers." Galt could have laid down his pen in 1821, his reputation as a novelist secure.

As it was, he was already working on two more Ayrshire novels. *Sir Andrew Wylie* was the first to appear, early in 1822. All of Galt's successes so far had been short one-volume novels. Blackwood (with an eye on the needs of the subscription libraries) wanted something more extensive and he persuaded Galt to expand *Wylie* to the fashionable three-volume length. Though this had no effect on the success of the novel (which ran quickly into a second edition) Galt was not pleased with the result. What he had planned was "the rise and progress of a humble Scotchman" from bare beginnings in Ayrshire to success in London. Blackwood insisted on a "good and striking story"—plot, intrigue, variety of incident, none of which were Galt's forte. The resultant novel is a patchwork of excellence (in the Scottish material) and complicated plotting which Galt himself confessed was "too romantic for my taste."

His next novel *The Provost,* published in 1822, was a very different matter. It is, in many respects, Galt's best book, tightly constructed, without loose ends or digressions, beautifully ironic in tone and admirably written. Coleridge possessed a copy in which he wrote "This and *The Entail* would alone suffice to place Galt in the first rank of contemporary Novellists." The central character is Provost Pawkie, who tells his own story of his rise from humble beginnings to total control of the burgh of Gudetown (which is Galt's Irvine, faithfully remembered in loving detail). The rich comedy of *The Provost* made it an immediate success, a second edition being called for within a month. It is a comedy with serious overtones recognised by few early readers. For all its ironic humour, Galt is offering a serious study of the manipulation of power, nonetheless real for its provenance being not one of the great centres but a small Royal Burgh. Coleridge's judgment was just.

Galt was to complete two more novels for Blackwood. *The Entail* was published in the last days of 1822. Once again, Blackwood persuaded his author to expand to three volumes. Once again, Galt had his misgivings, and the third volume shows signs of romantic filling-out. But the reader can take this intrusive material in his stride. *The Entail* is a powerful and tragic study of obsession. Claud Walkinshaw, an orphan, grows up in Glasgow in poverty. After twenty years as a pedlar he returns to the city a successful cloth-merchant. Obsessed with repossessing the lands lost by his grandfather, he acquires the farm of the Grippy and entails it, ruthlessly manipulating his family in his mad need to pass on his property intact. He dies, frustrated, in a scene which for irony and horror has few equals in literature. His widow "the Leddy," hitherto only a chattel, emerges after his death as a powerful, loquacious and warmly human matriarch. The serious critics of Galt's day were in no doubt that this was a major work. Christopher North, Scott, Jeffrey and Coleridge united in its praise. To Lord Byron, Galt's old travelling companion, "the portraiture of Leddy Grippy was perhaps the most complete and original that has been added to the female gallery since the days of Shakespeare." Linguistically, too, the book is a triumph. Never (not even by Burns) have the resources of Ayrshire Scots been used with such precision and subtlety.

Galt's final novel for Blackwood followed after a lapse of some years. After *The Entail,* the two men fell out. Galt had come to resent what he called Blackwood's "interference" in his writing and he went to another publisher. But they made it up, and in 1826 Galt wrote the final novel in the series he had come to think of as Tales of the West. His mind was now on other schemes and this was intended to be his last novel. *The Last of the Lairds* is sheer high comedy, a study of an eccentric Ayrshire landowner, bankrupt but undefeated, who contrives to emerge in comic triumph. The book had a curious history. Galt (in late 1826 on his way to an appointment in Canada) left the manuscript with Blackwood, who proceeded to "interfere" once again. Alarmed at the book's "vulgarity" he turned the manuscript over to Dr D. M. Moir, who gave it a radical overhaul, converting Galt's salty novel into a pleasant pastoral. The original text (from Galt's own manuscript) was not published till 1976.

Yet, in spite of their bickering and their sometimes uneasy relationship, the two men needed each other. Blackwood needed a novelist under his imprint who would match up to his rival Constable's imprint on Sir Walter Scott. Galt, after half a lifetime of hackwork, needed a publisher who could recognise a novelist when he saw one. The six Scots novels, written in Ayrshire Scots for Blackwood between 1820 and 1826, remained in print as the "Works of John Galt" under the Blackwood imprint for over a hundred years. They established Galt's place in Scottish fiction.

3

It is possible to depict Galt's career so far as a long apprenticeship followed by years of triumphant success. The pattern broke down on the completion of the Blackwood novels. Galt in 1823 shifted publishers. Oliver and Boyd published his next carefully-researched novel, *Ringan Gilhaize,* written as a riposte to Scott's *Old Mortality* of 1816. Some of Galt's ancestors had fought as Covenanters, and *Ringan Gilhaize* is a sympathetic study of men whom Scott had dismissed as "wild western whigs." It is all the more remarkable, since Galt himself was essentially a man of the eighteenth century Enlightenment and an agnostic. His dour Calvinist warriors had required as much creative imagination as his minister of Dalmailing and Galt always regarded *Ringan Gilhaize* as his best achievement.

Galt completed several other historical novels for Oliver and Boyd. They are of little account, written without conviction or pressure other than financial. Galt, indeed, was tiring of his dependence on his pen. His skill as a parliamentary lobbyist had induced a group of Canadian claimants in 1820 to appoint him their agent. He found himself increasingly involved in Canadian affairs and this involvement was to lead in 1826 to his appointment as Superintendent for the Canada Company in Ontario. He was in Canada for part of 1825 and from 1827 till mid-1829. This episode in his life had little to do with his literary career. At a later date it resulted in some routine fiction, one of which, *Bogle Corbet,* has recently been reprinted in Toronto as an "early Canadian novel." The Canadian years were important to Galt, and to Canada. They were of slight significance to him as a writer. An excellent account has recently appeared in H. B. Timothy's *The Galts: A Canadian Odyssey,* Toronto, 1977.

The Canadian episode was, like all of Galt's ventures into the world of affairs, a disaster. It began in high hopes. Galt worked like a beaver in Canada and laid a firm foundation for the Province of Ontario. But his independence and plain-speaking was too much for his superiors and he was recalled. Galt then suffered one of these dramatic reverses that are always possible in the world of business. From a position of influence and apparent wealth (a fine salary, a small estate, his own carriage, his motto painted on its door) he found himself deposed and dispossessed. On his return to England, one of his creditors sued him for a quite minor debt. The others closed in. Galt was committed to the debtors' prison of the King's Bench and, in his own words, "retired from the arena of business like a vanquished bull."

It was Galt's last business venture. Thereafter he had to write for his living, often with results inimical to his literary reputation. He traded himself out of his immediate difficulties by writing a three-volume novel, *Lawrie Todd,* for the publishing firm of Colburn and Bentley and thereafter he worked for them for some years turning out three-decker novels—in his own bitter words—"like an upholsterer." He returned to periodical writing, in *Blackwood's,* in the new *Fraser's,* in any journal that would take his writing. It was hard and seldom congenial. But it brought in a thousand pounds a year.

Galt's resilience was such that even while he was grinding out these pot-boilers, he was planning work more worthy of him. His *Life of Byron* of 1830 is a workmanlike job, based on personal knowledge. His final emergence from commercial bondage came with the publication in 1832 of his political novel *The Member,* a beautifully written study of men in power. Galt signalled his intentions clearly to those readers who could read his code. His name does not appear on the title-page. *The Member* is simply "by the author of The Ayrshire Legatees etc., etc." It was, Galt implied, the author of the vintage Blackwood novels speaking once again in his authentic voice. When the novel was reprinted in 1975 (after being out of print for more than a century) one of the reviewers found it came "close to the sublime on many pages." *The Member* was a fitting finale to Galt's career as a novelist.

In his latter years Galt made no further attempts to write novels. For a time he suffered from a crippling illness and he occupied his days of immobility by putting together a two-volume *Autobiography* which appeared in 1833, following this up the next year with a parallel *Literary Life.* Galt then decided the time had come to quit the London scene and he left in 1834 to spend his final years in the family house in Greenock. He was in retirement but not in retreat. Between 1832 and 1836 he began on what was for him a new genre, the novella or long short-story. William Blackwood died in

1834 and *Blackwood's Magazine* was no longer open to him. But there was still *Fraser's* and a new hospitable journal *Tait's Edinburgh Magazine*. For these Galt wrote a group of remarkable stories, some of them a kind of coda-variation on the novels of the great Blackwood period. Their republication in 1978 from the back-files of these journals has meant yet a further reassessment of Galt. Stories like the surrealistic *Tribulations of the Rev. Cowal Kilmun* and the masterly *A Rich Man* (Galt at his vernacular and ironic best) must now be added to the corpus and given their proper place in Scottish fiction.

4.

Irvine owes much to Galt. He never forgot it and in a very real sense he put the old Royal Burgh on the map. The old Royal Burgh was not ungrateful. There is an entry in the Town Council's Minute Book for 16th September 1825:

> Baillie Fullarton mentioned that the requisite committee of the Magistrates and Council had last week conferred the freedom of the Burgh upon John Galt Esquire now of the City of London he having made oath de fideli and paid the Stamp Duty; of which the meeting approved.

The Minutes for the day are firmly signed "Robt. Fullarton B."

No one was more astonished at the short ceremony than John Galt. Robert Fullarton, Baillie, was the old man he remembered from his far-off Irvine boyhood, the model for his indestructible Provost Pawkie of *The Provost;* and there was the same old man, still pulling the wires, still (in a good legible hand) signing the Minutes, still capable of making a presentation speech of which Galt reported "Provost Pawkie himself could never have said anything half so good." Faced with the demand to pay the Stamp Duty on his own Burgess Ticket, I am sure Galt (having just taken the oath de fideli to his native town) paid up with a good grace.

THE SCOTTISH ENLIGHTENMENT
IN THE AGE OF GALT

ANAND C. CHITNIS

I

The sheer richness of that era described as "The Scottish Enlightenment" is regularly brought home to our own time by the plethora and regularity of bicentennials such as that of John Galt. Any definition of the "Scottish Enlightenment" inevitably brings problems and leaves particular specialists dissatisfied, but for purposes of historical analysis, it is important to distinguish between what Christopher Smout calls "The Golden Age of Scottish Culture" and the more particular part of that "golden age" which can be called the "Enlightenment." In the generation after the Treaty of Union appeared the first expressions of painting, printing, music, portraits in paste, architecture, poetry, prose and philosophy that were to continue to appear for over a hundred years. They were accompanied in the same century by other work of practical or theoretical academic endeavour, by agricultural improvement, early industrialisation, trade, inventions, a concern for medical discoveries and education, and the catalogue of achievements associated with canals, bridge-building, marine engineering, lighthouse building and shipping. The totality of these and other Scottish works, in so many different areas of human endeavour, and making their appearance within a relatively circumscribed time-span (c 1730-c 1830), can justify the ascription "golden age." The era was qualitatively and quantitatively different from what went before and what followed, although its origins lay in the late seventeenth century and its impact was felt throughout the nineteenth.

The Scottish Enlightenment was a particular part of the whole. Its content was high culture, that is the intellectual contributions to philosophy, science and medicine. Its social background, from which it derived so much and to which it

31

gave so much, lay in the resorts of the elite in Scottish society, the gentry who patronised the *literati* and who were deeply interested in their concerns, the lawyers who were so crucial a force in politics, the economy and society, the churchmen, the academics and those professionally engaged in the business of philosophy, science and medicine. Consequently, any consideration of the Scottish Enlightenment must devote itself to the interaction between the ideas and the social institutions of the enlightened. Any definition of enlightened will point to certain common characteristics, the philosophical or thoughtful stance ("the search for principles and common elements at work in all times and in all places"),[1] the concern for a particular notion of progress, the belief in man's ability both to understand and shape his social and natural environment and the co-operation of the enlightened in intellectual ventures such as the societies and universities of eighteenth and early nineteenth century Scotland. The philosophical tradition of the *literati* was in marked contrast to another strand in Scottish cultural development, the antiquarian, represented most vigorously in the late eighteenth century by the Earl of Buchan and his attempt to rival the Philosophical Society of Edinburgh with his Society of Antiquaries.[2]

Because the Scottish Enlightenment was an integral part of a greater social ferment, it inevitably interacted with it and so in practice it is often hard to distinguish between a contribution that belongs to the enlightenment and one that belongs to the "golden age" as a whole. Literature is clearly in this ambiguous position: arguments can be adduced either to view certain Scottish literary works as part of the Enlightenment or to dismiss their philosophical content and relegate them merely to the "golden age," to view them as an expression of that politeness which was of such concern to many in Scotland in the so-called "age of improvement." On the other hand, their very ambiguity gives them a considerable value as mediators between the enlightenment and the "golden age," and the work of John Galt reflects most usefully Scotland in the age of improvement as well as Scotland in the age of Enlightenment. There are various themes of an intellectual and social nature discussed in his work that highlight that interaction between ideas and society which give the Scottish Enlightenment its distinctive character.[3] Galt's novels are also

"The Penny Wedding," Sir David Wilkie's painting in the
Royal Collection, reproduced by Gracious Permission of
Her Majesty The Queen.

There were close links between Galt and Wilkie and, though difficult
to prove, there are grounds for the belief that Galt provided Wilkie
with the idea for this painting.

"Pitlessie Fair" by Sir David Wilkie, Scottish genre painter and contemporary of Galt. Both drew on scenes of Scottish rural life for their inspiration. Reproduced by permission of the National Gallery of Scotland.

valuable in illustrating the local interaction between ideas and society in late Enlightenment Scotland and how the end of both the enlightenment and the "golden age" were quite evident by the mid-1820s. This short study seeks to elaborate generally on two social and intellectual themes that Galt mentions in his novels of the 1820s, namely philosophic history and Moderatism, and to give some consideration to the last years of the Enlightenment in Scotland during which Galt wrote.

II

Perhaps the matter of central concern in any considera-tion of the Scottish Enlightenment and John Galt is the whole matter of philosophic or theoretical history since the author was very much aware of the genre and considered that he was applying it to a circumscribed locality. Philosophic history was a major intellectual study of eighteenth century Scottish philosophers and through it, they could elaborate on their favourite theme of man and society. It has been shown that the Greenock Library would have given Galt, before he left the town in 1804, the chance to read a wide selection of the important works of the Scottish *literati* of the eighteenth century: William Robertson's histories, David Hume's Essays, the two major works of Adam Smith, the works of Adam Ferguson and those of such continental practitioners of philo-sophical history as Montesquieu.[4] Montesquieu had pointed to the importance of such environmental factors as climate and soil in determining the government, laws and other social institutions of different countries: "different climates produce different wants, different wants different styles of life, different styles of life different laws. Institutions like slavery, or polygamy, or parliamentary government arise in response to climatic requirements."[5]

The Scots' philosophers were also concerned with explaining the relationship between the institutions of society and their circumstances, but unlike Montesquieu's essentially static conception of society, they saw society as dynamic and they believed, above all, that the form of economy dictated the nature and form of social institutions. The concern they passed on to Galt for local application, was for progress and improvement, the implications of the transition of a society from rudeness to refinement. The Scots believed in the natural sociability of man; to quote but one, Adam Ferguson: "Man is made for society and the attainments of reason."[6] They observed, too, that man had been prompted to develop from a primitive to a sophisticated state by the naturally endowed faculty of activity. He thus desired to satisfy his wants by improving his material conditions. As John Millar, the Glasgow professor of law, put it: "Never satisfied with any particular attainment, [man] is continually impelled by his desires from the pursuit of one object to that of another; and his activity is called forth in the prosecution of the several arts which render his situation more easy and agreeable." For Adam Smith, active powers

> first prompted mankind to cultivate the ground, to build houses, to found cities and commonwealths, and to invent and to improve all the sciences and arts which ennoble and embellish human life, which have entirely changed the whole face of the globe, have turned the rude forests of nature into agreeable and fertile plains, and made the trackless and barren ocean a new fund of subsistence, and the great high road of communication to the different nations of the earth.[7]

The Scots also believed in the uniformity of human nature in all times and places.

The historical analysis of the Scottish Enlightenment traced the passage from rudeness to refinement through four stages, hunting, pasture, husbandry and commerce. The stages were progressive but did not imply betterment since barbarism could recur. Just as John Millar could point to Scotland after 1603 and the departure of the Crown as an instance of retardation and Adam Ferguson to the latter days of the Roman republic when there was a relaxation of the military and political virtues and a regression of human nature so, too, was John Galt, within his own limits, to show in *The Entail* how economic progress could corrupt the human heart. In tracing the history of man, philosophic history was inevitably faced with the absence of unrecorded facts and that gave it its theoretical character since the missing facts were supplied by conjecture. Philosophic history was also all inclusive and not confined to certain topics. To paraphrase David Hume, wars, treaties and successions were not enough; history was useless and unintelligible without equal consideration being given to "manners, finance, arms, trade, learning."

John Galt is writing of a Scotland undergoing an era of marked economic improvement and change. In philosophic history, the way in which a society earned its living was the most fundamental determinant of its character and institutions. In the hunting stage, for example, communities would be small and based on the family. As private property arose (such as cattle), there would be a stimulus to the establishment of government to protect that property. That government would necessarily be the creature of the propertied classes and would frame laws in their interest and against those who threatened them. Property would also introduce distinctions in society between man and man which did not exist in the primitive stage when all were equal in their poverty. Thus property permitted the rise, perpetuity and heredity of class distinctions and could stimulate men to further exertions. As Lord Kames noted "Without private property there would be no industry, and without industry men would remain savages forever." For Adam Ferguson, the possession of property is what distinguishes savage and barbarous societies from those that are refined.[8] The *literati* showed a considerable acquaintance with past history, classical authors, forgotten peoples and even surprising living examples of stages long past to eighteenth-century Europeans (the North American Indian) in illustrating their theories about the rise and development of institutions and relationships in society.

The mechanisms of progress from one historical stage to another included man's active powers, his efforts to improve his condition. Another was heterogeneity of ends, that in attempting to secure one objective man, in fact, set in train another unintended end. Adam Smith gave an example of this when he wrote of the accumulation and domestication of animals which contributed to the transition from the hunting to the pastoral stage. Such accumulation and domestication introduced the inequality of wealth into society and also government, to protect that wealth. Along with these developments arose the influence of the propertied over the property-less. Similarly, once land arises as an important

35

feature of the agrarian stage it, too, causes different and unintended developments such as the rise of feudalism.

Likewise there were factors in the agrarian stage which caused the emergence of the commercial: Smith showed that as subsistence precedes any development in society such as luxury, the cultivation and improvement of land which provide subsistence must precede towns. Towns "furnish only the means of conveniency and luxury" and arose from surplus rural produce. He went on to show how the cultivation of land required the activities of certain artificers, smiths, carpenters, wheelwrights, ploughwrights, masons, bricklayers, tanners, shoemakers, tailors. These specialists frequently needed each other and as they did not have to reside in one locality, unlike the farmer, they tended to congregate near each other, thus forming a town. They were then joined by those butchers, brewers, bakers and others who supplied their needs. Thus two developments in agrarian society prompted the formation of towns (the centres of activity in the commercial stage), surplus and the demand for specialist tradesmen.

Smith, Ferguson and Millar pointed to a further contributory factor within the agrarian stage which fostered the commercial, the cultivation of "arts." For Smith, the arts arose out of improving and multiplying the materials needed for man's necessities. Ferguson considered art natural to man, a basic skill that he came to refine. Hume found that the arts reinforced man's social inclinations so that cities became attractive places for conversation and for the pursuit and communication of knowledge. When these circumstances came to prevail, the whole basis of the subsistence of the labouring part of the population changed and trades, professions and independent labour arose.[10] Such were the salient features of philosophic history which Galt portrayed on a local scale a generation or more after its major Scottish practitioners had passed on, and his Canadian experience would have deepened his knowledge of the comparative progress of different societies.

III

At the very beginning of *Annals of the Parish*, Rev. Micah Balwhidder draws attention to a central problem facing the late eighteenth century Kirk, namely patronage. He describes his placing in the parish of Dalmailing by the patron in 1760:

> The people knew nothing whatsoever of me, and their hearts were stirred into strife on the occasion, and they did all that lay within the compass of their power to keep me out, insomuch that there was obliged to be a guard of soldiers to protect the presbytery; . . . The people were really mean and vicious, and flung dirt upon us as we passed, and reviled us all, and held out the finger of scorn at me.

Balwhidder could only enter the kirk by the window but he determined to counter the feeling against him by setting out next day to visit his parishioners. The very man who had the day before protested "Verily, verily I say unto you, he that entereth not by the door into the sheepfold, but climbeth up some other way, the same is a thief and robber" changed his tune when he saw the visitations taking place. "There was no ane in the parish mair against you than mysel';" he said, "but this early visitation is a symptom of grace that I couldna have expectit from a bird out of the nest of patronage."

The early introduction of the problem of patronage into the book points immediately to the domination of the Kirk at that time by the Moderates and the Moderate party, to whom the present study now turns. Galt would have been exposed to many a sermon from Moderate ministers, one quarter of whom were trained at Glasgow when Francis Hutcheson and William Leechman were powerful influences between 1729 and 1785. Divinity students would have imbued the social philosophy of the day and the Moderates among them found appealing the integration of all facets of life that lay at its core. The Kirk was in and of society and not separated from it.

Patronage came and went. It had been accepted from 1567, restored at the Restoration, abolished at the Revolution and restored again in 1712. As an institution, it necessarily involved the Kirk in eighteenth century politics. Patrons of livings filled vacancies and they might consult with congregations in so doing. Thereafter, the nominee was presented to the presbytery who ordained and inducted him if his qualifications were satisfactory. The duty of the heritors was thus confined to make provision out of teinds for the poor, for education, for the maintenance of the kirk fabric and surroundings, the pulpit and the manse. The third quarter of the eighteenth century was marred by numerous forced settlements of the type described at Dalmailing. The patrons were opposed to popular pressure in the parishes to repeal the act of 1712 and to substitute instead popular election of the minister or election by the heritors and elders. The Government would not agree to any repeal of the act because they were dependent on the patrons for electoral support. Popular beliefs thus grew up that Moderate ministers were forced on unwilling, evangelical congregations, that invariably they were more concerned with the worldly than with the spiritual, and that they were the agents of the ruling class to "improve" congregations.

The General Assembly also involved the Kirk in eighteenth century politics since it was one of the very few forums in which various interests involved in the general life of Scotland were represented. Such representation was largely through the lay elders, a significant number of whom were lawyers. Lawyers were central to much of the economic, social and political life of Scotland at the time.[11] A wide range of matters were discussed at the Assembly and the Government were concerned that only an impression of harmony should be given in the post-Jacobite era. Thus, when Micah Balwhidder preached before the Commissioner in Chapter XX of the *Annals of the Parish* (the Commissioner being the Government representative at the Assembly) he was justifiably concerned, even as late as 1779, with his text being misconstrued as an excuse for making political observations. He was rightly anxious when the local Dalmailing landowner, Lord Eaglesham, told him afterwards "that, in speaking of the king's servant as I had done, I had rather gone beyond the modern moderation."

The immediate origin of the Moderate party in the Kirk was the clergy's demand in 1749-1750 that their stipends should be augmented. Such a demand exacerbated the already tense situation that existed between patrons and heritors since the latter would have been required to find the money for the increase at the very time when the enforcement of the patronage act made their impotence in choosing the man they paid very clear. From the Government's point of view, to require the landed interest to find the money for the increase would lead to their disaffection and their withdrawal of political support for the Newcastle-Pelham ministry. Consequently, the pay demand was refused and the stimulus given to clerical leaders to form a party that would assert the independence of the Kirk of lay control. Something of the atmosphere of the age as far as this matter of the financial relationship between minister and heritors is concerned can be gathered from Chapter XXVII of *Annals of the Parish*. In 1786, Balwhidder's manse was in grave disrepair and the "pawkie" counselling of his father-in-law led to the building of a new one and thereafter, to an augmentation of his glebe and income. These activities of Balwhidder to preserve "what was due to the establishment and the upholding of the decent administration of religion" soon showed him how austerely the heritors treated their minister and how they reacted to his success in obtaining from them both the new manse and an increased stipend:

Few of them would come to the church, but stayed away, to the detriment of their own souls hereafter, in order, as they thought, to punish me; so that, in the course of this year, there was a visible decay of the sense of religion among the better orders of the parish, and, . . . their evil example infected the minds of the rising generation.

The Moderate leadership believed that they would never be able to free the Kirk from external control until there was clearly seen to be order in its affairs. Such disputes over heresy charges in the 1750s against the like of Hume and Kames and the attitudes displayed towards the writing of *Douglas* by John Home, scarcely gave that impression of harmony in the Scottish Kirk so dearly sought by the London government. The Moderates saw a need, therefore, to assert control over the opposite tendency in the Kirk, the Evangelicals, and they were clearly helped a good deal by a number of Evangelical secessions which weakened the opposition to them.

Imbibing as so many of them had the social philosophy of the day (and the Moderate leader up to 1780, William

Robertson, was one of its leading practitioners) the Moderates believed good order was essential both in society and in the Kirk. The Kirk was a society within society. It had its own courts which were instruments of discipline and its members had to submit to those courts. They insisted that they were returning to the first principles of Presbyterianism when they tried to revive the authority of the General Assembly and insisted that its decisions be carried out by synods and presbytries. The area of dispute over which the principle of order was fought was patronage. Robertson's view was that patronage was the legal method of appointing ministers to vacant parishes and there was little prospect, in the short term, of altering that method. The Kirk would be in a stronger position to assert control over its own affairs if it accepted and enforced the patronage system. There was also a benefit to be gained from abiding by the law of the land: the legal system of ministerial appointments made possible the placing of particular kinds of clergymen, those, for example, of a more enlightened education who might not be chosen by the expression merely of popular will. The mechanisms of clerical appointment could thus make the Kirk an agency of improvement. But this was a side benefit of abiding by the law, of re-introducing the discipline and authority of the General Assembly over presbyteries and synods, and thus freeing the Kirk of external and political manipulation.

The document that proclaimed the Moderates' views and also showed their familiarity and acceptance of the social philisophy of the day was *Reasons of Dissent from the Judgment and Resolution of the Commission, 11 March 1752, resolving to inflict no censure on the presbytery of Dunfermline for their disobedience in relation to the Settlement of Inverkeithing.*[12] It was composed by Robertson and others who opposed the decision to censure neither a kirk session nor a presbytery who had refused to accept the presentation of a minister and to induct him, despite being instructed to do so by the General Assembly. In the course of the document, it was professed that man is a social being, that in society regulations for good order have to be framed and accepted, and any decision not to reprimand a failure to obey laws is an acceptance by society of disorder. Society was a union of peoples and such a union required subordination to authority.

The Kirk, too, was a society within society that also set up authority: there could not be any private judgment in those matters that were tantamount to Independency, anarchy and confusion. Two fundamental principles of Presbyterian church government were parity of ministers and subordination of judicatures. The second especially guaranteed against anarchy and confusion and under it there was a supreme court whose judgments were absolute and final. The General Assembly was that supreme judicature in the Kirk and if lesser courts disobeyed the Assembly with impunity, then the entire Presbyterian constitution was overturned. As was stated, "if presbyteries assume to themselves a right of superseding at pleasure the authority of the general assembly, enjoining a settlement to be made effectual, no man can see an end of this confusion."

The Moderate party organised itself at General Assemblies from the early 1750s. By the 1760s, they controlled many positions of power and influence and Robertson especially was elected Moderator several times. Their control over church courts was not as complete as might have been assumed and they never had a dependable majority in the presbyteries of the late eighteenth century except in a few lowland and east coast areas. Even in Galt's Ayrshire presbyteries were reasonably balanced between Moderates and Evangelicals. In 1780, only twelve out of twenty-nine clergy in the presbytery of Ayr actively and consistently supported Moderates measures, and in 1784, the presbytery actually passed an overture attacking patronage.[13] But by 1780, Robertson had retired and the early idealism of the Moderates of his ilk retreated in the face of the new social and political climate that came to prevail. Certainly from 1790, the Scottish Enlightenment entered a new phase.

IV

Galt's novels were published in the latter years of the Scottish Enlightenment, and there are several instances in his books that point to salient features of those years. A first instance is the concentration on the West of Scotland. It is clear that in its heyday, the Scottish Enlightenment was pre-

41

dominantly the Edinburgh Enlightenment. Of course there were figures elsewhere like Adam Smith and Thomas Reid, but the overwhelming weight of activity and individual *literati* were to be found in the capital city with its law courts, university, medical school, publishing houses and societies that interacted on a scale unsurpassed by any other Scottish town. But throughout the eighteenth century, the economic fortunes of Glasgow were on the rise. There is a nice contrast to be drawn between the city fathers of Edinburgh and Glasgow in the eighteenth century: the one developing numerous plans to recapture for their erstwhile capital, now bereft of parliament as well as crown, a social elite and intellectual life that came with the investment in the University, the Infirmary and, above all, the New Town. The other was not interested in the same matters, so much so that its distinguished scientists Joseph Black and William Cullen left Glasgow for the lusher academic pastures of Edinburgh. What did interest Glasgow increasingly was commerce and business, perhaps the real not the conjectural world. Galt, of course, was particularly familiar with the West of Scotland spirit, because of his own involvement in the world of business and his association with men like Kirkman Finlay, whose activities laid the basis of Victorian might of Glasgow. Galt's novels, then, point us in the direction that the improved Scotland had taken with the development of commerce and industry. In *The Ayrshire Legatees* he noted that "at Greenock I saw nothing but shipping and building; at Glasgow, streets spreading as if they were one of the branches of cotton-spinning; and here, [Edinburgh] the houses grown up as if they were sown in the seed-time with the corn by a drill-machine, or dibbled in rigs and furrows like beans and potatoes" (Chapter I, Letter III). The world of industrialisation, while continuing to provide for an improving Scotland, was in many ways inimical to the enlightened Scotland of the middle fifty years of the eighteenth century.

In Chapter XXXV of *Annals of the Parish*, Micah Balwhidder gives a hint of the new world as it appeared in 1794. Christian practice was on the decline, the kirk was a shelter on a rainy Sunday rather than a source of religious insight. He was struck by the secularisation of Christian virtues and preached on the subject:

I dealt with brotherly love, bringing it home to the business and bosoms of my hearers that the Christianity of it was neither enlarged nor bettered by being baptised with the Greek name of philanthropy. . . . I told my people that I thought they had more sense than to secede from Christianity to become Utilitarians; for that it would be a confession of ignorance of the faith they deserted, seeing that it was the main duty inculcated by our religion to do all in morals and manners to which the new-fangled doctrine of utility pretended.

The era of enhanced commerce and industry was accompanied by an era of heightened political feeling. Politics had never been far from the surface in eighteenth-century Scotland as the issues of patronage and the sensitivity to the proceedings of the General Assembly showed. But in the last decades of the century, the rise of numerous issues caused sides to be taken on the many controversies that dominated political life, parliamentary reform, patronage, the American colonies and war, Roman Catholic emancipation, Ireland and pre-eminently the French Revolution. So wary did common folk become that the incident Galt describes in Chapter XII of *The Provost* is quite comprehensible. A supposedly French spy is caught in the town during the time of the American war and it takes a little while and more embarrassment to discover that, in fact, he is a confectioner, coming to work in Glasgow and the map in his luggage was the outset of a fashionable table, Arran being roast beef, the craig of Ailsa being plum pudding and Plada a butter boat.

The impact of the French Revolution on Scotland was far-reaching. The Government became even more keen to control influential areas of Scottish life, not only the few parliamentary seats and electors, but the Kirk, the legal system and professorial appointments in the universities. The result was serious for these social institutions which had been crucial for the maintenance of the Enlightenment in Scotland. Those Whig professors who criticised the repression of Pitt and Dundas were reported to the Bench and had to be cautious in their writings and lectures. Talk of reform was not distinguished from talk of sedition. The judges savagely repressed allegedly democratical activities that came before

43

them for retribution. The Kirk split between Moderates and Evangelicals saw the Moderates siding with the Tory government and the Evangelicals with the Whig opposition. The earlier Moderates' concern to dissociate themselves from inordinate state interference was effectively reversed as was their alliance with intellectuals: in 1805 they opposed vigorously a candidate for an Edinburgh chair who had quoted Hume on causation approvingly in a footnote. Micah Balwhidder reckoned his discourse on the French Revolution was "one of the greatest and soundest sermons that I had ever delivered in my pulpit" (*Annals of the Parish,* Chapter XXXIV, 1793). The following Sunday, many were at church who had not been for years:

> The democrats, who took a world of trouble to misrepresent the actions of the gentry, insinuated that all this was not from any new sense of grace, but in fear of their being reported as suspected persons to the king's government. But I could not think so, and considered their renewal of communion with the church as a swearing of allegiance to the King of kings, against that host of French atheists who had torn the mortcloth from the coffin, and made it a banner, with whom they were gone forth to war against the Lamb. The whole year was, however, spent in great uneasiness, and the proclamation of war was followed by an appalling stop in trade.

(Galt's last point here well illustrates how the two developments, of commerce and of the French Revolution, were much intertwined in their effects.)

The same chapter gives an excellent example of the debate in Scotland over the French Revolution and the paradoxical responses it called forth. Two weavers were brought before the local justice of the peace on suspicion of high treason. The magistrate, immediately they were brought in

> began to ask them how they dared to think of dividing, with their liberty and equality of principles, his and every other man's property in the country. The men answered him in a calm manner, and told him they sought no man's property, but only their own natural rights: upon which he called them traitors and reformers. They denied they were

traitors, but confessed they were reformers, and said they knew not how that should be imputed to them as a fault, for that the greatest men of all times had been reformers. "Was not" they said, "our Lord Jesus Christ a reformer?" —"And what the devil did he make of it?" cried [the magistrate], bursting with passion. "Was he not crucified?" . . .
I never from that day could look on [him] as a Christian, though, surely, he was a true government man.

The exaggerated politicising of the areas and institutions of Scottish life that had earlier encouraged new thought contributed powerfully to the demise of the Scottish Enlightenment. Tories and their patronage came to rule the roost in Edinburgh intellectual circles who bore little resemblance to their predecessors. Nowhere was this more true than in the Edinburgh chair of moral philosophy whose holder in Galt's heyday was John Wilson, the "Christopher North" of *Blackwood's Magazine*: as a moral philosopher, Wilson was not to make the contributions of an Adam Ferguson or a Dugald Stewart. Of course, it must also be noted that the developing economic life of Britain in the early nineteenth century meant that wider employment opportunities were made available to talented Scots. Instead of remaining in Scotland to take the few posts there available commensurate with their talents, such as university chairs, many were able to go south to places as M.P.s, journalists and specialists in various areas of developing public life that had simply not been open to students of earlier generations. Their loss was felt in the calibre of personnel left to man the Scottish institutions and in the tenor of debate which engulfed Scotland.
Perhaps the periodicals best exemplify the nature of the debates and the relationship between the Enlightenment and society in the later years of the movement. In 1802 had been founded the Whig *Edinburgh Review*. It was followed in 1809 by the *Quarterly Review* specifically because Walter Scott and others loathed the political principles of the *Edinburgh*. In 1817, the publisher William Blackwood began his *Edinburgh Magazine* and he soon engaged Wilson and J. G. Lockhart as the principal writers for his venture. It was Lockhart who two years later was to berate the Edinburgh

reviewers as "the legitimate progeny of the sceptical philosophers of the last age" and their journal as "an infidel work." [14] Such was the company that Galt kept, his literary associates were at the core of the Tory reaction to contemporary events and reforming opinion. Galt's own Conservatism is evident in *The Ayrshire Legatees,* where he has several unflattering pen-portraits of Whig politics and politicians including Earl Grey of whom he noted that on first hearing he appears "a very supercilious personage, and this unfavourable impression is liable to be strengthened by the elegant aristocratic languor of his appearance" (Chapter IX, Letter XXIX).

From 1815 evidence that confidence in the Scottish Enlightenment had been lost could be seen in a number of criticisms that were published. Lockhart's *Peter's Letters to his Kinsfolk* (1819) is the best known, but there were others such as Michael Russel's *Remarks and Explanations connected with the "View of the System of Education at present pursued in the Schools and Universities of Scotland"* (1815) and Robert Mudie's *The Modern Athens: a Dissection and Demonstration of Man and Things in the Scotch Capital* (1825). Even Galt could not resist his sly observations on Enlightenment Edinburgh in *The Last of the Lairds* published in 1826. Chapter II is a satire on the philosophers and political economy (which was "neither honour for the rich nor charity for the poor") and discusses the conspiracy of the Government and the people to overthrow the gentry by altering the value of money. Contemporaries would not have missed the allusions: for example, Francis Horner, the son of a Glasgow linen merchant and devoted pupil of Dugald Stewart, had been one of those young Scots, well-versed in political economy, to go south to be given a parliamentary seat and to rise to the chairmanship of the bullion committee until his premature death in 1819.

A belief common to the critics was that the traditional Scottish philosophical education was shallow in its content compared with the classical education offered by the English universities. Witness Lockhart:

The style of education and exertion to which [the Edinburgh student] submits are admirably fitted for sharpening

46

and quickening the keenness of his understanding, but do not much tend to fill his mind with a store of thoughts, feelings, and images, on which it might repose itself, and in which he might possess forever the means of a quiet and contemplative happiness. He is made a keen doubter, and a keen disputer; and in both of these qualities there is no doubt he will at first have pleasure. But in neither is he furnished with the elements of such pleasure as may endure with him, and increase with him throughout a laborious and, above all, it may be, a solitary life.[15]

Michael Russel had been a schoolmaster in Scotland, became a journalist and later editor of the *Sunday Times*. His attack was on grounds that were seldom if ever expressed in the heyday of the Enlightenment when Scottish education and philosophy were clearly of a high order. He bemoaned the deficiencies of the Scottish universities in classical education and also the professorial emphasis of the teaching system:

It is folly, then, to tell the world in these days, that instruction in what is called logic and morals, is to be valued, according to the excellence of the lectures which any particular Professor or seminary may have happened to get credit for with the public. The character of a school . . . ought to be estimated chiefly from the nature of its discipline, and according to the provision which is made for regular attendance, and for animated and constant exertion, on the part of the pupil,—not, in short, from what the teacher achieved, but from what the student is induced to achieve.[16]

For Mudie, the Northern Athens, which had long and justifiably boasted of its schools of philosophy and medicine, had now been depressed by its general circumstances and by the way the patronage system had worked. "I did not hear," he wrote in 1825, "that any of the Athenian professors have put in a single claim for immortality" with the exception of a natural philosopher and a natural historian.[17]

The post-war circumstances had laid the citadel of the Enlightenment open to such attacks. The increased politicisation of the law and clerical and professorial appointments, and

the creation with industrialisation of wider employment opportunities for Scottish students impoverished Scottish intellectual
life. A good deal of form without substance was left except
in some fields of science and medicine. The financial difficulties of Walter Scott, Archibald Constable, the publisher, and
even the city of Edinburgh itself give economic clues to an
intellectual state of affairs and Scotland's Victorian greatness
was to lie in the west with the development of industry and
commerce. A renewed defence of traditional Scottish form
and practice in high education was not to appear until after
c 1830 as Dr George Davie has shown in *The Democratic
Intellect: Scotland and her Universities in the Nineteenth
Century.*

The Whig *Edinburgh Review* did not omit to concern
itself with post-Enlightenment concerns: its editor, Francis
Jeffrey, for example, challenged the philosophers' capacity
to analyse the mind and mental processes in the same way as
matter. The mind was susceptible only of observation, whereas
matter could be physically examined. Experiments on matter
gave control and power over it, those on mental processes
did not give such control.[18] *The Review* also in the 1820s was
a powerful medium for applying the social philosophy of the
Enlightenment to practical problems then being faced.
Nowhere is this seen more clearly than in the campaign during
that decade to establish a Scottish-type university in London
and mechanics' institutes. The natural evolution of society
was to be encouraged at a time of industrial depression and
working class unrest. In the opinion of writers such as Henry
Brougham and J. R. McCulloch it was best done by educational means: the pursuit of knowledge by working men
would make them reluctant to support rash and sudden inno-
vation; they could be taught how inventions and public
tranquillity serve their interests; they could be instructed in
political economy so that they could understand the cyclical
booms and slumps of the commercial era.[19]

Jeffrey and Brougham appreciated, though, that the
development of working-class education could lead to the
"mutual exchange of property and condition," the very
antithesis of the natural evolution of society, unless measures
were also taken to instruct the middle classes. Most of them in
England were *personae non gratae* at the universities of

Oxford and Cambridge which admitted only Anglicans. So there was a crying need for a university in London, specifically for the "richer classes," which would "endeavour to maintain their intellectual superiority by improving their understandings, and especially by making themselves thoroughly acquainted with those branches of knowledge on which they and their immediate dependents are most likely to come into collision."[20] As Adam Smith had pointed to such features of advanced society as the division of labour, so did his successors attempt to mitigate the evils of that society by educational means which contributed to the stability of Britain in the early nineteenth century. The *Edinburgh Review* rather than the Tory journals, was an instrument they used. Such was the relationship between the philosophic history of the Enlightenment, which Galt popularised, and society by the 1820s. The periodicals and their publishers represent the state of Scotland at the time: highly politicised, critical and lacking confidence in the ability to maintain the Scottish reputation for knowledge and yet attempting to adapt the philosophy of the Enlightenment to meet the challenges posed by industrialisation.

NOTES

1. Andrew Skinner, "Economics and History—The Scottish Enlightenment," *Scottish Journal of Political Economy*, XII (1965), p 4.
2. See Steven Shapin, "Property, Patronage, and the Politics of Science: the Founding of the Royal Society of Edinburgh," *The British Journal for the History of Science*, VII (1974), pp 16-18.
3. I accept the criticism of Professor John MacQueen that I drew too fine a distinction between philosophy proper and philosophy as expressed in novels and other literature in my book, *The Scottish Enlightenment: A Social History* (Croom Helm, 1976). I think there is a difference between "enlightenment" and "golden age" and in my enthusiasm to make that difference clear, I rode roughshod over the content of some literary works. I trust this short study compensates in some degree. (*British Society for Eighteenth-Century Studies Newsletter* (October, 1977), pp 30-31).
4. See that most helpful lecture, Erik Frykman, "John Galt and Eighteenth Century Scottish Philosophy," The John Galt Lecture for 1953, *Papers of the Greenock Philosophical Society* (Greenock, 1954), pp 7-10.
5. Peter Gay, *The Enlightenment: an Interpretation*, 2 vols. (New York, Alfred A. Knopf, 1966 and 1969), II, p. 329.

6. Adam Ferguson, *Principles of Moral and Political Science,* 2 vols. (Edinburgh, 1792), I, p 199. In my subsequent discussion, I am concerned with the shared opinions of eighteenth century Scottish philosophers and not their points of dispute. My approach will, therefore, make them appear more at one in their analyses than in fact they were.

7. John Millar, "The Origin of the Distinction of Ranks," in William C. Lehmann, *John Millar of Glasgow 1735-1801: his life and thought and contribution to sociological analysis* (Cambridge U.P., 1960), p 218. The Smith quotation is from the *Theory of Moral Sentiments* and given in Adam Smith, *An Inquiry into the Nature and Causes of the Wealth of Nations,* ed. Andrew S. Skinner (Pelican, 1970), p 23.

8. Henry Home, Lord Kames, *Sketches of the History of Man,* 3 vols. (Edinburgh, 1807), I, p 97 and Adam Ferguson, *An Essay on the History of Civil Society 1767,* ed. Duncan Forbes (Edinburgh U.P., 1966), pp 11-12, 82 and 125.

9. Adam Smith, *Lectures on Justice, Police, Revenue and Arms,* ed. Edwin Cannan (Oxford, Clarendon Press, 1896), p 15 and *Wealth of Nations,* pp 480-481.

10. Smith, *Lectures on Police etc.,* p 160; Ferguson, *Civil Society,* pp 167-168; David Hume, *Essays, Moral, Political and Literary,* ed. T. H. Green and T. H. Grose, 2 vols. (London, Longmans Green, 1875), I, pp 301-302; and Millar, "Origins of the Distinction of Ranks," pp 285, 289 and 280.

11. See Chitnis, *Scottish Enlightenment,* Ch. 4.

12. Published in full in *Scots Magazine,* XIV (1752), pp 191-197.

13. See Ian D. Clark, "From Protest to Reaction: The Moderate Regime in the Church of Scotland, 1752-1805," *Scotland in the Age of Improvement,* eds. N. T. Phillipson and Rosalind Mitchison (Edinburgh U.P., 1970), pp 213-214.

14. J. G. Lockhart, *Peter's Letters to his Kinsfolk,* 3rd ed., 3 vols. (Edinburgh, 1819), II, pp 128 and 135.

15. *Ibid.,* I, pp 200-201.

16. Rev. Michael Russel, *Remarks and Explanations connected with the "View of the System of Education at present pursued in the Schools and Universities of Scotland"* (Edinburgh, 1815), pp 75-76.

17. [Robert Mudie], *The Modern Athens: A Dissection and Demonstration of Man and Things in the Scotch Capital* (London, 1825), pp 210 and 221.

18. Francis Jeffrey, "Stewart's Life of Dr Reid," *Edinburgh Review,* III (1804), pp 273-277 and "Stewart's Philosophical Essays," *Edinburgh Review,* XVII (1810), pp 173-186.

19. See, for example, *Edinburgh Review,* XLIII (1825-1826), p 245 and XLVI (1827), pp 38 and 234-235.

20. See, for example, *Ibid.,* XLII (1825), pp 223 and 386. The quotation is from XLIII, p 11.

ANNALS OF THE PARISH
AND HISTORY

CHRISTOPHER A. WHATLEY

John Galt's *Annals of the Parish* has long been recognised as
a useful literary introduction to the period 1760 until 1810,
when Scotland was experiencing marked social and economic
changes associated with the Industrial Revolution. Not only
did the great Whig historian G. M. Trevelyan refer to the
quality of Galt's record in *Annals,* "that little story book,
first published in 1821, which still remains the most intimate
and human picture of Scotland during . . . the reign of
George III,"[1] but so too did the Marxist historian Professor
E. J. Hobsbawm, albeit in a footnote in his *Industry and
Empire.*[2] Unfortunately such references are generally brief
and even writers who have dealt most sympathetically with
Galt's "social realism" have not fully explored the mass of
contemporary material and allusions which Galt gathered and
re-formed for his artistic purpose. Perhaps it has been difficult
for those who are primarily critics of literature to appreciate
fully the significance of Galt's selection of historic events. On
the other hand, it might have been assumed that this particular
task had been fulfilled by publications such as W. M.
Brownlie's *John Galt: Social Historian,* published over twenty-
five years ago.[3]

The question of how far *Annals* can be considered as an
accurate description of Scotland during the late eighteenth
and early nineteenth centuries is an important one. Galt
himself claimed that he wanted to produce, for Scotland,
"what the *Vicar of Wakefield* is for England" and elsewhere
in his *Autobiography* he stresses the non-novel-like qualities of
his work. Indeed he may well have been "embarrassed
by the very term novel"[4] according to Keith Costain, who
argues that *Annals of the Parish* (and possibly *The Last of
the Lairds*) were "theoretical histories," a term which Galt
himself used but which has not been followed through by
critics until recently. The term and concept appear to have
been borrowed by Galt from the eighteenth century Realist

School of Scottish philosophy. The group, which included amongst its adherents Thomas Reid, John Millar and Dugald Stewart, believed that "the study of History was the study of progress" and that societies developed and improved in a series of stages, with the commercial and industrial era being a later and superior part of this process. *Annals of the Parish* was Galt's attempt, by artistic means, to illustrate his philosophic position, and through the eyes of Micah Balwhidder we are exposed to the Realist view of history, with change taking place not because of human planning, but caused by non-rational impulses and Providential design.

Clearly it is vital that we should explore the possibility that Galt took seriously his own view that a work of fiction should be "a vehicle of instruction, or philosophy teaching, by examples," thereby tempting him to take a less than accurate view of change and "progress." How far are the claims for Galt's "social realism" and "fascinating social history" the result of Galt's own preconceived notions of the period coinciding with similar views of history held by his twentieth century admirers? In the light of this possibility then, how accurate is Galt's "evidence"?[5]

Except in the very widest sense, it cannot reasonably be claimed that *Annals* is a valid primary source. The tale begins in 1760, nineteen years before the author was born, and while Galt later claimed that he remembered events from when he was "less than two years of age" he also confessed that "I have not a very good general memory."[6]   He left Irvine when he was about ten years old, in 1789 or 1790 (and it is on Irvine and its locality that the story *appears* to be based) and by the time he began work on the book in any conscious sense, probably in 1812, he had been away from the area for about twenty-three years. By then his childhood memories must have been somewhat distorted by the passage of time. The gaps appear to have been filled in by contemporary printed material and the recollections of family and friends. This however may be of some significance for those interested in the period in that some of the attitudes, concerns and *bêtes noires* in the novel may reveal a great deal about early nineteenth century views of the very recent past.

While it is true that Galt used much local material and many Ayrshire names in *Annals,* it is not local history—

certainly one could not better understand the development of any single parish through reading Galt's work. Attempts to trace the history of a specific Ayrshire parish through fifty years of the life of the Reverend Micah Balwhidder are doomed to failure and disappointment. Simply, this is because Dalmailing does not exist. It is an amalgam of several north Ayrshire parishes—Kilwinning, Irvine and Dreghorn provided some of the raw material of the book, while Sorn parish and its cotton mill at Catrine seems to have provided the model for Galt's Cayenneville. Bound into this fabric are shreds of events and personalities from the wider Scottish stage. In spite of this, it is a mark of Galt's achievement that he has managed to create a world which people are prepared to believe in. A slavish attempt to follow the real developments in one Ayrshire village would have seriously limited the scope and range of incidents upon which Balwhidder could comment, and more importantly perhaps, Galt's task of portraying progress would have been more difficult. After all, in the words of Micah Balwhidder himself, his parish "was but a type and index to the rest of the world." (Chapter XLV).

For the historian however, this is less than satisfactory. The industrialisation of South West Scotland was not typified by the creation of a host of cotton spinning villages like Cayenneville—indeed there was only one large cotton works in the whole of the county of Ayrshire during the period 1760 to 1810, and that was at Catrine.[7] The more typical Ayrshire village experienced an intensification of the domestic hand-loom system, with spinning being carried on in small "jeanie" houses, employing only small numbers of people under one roof. In other words, Galt's "typical" parish, in the context of Ayrshire, is atypical, and as an illustration of economic change in the area can be misleading.[8] *Annals* then requires close scrutiny, to discover how far it is useful as a record of this key period for Scottish history.

II

By using Ayrshire names in particular Galt early establishes a localised setting. Present at Micah Balwhidder's placing in Dalmailing is Mr Given, "the minister of Lugton," which is neither a parish nor a church, but is a small township near the Renfrewshire boundary as well as being the name of a river which runs through Kilwinning parish and the estate of the Earls of Eglinton. Another local river, the Annick, is utilised in Chapter XVI, when "Mr Sprose of Annock," that "vehement and powerful thresher of the mind" is introduced. The surname Rickerton, given to Rab, one of the three "bastard bairns," sounds very much like Riccarton, a parish near the manufacturing town of Kilmarnock, which was some seven miles from Irvine. In Chapter VI "Douray moor" is considered to be a promising place for sinking coal pits—and indeed the Doura area was one which provided much coal for the then expanding Irish demand for that mineral. While such references might not have meant much to his readers when the book was first published in 1821, the Ayrshire setting would have been firmly established by his loosely disguised "Delap" cheese—Dunlop cheese was one of the district's most famous products whose reputation, Balwhidder rightly claims, had "spread far and wide over the civilised world" (Chapter VI). These few examples (and there are many more in *Annals*) are sufficient to demonstrate the means by which Galt begins to achieve his purpose, the creation of a world so convincing that "theoretical history" is not an awkward intrusion but the ordering of known facts.

Elsewhere[9] critics have shown the variety of ways names are used by Galt—crudely sometimes, as a form of labelling. By calling the engineer at Cayenneville "Mr Cylindar" in Chapter XLII he does further persuade the reader that he has closely observed the personnel of a manufacturing village, although it could be argued that this could have been done in a more subtle fashion. Even more clever (or perhaps more grotesque) is the change which the name of the cotton spinning community undergoes, from Cayenneville to, in 1806 (Chapter XLVII) "Canaille," because according to Balwhidder, "the country folk" were not used to the former "langnebbit" words. It seems to be far more likely that the French equivalent of "mob" was deliberately used as the cotton mill had been the major source of unrest in the area during the French Revolutionary and Napoleonic Wars when Catholics, Irish, Jacobins and other less than worthy elements were finding work there, so corrupting the "honest simplicity" of "our good old hameward fashions." In 1809

Balwhidder viewed with dismay the full impact of the changing world when the "Canaille Meeting-house" was opened and the kirk seats remained empty.

<h1 style="text-align:center">III</h1>

It is not only by using local place names that Galt creates his local setting. Displaying a remarkable knowledge of the West of Scotland economy in the late eighteenth century he mentions a host of factors which strengthen the factual basis of his account. The central importance of the coal trade between the north Ayrshire ports and Ireland is recognised, firstly in Chapter IV, when Charlie Malcolm's brother Robert goes to sea "with an owner that was master of his own bark, in the coal trade at Irville." Then in Chapter VIII, Lord Eglesham's fall into a midden is partly caused by the road to the harbour being blocked by coal carters taking their loads there for shipment. In Chapter X, the trade is even more firmly (and accurately) fixed between "Irville and Belfast." On the other hand one might have expected that a writer of Galt's apparent punctiliousness would have noted the difficulties of shipping coal at Irvine harbour during this period, when ships had to be loaded outside the harbour from lighters as a sand bar at the river mouth often prevented ships entering the port itself.

Glasgow and its colonial trade also receives justified attention. In Chapter I, Mr Maitland, "now the Lord Provost of Glasgow" and "a great Glasgow merchant," is woven into the tale, thereby acknowledging the ascendancy of the merchants and their Virginia and other trade, success in which often facilitated their entry to the political life of Glasgow and the surrounding counties.[10]

Not only are industrial and commercial affairs included in the pastiche, but so too are agricultural developments. Sometimes these are linked to Glasgow itself, as in 1789 (Chapter XXX) when a thrice-weekly stage coach service was begun between Ayr and Glasgow, taking in Dalmailing and Cayenneville en route. Stimulation was thus provided for the dairying industry and Mrs Balwhidder, for example, was able to "send a basket of her fresh butter" to Glasgow. *Old Statistical Account* writers and other contemporary sources provide ample reinforcement of the suggestion that contact with the rising markets of the larger towns was a great boon to the Ayrshire producers of butter and cheese. By 1811 William Aiton was able to report that, "All the milk, made at more than a mile and a half, and not more than ten miles from Glasgow, is converted into butter and butter-milk, and sold in that city."[11] Earlier, in Chapter XIII, the new toll-road was being planted along its sides with hedges, which were themselves part of the process of agricultural enclosure which had been a dominant concern of Ayrshire farmers from the early 1760s.[12] The important and advanced rôle which the Lothians played in the advancement of Scottish agriculture is also acknowleged by Galt. The aptly (if crudely) named Mr Coulter in 1766 leased a farm in the neighbourhood of Dalmailing; "He was from far beyond Edinburgh, and had got his insight among the Lothian farmers," and followed strict and successful crop rotations, which were subsequently imitated by the local farming community.

Galt brought the consequences of such closely observed changes right into the heart of the Balwhidder household. The coincidence of transport improvements, "and the traffic thereon with carts and carriers," and the growing numbers of young men who were sailors in the colonial trade and brought home sugar (and coffee beans) encouraging the planting of "grozet and berry bushes" whose produce was made into jam and jelly. The results were twofold—the confectionery cured both coughs and sore throats, and Mrs Balwhidder was plagued with people borrowing her brass pan.

IV

Frequent usage of place names and generally accurate references to the economic circumstances of the West of Scotland during the period covered in *Annals* provide a convincing setting, which, as the latter example demonstrated, Galt was able to use to good effect; this does not however necessarily provide the historian with anything more than yet another confirmation of well-known trends and events which marked the Industrial Revolution in Scotland. Perhaps by examining in some detail specific and identifiable happenings and characters we can better ascertain how far Galt was merely using a commonplace but convincing background as a basis for his "theoretical history."

In some instances Galt does remain remarkably true to markers of economic and social change whose validity is borne out by examination of extant records. For example, Chapter II, which covers the year 1761, opens with a reference to "the great smuggling" which was indeed rife near "the Laigh Lands around the Troon and the Loans." Customs and Excise Letter Books provide ample testimony to the popularity of the deserted sandy beaches in Dundonald parish for smugglers of illicit brandy, salt and other goods which carried high import duties.[13]

In other instances though, ascertainable events and dates are at least distorted by Galt. In Chapter VIII, he manages to link his philosophic belief in the rôle of Providence in historic development with a specific, and in terms of the industrialisation of the area, an important event. Lord Eglesham, struggling to pass through the "clachan," with its narrow road, middens and coal carts, had an accident in which he was thrown, "head-foremost, into the very scent-bottle of the whole commodity." Presumably shocked into action, he determined to apply to Parliament "to put down the nuisance." The outcome of the fortuitous accident is the construction of the improved trust road. 1767, the year of the accident, does seem to have been deliberately chosen, as it was then that the Board of Ayrshire Trustees (set up under an Act of Parliament of 1766) decided which roads would be improved first, and in fact those which linked the main northern towns were earmarked for early widening, straightening and so on.[14] It is however with this sort of example, which is generally accurate, that doubts about Galt's veracity begin to arise. The Act of Parliament which Lord Eglesham swore he would obtain was in fact secured in 1766, a year before the fall into the dunghill. To have been bound by such chronological constraints however would have severely reduced the necessity for divine intervention in the affairs of the town, and subsequently man's heart would not have been so humbled.

Similarly, Balwhidder attributes the shanking of three new "coal-heughs" on Douray moor in 1765 to the (God-given?) cold winter and a subsequent dearth of fuel. Previously, he reflects, coal mining in the "circumjacent parishes" had been considered a "gowk's errand." Yet Ayrshire's economic history from the turn of the eighteenth century had been largely a catalogue of coal mining ventures (admittedly often unsuccessful) especially where, as in the case of Dalmailing, access to the sea and Ireland was possible. Even Irvine Town Council itself had in 1762 (three years before Galt admits to this sort of activity in the area) set down shanks in the common "green," inspired not by a cold winter but by the anticipation of profits to be made from coal sales, and the action of "private" coalmasters, who had raised their prices.[15]

Further exploration of Galt's carefully selected material demonstrates quite clearly that he was prepared to exploit and re-work both events and people in order to suit his literary (and philosophic) purpose. This is particularly obvious where some of the major concerns are the focus of attention—the disintegration and degeneration (admittedly temporary) resulting from the erection of the factory at Cayenneville, and the harmful effect or influence of the French Revolution. We have already witnessed some slight assistance which Galt was prepared to give to the divine forces, in the form of alterations of awkward dates.

From a literary point of view, there is nothing unnatural or harmful in this process. Indeed it probably adds to the quality of *Annals*, and nowhere more effectively than where Balwhidder observes the disturbances which centred in Cayenneville during the French Revolutionary Wars. Immediately after the factory was built in 1788 Micah Balwhidder discovered, "signs of decay in the wonted simplicity of our country ways" (Chapter XXIX) largely caused, he thought, by the "unsatisfied and ambitious spirits" amongst the cotton-spinners and muslin weavers who were "nightly in the habit of meeting and debating about the affairs of the French, which were then gathering towards a head." While this approach is superficially plausible, historical credibility does appear to be stretched in that working-class concern for the French appears to have been extremely limited prior to 1790.[16] Evidence from the model for Cayenneville, Catrine cotton works, suggests that a mood very different from that portrayed by Galt was predominant there. In the 1790s the parish minister delighted in watching the workers tilling their potato plots in the evenings. Sometime during 1794 a church was built (ignored by Galt) in the village—and in order to maintain industrial peace the company adopted a policy of employing female rather than male spinners, the former being less inclined to unionise or strike.[17] It is in Chapter XXXIV that Galt's powers of amalgamation, distortion and re-creation reach a climax. Balwhidder dreams a "very remarkable dream," which is almost unmistakedly inspired by the writings of the virulent anti-revolutionary Edmund Burke, whose *Reflections on the Revolution in France* has, since its publication in 1790, provided British conservatism with its anti-radical rationale. Virtually the whole of Chapter XXXIV from *Annals* is written in Burkean tone and style reflecting the latter's belief that:

> . . . out of the tomb of the murdered monarchy in France has arisen a vast, tremendous, unreformed spectre, in a far more terrifick guise than any which ever yet have overpowered the imagination, and subdued the fortitude of man.[18]

Following his dream, which he later interpreted as a fore-warning of the execution of the French Monarch, Balwhidder preached, "one of the greatest and soundest sermons that I had ever delivered from my pulpit." We will never know if it matched Burke.

This incident is rapidly followed in *Annals* by the trial of two weavers from Cayenneville, suspected of having committed high treason. Conveniently, Mr Cayenne, the former American colonist who had had the cotton mill built on his property, had been made a Justice of the Peace. Following the plea by one of the defendants that the Lord Jesus Christ had also been a reformer, Mr Cayenne (whose colonial background and purchase of an Ayrshire estate would suggest that, initially at least, Galt had modelled him on the example of Claude Alexander of Ballochmyle) demanded: "And what the devil did He make of it?" and then "bursting with passion" inquired, "Was He not crucified?"

1793 had been the year of the trial, in Edinburgh, of a number of Scottish radicals—and it was there that Galt had discovered his model for Justice Cayenne, in Lord Braxfield, the infamous Scottish "hanging judge," whose answer to a plea similar to that of the Cayenneville weaver had been, "Muckle he made o' that, he was hanget."[19] For *Annals* Galt has merely (and ironically given the importance of colloquial Scots in the book) removed Braxfield's "exaggerated" Scots accent.

It is not only Mr Cayenne who, under Galt's direction, becomes a polyglot creation. In at least six chapters the story revolves around members of the Montgomerie family, that is the Earls of Eglinton, who were the major landowners in the Kilwinning-Irvine district. For the purposes of his tale, Galt has altered the name to "Eglesham," probably a mis-spelling of Eaglesham, the planned village in Renfrewshire which was also owned by the Eglintons and where, in fact, they had their landowning roots. So while it is clear that Galt is here referring to the Earls of Eglinton, thereby giving the novel some additional realism, this does create another pitfall for the unwary reader who seeks to link characters from *Annals* with the real thing. In fact the Eglinton family is used throughout the book (and in *The Provost*) not as a group of people whose existence adds to the novel's weight, but largely as a symbol of landed power and influence in the parish. It is doubtful, after having worked one's way through *Annals,* if a reader would feel that in Lord Eglesham Galt had created one of the memorable personages of Scottish literature. Even the model has been hacked and recast to fit the needs of the tale. In 1781, Lord Eglesham met his death at the hands of Mungo Argyle (the actual assailant was Mungo Campbell, the family of that surname being the Dukes of Argyle) following a dispute on the shore. Actually the 9th Earl of Eglinton was murdered in 1769, twelve years earlier. By 1781 it was Archibald, 10th Earl of Eglinton, who was head of the Montgomerie domains—and yet Galt makes no mention of the changed circumstances. In other words, Galt has, in this instance, fused two "real" characters to form a rather transparent, but, in terms of the plot, essential, Lord Eglesham.

Although Galt was a "moderate Tory" he was no supporter of the aristocracy[20]—and indeed he was not prepared to credit them with anything other than a restrictive attitude towards improvements in Dalmailing, referring in Chapter XXIX to the displeasure felt by some of the "ancient families, in their turreted houses" when Cayenneville and especially "the handsome dwellings" for the weavers were built in 1788. The portrayal of the landed gentry as an idle and wasting class is not accurate—and perhaps Galt's approach here tells us more about early nineteenth century views of the aristocracy than it does about the economic rôle of landowners in the eighteenth century, throughout Scotland. Professor T. C. Smout[21] and subsequent historians have shown quite conclusively that the rôle of landed activity and capital was of fundamental importance to the industrialisation process—and that the division between the new bourgeoisie and the old landed order is not justified in an economic sense, certainly before 1820. Galt however was unable to separate their political from their economic rôle, and so ignored the massive contribution which the landowners made in Ayrshire, in agriculture and estate improvement, in coal and other mineral mining, in road and harbour development, in encouraging and risking capital involvement in a host of enterprises—and in the north Ayrshire area itself Galt must have been aware of the achievements of people like Robert Reid Cunninghame of Auchenharvie, who managed the Stevenston coal mines from around 1770 until 1814, the Duke of Portland, who began the construction of Troon harbour and linked this with his Kilmarnock coal mines by rail, and the Earls of Eglinton themselves, who, under the 10th Earl in particular, made major advances in the Kilwinning and Ardrossan area, developing coal mining and the harbour and town of Ardrossan.[22]

V

The historian then, is forced to take issue with those literary critics who have talked about Galt's "realistic folk history"[23] and his "factual" tales of Scottish life.[24] Careful reading of *Annals of the Parish* reveals a number of historical flaws, where Galt was prepared to overlook actual dates and circumstances in order that the tale should follow his preconceived pattern. This is hardly surprising, given that he wished to produce a "theoretical history," or even if his aims were more modest, and concerned merely with producing a simple picture of "the real."[25] The achievement of such noble ends is fraught with difficulty as writers both before and particularly since Galt have discovered—Galt himself

61

may have overlooked the potential problems—and David Craig has shown clearly the weaknesses in Galt's attempt to provide a comprehensive picture of parish life in Scotland.[26]

Scotland and indeed Ayrshire was not such an easily recorded unit, to be reproduced in the space of several thousand words. It is the diversity of characters and events, the differing regional and even parochial specialisation and produce which has given us so many interpretations of Scottish economic and social history since the Industrial Revolution has been considered a worthy subject of study. It would be virtually impossible for Galt to satisfy any historian.

Even so, read with care and full awareness of the subjectivity of historical interpretation, one can recognise that John Galt was one of Scotland's finest social commentators. In terms of Scotland's literary development one only has to place *Annals* beside much of the work of Sir Walter Scott to see that in relative terms at least, Galt deserves to be included in the category of "realist." *Annals of the Parish* does deserve the attention of students of Scottish history interested in the period 1760 to 1810, not least because few other writers have had the courage to embark on such a course.

NOTES

1. G. M. Trevelyan, *English Social History* (1965 ed.), p 456. Trevelyan uses *Annals* rather than other documents, so apt was the work.
2. E. J. Hobsbawm, *Industry and Empire* (1968 ed.), p 367.
3. W. M. Brownlie, "John Galt: Social Historian," *Papers of the Greenock Philosophical Society* (Greenock, 1952); *see* also J. MacQueen, "John Galt and the Analysis of Social History" in A. Bell (ed.), *Scott Bicentenary Essays* (Edinburgh and London, 1973), pp 332-342, which looks at social and economic developments analysed in *Annals*.
4. K. Costain, "Theoretical History and the Novel: the Scottish Fiction of John Galt," *English Literary History,* Vol. 43, No. 3 (Fall 1976), pp 342-365. The views expressed here are fairly controversial. Other essays in this volume, particularly on *Ringan Gilhaize,* point to the inclusion of that work too in the category of "theoretical history."
5. A. F. McJannet, for example, in his *Royal Burgh of Irvine* (Glasgow, 1938) used Galt rather uncritically. Referring to the Volunteers he wrote, "The young ladies of the parish, writes Galt, presented the corps with a stand of colours, all glittering with gold, and the kings arms in needlework," p. 368.

6. J. Galt, *Autobiography*, 2 Vols. (1833), p 2.
7. C. A. Whatley, "The Process of Industrialisation in Ayrshire, c. 1707-1871," unpublished University of Strathclyde Ph.D. thesis (1975), pp 347-9.
8. It might have been best to have chosen a Renfrewshire or even a Galloway parish as they were often based on the existence of a cotton factory. On the other hand they would not normally have had a coal trade or strong seafaring links, as Dalmailing had.
9. D. Craig, *Scottish Literature and the Scottish People, 1680-1930* (1961), p 160; E. Frykman, *John Galt's Scottish Stories, 1820-1823* (Uppsala, 1959), p 94.
10. See, for example, T. M. Devine, *The Tobacco Lords* (Edinburgh, 1975).
11. W. Aiton, *General View of the Agriculture of the County of Ayr* (1811), pp 446-50.
12. Whatley, *op. cit.*, p 15.
13. The Customs and Excise Letter Books of the Irvine area are held in the Scottish Records Office, Edinburgh.
14. A. K. Goodwin, "Road Development in Ayrshire, 1750-1835," unpublished University of Strathclyde M.Litt. thesis (1970), which examines this subject in detail.
15. Court of Session Papers, Signet Library, Edinburgh, Irvine Town Council and William Glen, Petition of the Provost and Baillies of Irvine Town Council, 1764.
16. T. C. Smout, *A History of the Scottish People, 1560-1830* (1969), p 442.
17. *Old Statistical Account*, Vol. XX, Sorn, p 117; British Parliamentary Papers, 1818, XCVI, House of Lord Committee on the Cotton Factories Bill, minutes of evidence, pp 67-79.
18. Quoted in C. Cruise O'Brien (ed.), E. Burke, *Reflections on the Revolution in France* (1969 ed.), p 9.
19. K. F. Miller (ed.), H. Cockburn, *Memorials of His Time* (Chicago, 1974), p 108.
20. See J. T. Ward's article on *The Member* in this collection.
21. T. C. Smout, "Scottish Landowners and Economic Growth, 1650-1850," *Scottish Journal of Political Economy*, Vol. II, 1964; J. T. Ward and R. G. Wilson (eds.), *Land and Industry* (Newton Abbot, 1971).
22. For an account of the activities of a host of Ayrshire landowners in the period, see J. T. Ward, "Ayrshire Landed Estates in the Nineteenth Century," *Ayrshire Archaeological and Natural History Collections*, Vol. 8, Second Series, 1967-69.
23. K. Wittig, *The Scottish Tradition in Literature* (1958), p 251.
24. Frykman, *op. cit.*, p 85. Perhaps the selection of this word from what is a long statement with which I am in broad sympathy is a little harsh. The point is that even the best critics throw in such words.
25. Craig, *op. cit.*, p 156.
26. *Ibid.*, p 160.

IRONIC SELF-REVELATION IN
ANNALS OF THE PARISH

KENNETH G. SIMPSON

Certain of John Galt's comments have encouraged the view that *Annals of the Parish* is of interest primarily as social history. Of the *Annals* Galt wrote:

> To myself it has ever been a kind of treatise on the history of society in the West of Scotland during the reign of King George the Third; and when it was written, I had no idea it would ever have been received as a novel. Fables are often a better way of illustrating philosophical truths than abstract reasoning; and in this class of compositions I would place the Annals of the Parish.[1]

That the *Annals* and *The Provost* were generally regarded as novels was unfortunate according to Galt, whose intention was "to exhibit a kind of local theoretical history, by examples, the truth of which would at once be acknowledged."[2] For his Scottish stories Galt endeavoured to create the illusion of actuality; and in attempting to demonstrate by quasi-factual techniques the processes of social change in particular communities he was certainly an innovator, as he was later to claim:

> Many, I am very free to allow, have vastly surpassed my endeavours in the historical novel, but I do not think that I have had numerous precursors, in what I would call my theoretical histories of society, limited, though they were required by the subject, necessarily to the events of a circumscribed locality.[3]

In the light of Galt's aims the choice of the chronicle form was a very natural one: it fosters authenticity and impersonality. At the same time it has important implications for the *Annals* as fiction, and the purpose of this paper is—without wishing to diminish its importance to historians—to suggest that *Annals* is also a major work of fiction: it is a consummate psychological study; it is a masterpiece of ironic writing; and it is a subtle development of an "objective" or "documentary" type of memoir firstly notably exemplified by Defoe and, like much else, splendidly sent up by Sterne.

Galt does not intrude as a presence within the *Annals*. He fulfils the novelist's obligation to select and order experience, but the artifice is not obvious, which is perhaps the highest tribute that one can pay to the achievement of the realist writer. That Galt saw his function as more than that of a recorder of experience, that he appreciated the rôle of the mind of the writer as synthesiser, is made plain in his claim:

> In the composition of The Provost I followed the same rule of art which seemed to me to prosper in the Annals of the Parish, namely, to bring impressions on the memory harmoniously together.[4]

On another occasion the recognition is even more explicit: re-reading the *Annals* he found:

> . . . in almost every page proofs of those kind of memorials to which I have been most addicted—things of which the originals are, or were, actually in nature, but brought together into composition by art.[5]

The writer's knowledge of human experience affords the material which is transformed by his mind into art.[6] For its expression Galt established a voice that is totally independent of himself as author, that of Micah Balwhidder. Mr Balwhidder emerges very early as no cipher, no bland persona, but a distinctive personality. Galt's eye for detail embraces the psychological, and in Balwhidder he offers a full and lively characterisation with remarkable economy.

Galt establishes Mr Balwhidder with the remit of annalist and affords him the authority which derives from his (Balwhidder's) experience. By thus clearly defining the function of his narrator and by achieving this degree of authorial detachment, Galt manages to circumvent some of the pitfalls which beset first-person narration. (In *Moll Flanders,* for instance, Defoe in his preface makes explicit didactic claims for his novel, yet Moll's behaviour and experiences undermine both the author's claim and those homilies which she, as penitent, is compelled to voice. As a result readers divide into those who see Defoe as naive victim of an irony which encompasses him as author, and those who regard him as master of a sophisticated irony. Essentially this is the difference between a narrowly didactic work which founders on the vivacious personality of its narrator (who takes over the book) and a more broadly ironic novel which includes among its targets narrowly didactic fiction). By his silence Galt carefully avoids such problems; and by choosing to dispense with any intermediary he increases the potential for ironic self-revelation.

In *The Ayrshire Legatees,* following the example of Smollett in *Humphry Clinker,* Galt exploited the possibilities of the epistolary mode of narration for ironic self-portraiture: the letter-writer unwittingly reveals contradictory aspects of himself in his correspondence. Like Smollett, he saw the ironic potential of the "multiple view," whereby a number of distinct individuals write independently about the same central experience or incident. In *The Ayrshire Legatees* not only do the members of the Pringle family respond as individuals to events in London but the reading of their letters among their correspondents in Garnock evokes distinctive reactions, and it serves to contrast Ayrshire parish life with that of the metropolis; and here Galt employs an editor to provide informative linking between letters. The result of these factors is a certain dissipation of the irony. *Annals of the Parish* does not suffer in this way and is less diffuse because Galt chooses the simple but admirable expedient of maintaining the one narrator throughout. The advantages for psychological penetration are considerable, and the sustained presence of the one narrative voice is the ideal medium for ironic self-revelation: there is time to reveal the complexities and contradictions of his personality, the discrepancies between word and deed, between event and personal view of it, time to savour the unwitting exposure of weaknesses. There is a certain, almost merciless, inevitability about the unveiling of Balwhidder's character.[7]

V. S. Pritchett, in an astute essay which remains the best short introduction to the *Annals,* remarked that "one is never quite certain whether the minister knows how comical he really is."[8] This applies equally to his participation in those incidents which he recounts and to his rôle as annalist.

Balwhidder characterises himself through the kind of commentary which—sometimes, allegedly, despite himself—he offers; but he is also characterised in his self-consciousness as narrator, and there is a fertile source of irony in the discrepancy between his theoretical conception of his function as annalist and his practical achievement. Despite repeated reminders to himself to eschew personal speculation and concentrate upon a record of fact (*e.g.* "But it is what happened that I have to give an account of." (Ch. 26, p 115),[9] Balwhidder's account reveals a strongly subjective colouring. Of this Galt was well aware; indeed it strengthened the illusion of authenticity in the writings of his "old doited author" whose "garrulous humour" he acknowledged.[10]

Some of the subjective elements in the recounting of events may be attributed to the distinct personality, rather than the age, of the annalist. The ironic discrepancy, then, is between his function and his nature, his task and his suitability for it. No writer can ever refine himself completely out of his work; Micah Balwhidder's attempts to do just that lead, in superb irony, to a highly personal record of events. Garrulous he certainly is, and self-important, and self-conscious. His awareness of his obligations as chronicler can be turned readily to the service of his own natural discursiveness and taste for the particular. In the joyfully detailed recollection of the return of Charlie Malcolm (". . . his coming was a great thing to us all, so I will mention the whole particulars" (Ch. 4, p 21)), there is an element of self-indulgence; and a comically minute account of how the minister came to be unable to preach on a particular Sunday prefaces the affair of Mr Heckletext, his unfortunate choice of deputy for the day (Ch. 13, p 63). Balwhidder's self-importance as annalist is gratified to an extent in that strict adherence to the year-by-year report means that developing situations can quite defensibly warrant a tantalisingly brief mention in one annal, only to be more fully recounted later. The annalist takes a none-too-secret pleasure in creating this kind of suspense:

It was during this visit to his lady mother, that young Laird Macadam settled the correspondence with Kate Malcolm, which, in the process of time caused us all so much trouble: for it was a clandestine concern, but the time is not yet ripe for me to speak of it more at large. (Ch. 10, p 54).[11]

In that the account is punctuated by the annalist's recognition of the problems arising therein, there is a distinct affinity with romantic irony. The self-conscious narrator repeatedly protests his need to suppress the personal, thus setting a standard against which to measure the irony of his inevitable failure. Balwhidder reveals his own values and characteristics despite his best intentions, and from time to time he feels obliged to make apology. Generally after apology or self-reproach the route to the avowed concern becomes as circuitous as before. The account of the year 1771 begins with a lengthy consideration of Lady Macadam's fondness for fashionable amusements that terminates in a sharp self-reproof: "but I must come to the point anent the affair" (Lady Macadam's discovery of her son's liaison with Kate Malcolm) (Ch. 12, p 59). There follows an unduly detailed description of the demure life of the manse on the evening on which he was summoned. To Balwhidder the annalist the intention is undoubtedly to set the scene from which he is summoned; but part of the motivation may also lie in a desire, of which he is not fully aware, to redress the balance after dwelling so long on extravagant and immoral pastimes by reverting to the sobriety and industry which his own household exemplifies. The effect of this tension between the function of annalist and the nature and calling of the particular annalist is to delay even further the progress to the facts that he wishes to present. Thus the pattern of the book is that of vacillation between record and reflection, fact and impression.

The *Annals* are as interesting as portrait of the personality and values of the annalist as they are as record of social change. Galt's psychological penetration is acute as he portrays a man trying to restrain his nature in order to make it fit the rôle that he has chosen for it. Sometimes Mr Balwhidder has recourse to a fund of native ingenuity in attempting to justify the direction which his chronicle has taken. On one occasion he has been unable to resist mentioning the bizarre death of a lady who is a cousin of his first wife, and, aware of having exceeded his remit, he makes a desperate attempt at justification:

This sore accident was to me a matter of deep concern and cogitation; but as it happened in Tarbolton, and no in our parish, I have only alluded to it to shew, that when my people were chastised by the hand of Providence, their pastor was not spared, but had a drop from the same vial. (Ch. 18, p 90).

In moments such as this Mr Balwhidder ceases to be the innocent, the unwitting victim of irony; instead he comes closer to being the *eiron,* or conscious dissembler, and seems to exemplify that quality which A. W. Schlegel discerned in some of Shakespeare's characters, that

facility of self-deception, the half self-conscious hypocrisy towards ourselves, with which even noble minds attempt to disguise the almost inevitable influence of selfish motives in human nature.[12]

Thus one of the subtlest ironies in the book is that which informs the discrepancy between Mr Balwhidder as he intends to appear and Mr Balwhidder as he does appear. On some subjects he attempts restraint and presumably believes himself successful; in fact he fails but remains innocent of the extent of his self-revelation.

Quite the most interesting example of this is his relationship with Mrs Malcolm. In the first annal the reader is alerted to the importance of this lady to Mr Balwhidder:

The An.Dom. one thousand seven hundred and sixty, was remarkable for three things in the parish of Dalmailing.— First and foremost, there was my placing; then the coming of Mrs Malcolm with her five children to settle among us; and next, my marriage upon my own cousin, Miss Betty Lanshaw. (Ch. 1, p 5).

The order here is not merely chronological (indeed it may not be chronological); rather, it reflects the writer's priorities. The marriage to Miss Betty Lanshaw seems to have been determined by a combination of general family agreement and the will of the lady herself, with the prospective bridegroom's attitude one of quiet acceptance; and, revealingly, the report of the marriage is virtually appended to the chapter and occupies about one-quarter of the space that is devoted to the account of Mrs Malcolm. Early in Mr Balwhidder's description of that lady there is passing mention of physical detail, suggesting an attraction:

> She was a genty body, calm and methodical. From morning to night she sat at her wheel, spinning the finest lint, which suited well with her pale hands. (Ch. 1, p 7).

There is soon further evidence of Mrs Malcolm's influence with the minister. In the second annal (Ch. 2, pp 11-15) he denounces tea-drinking, but by the third he has accomplished something of a *volte-face*:

> . . . here I am bound in truth to say, that although I never could abide the smuggling, both on its own account, and the evils that grew therefrom to the country-side, I lost some of my dislike to the tea, after Mrs Malcolm began to traffic in it, and we then had it for our breakfast in the morning at the Manse, as well as in the afternoon. (Ch. 3, p 19).

There follows an attempt at vindication: "But what I thought most of it for, was, that it did no harm to the head of the drinkers, which was not always the case with the possets that were in fashion before," but by this point the reader is left in no doubt as to the real cause of the minister's relenting; and, as if in an attempt to recover his professional standing, the Rev. Balwhidder reassures us: "I never lifted the weight of my displeasure from off the smuggling trade, until it was utterly put down by the strong hand of government." All unwittingly he has revealed more about himself than he ever intended.

Mrs Malcolm appears regularly as a model of Christian forbearance and faith.[13] There are occasions where contemplation of her example colours his entire mood (*e.g.* Ch. 25, pp 113-114, where he uses the reward of her saintliness with latter-day contentment as an index to the world; and Ch. 23, pp 108-110, where he is so moved by the affliction of Mrs Malcolm on the death of her son that he approximates to the man of feeling).[14] On an earlier occasion Mr Balwhidder remarks that he cannot speak of the Malcolm family reunion on the return of Charles, "not being present" (Ch. 17, p 83), and one hears not the annalist's passing apology, but, rather, a note of real personal regret at being unable to participate. There is further testimony to the significance of the family to him in that he thinks fit to develop his account of the death of Mrs Malcolm into a short history of the family's fortunes thereafter—this in defiance of the historical scheme of his narration, as he concedes. The repeated encomia on Mrs Malcolm betoken an interest which is, one suspects, more than spiritual.[15] That Mrs Malcolm is mentioned more often than all the Mrs Balwhidders together is perhaps evidence of where the minister's heart truly lies.[16]

Ironically Mr Balwhidder's situation as narrator here parallels that which he must maintain in life: in a close community such as Dalmailing the minister's behaviour is subject to the closest of all scrutiny; thus what he may feel towards Mrs Malcolm must be kept to himself. This may be one of the aspects which Galt had in mind when he wrote that, contemplating a Scottish equivalent of *The Vicar of Wakefield,* he "began to observe and to conjecture in what respects the minister of a rural parish differed from the general inhabitants of the country"; and a little later he referred to his "intention of writing a minister's sedate adventures"[17] (with "sedate" bearing more than a hint of irony, given the mishaps —several of them farcical—in which the Rev. Balwhidder, following in the footsteps of Parson Adams and Dr Primrose, becomes embroiled).

Galt may have had in mind also the sense in which the very situation of a minister in a small community at that time encouraged self-importance. In the earlier years of Mr Balwhidder's incumbency his parish often appears as a comic backwater.[18] The limitations of his society stimulate self-esteem. His sense of his importance to the reader as annalist is equalled by his sense of his importance to his flock as pastor, with the result that the account of the community is largely an account of self in relation to community. (In fairness, however, one must concede that there is in *Annals* a level of social observation which is lacking in, for instance, *The Vicar of Wakefield*: unlike Dr Primrose, Mr Balwhidder is seen participating within the life of the community).

71

Galt makes plain through Balwhidder's chronicle the extent to which his circumstances have fostered the degree of ego-centricity which he manifests. The minister's earliest problems are parochial (though that is not to demean their magnitude to him)—winning over his parishioners (which appears to become the *raison d'être* of Mrs Balwhidder the first), and coping with the heritors. For almost half his tenure Mr Balwhidder encounters nothing which challenges him intellectually. He notes with pride in the first sentence of his introduction:

> In the same year, and in the same day of the same month, that his Sacred Majesty King George, the third of the name, came to his crown and his kingdom, I was placed and settled as the minister of Dalmailing (p 1).

In view of the extent of the hostility to him, which he duly records, "settled" denotes a certain innocence; but at the same time it conveys exactly his own values—he arrives with fixed and limited views and Dalmailing life does nothing to make him change them, but rather strengthens him in them. His situation conduces to naive complacency, myopia, and an ignorance of the ways of the world. The one brave venture from the parish, the visit to the General Assembly, proves just how parochial and outdated he is. It is a chastening experience.

Normally the world comes to Mr Balwhidder in small and palatable doses, courtesy of the *Scots Magazine*. His limited experience leads him to boast and exaggerate on behalf of his own community: Lady Macadam "could read and speak French with more ease than any professor at that time in the College of Glasgow; and she had learnt to sew flowers on satin, either in a nunnery abroad, or in a boarding-school in England" (Ch. 4, p 23) (as to which, it matters not—they are equally remote in Dalmailing terms); and the cheeses of Mr Kibbock, father of the second Mrs Balwhidder, "have under the name of Delap-cheese, spread far and wide in the civilized world" (Ch. 6, p 32).[19]

Until the wider world forces its countenance before them, Dalmailing and Mr Balwhidder are interested in world affairs only insofar as they may claim to have a stake in them: for some time the American Rebellion is meaningful only in

terms of the safety of Charles Malcolm and Captain Macadam
(Ch. 16, p 75). To Mr Balwhidder Dalmailing is the fixed
point, the centre around which world events revolve and in
whose terms they must be seen; and he is the centre of Dalmailing. Thus he habitually reduces major events by affording
them equal attention with (or often less than) the parochial.
The effect is not to devalue the events in themselves but to
display his severely limited perspective. Mr Balwhidder has
an eye that is observant of the details of parish life (it helps
warrant comparison of Galt with Balzac),[20] but he lacks dis-
crimination, and his account is thus authentic in terms of the
life of the community and the psychology of the chronicler.

Coleridge offered an acute judgment of *The Provost* which
might be applied equally readily to the *Annals*. He discerned
and relished "the unconscious, perfectly natural, Irony of
Self-delusion, in all parts intelligible to the intelligent Reader,
without the slightest suspicion on the part of the Autobiographer."[21] This "irony of self-delusion" is central to Galt's
comedy. Examples abound; for instance, here is Mr Balwhidder on a lone evening walk contemplating the material of
his next sermon:

> Taking my walk alone, and thinking of the dreadfulness of
> Almighty Power, and how that if it was not tempered and
> restrained by infinite goodness, and wisdom, and mercy,
> the miserable sinner man, and all things that live, would
> be in a woeful state, I drew near the beild where old widow
> Mirkland lived by herself, who was grandmother to Jock
> Hempy, the ramplor lad that was the second who took on
> for a soldier. I did not mind of this at the time, but
> passing the house, I heard the croon, as it were of a laden
> soul, busy with the Lord, and, not to disturb the holy
> working of grace, I paused, and listened. (Ch. 18, p 85).

Mr Balwhidder deludes himself into conceiving in the best
possible light his motivation in stopping; to the reader it is
plain that the reason lies in simple curiosity, rather than
religious sense.

By following scrupulously the flux of Mr Balwhidder's
thought Galt has him betray the contradictions within him
and the extent of his self-delusion. Here is his attempt, on
recording her death, to pay homage to his second wife:

I laid her by the side of my first love, Betty Lanshaw, my own cousin that was, and I inscribed her name upon the same headstone; but time had drained my poetical vein, and I have not yet been able to indite an epitaph on her merits and virtues, for she had an eminent share of both. Her greatest fault—the best have their faults—was an over-earnestness to gather geer; in the doing of which I thought she sometimes sacrificed the comforts of a pleasant fireside, for she was never in her element but when she was keeping the servants eydent at their work. But, if by this she subtracted something from the quietude that was most consonant to my nature, she has left cause, both in bank and bond, for me and her bairns to bless her great household activity (Ch. 37, pp 153-154).

As a eulogy, this begins to disintegrate when he remarks that he has "not yet been able to indite an epitaph on her merits and virtues"; he further undermines his ostensible purpose by expatiating on "her greatest fault" (by the superlative, implying the existence of others); and the effect is completed when the final tribute reflects less than favourably on himself in demonstrating his own fusion of economic sense and religious sentiment. The basis of such irony is in the innocence of the speaker as to the import of what he is saying; he is blissfully unaware of the extent of his self-betrayal.

Equally he is intermittently the victim of the irony of events. He has wildly extravagant literary aspirations (extravagant in that they disregard entirely the question of his capacity for such a task) to write either "an orthodox poem like Paradise Lost, by John Milton (treating) more at large of Original Sin, and the great mystery of Redemption," or "a connect-treatise on the efficacy of Free Grace" (Ch. 5, p 28). These come to nothing because, he claims, "some new thought ever came into my head," and because the high living of the maidservants (culminating in one's becoming pregnant—a splendid ironic detail in the light of his proposed subject-matter) has necessitated his looking for another wife. Similarly, what is heralded in the record of the raising of the volunteers as "a sad disaster" amounts to the farcical mishap of his falling over the prostrate Dr Tanzey (Ch. 44, p 182).

There are moments when the comic juxtaposition of the

serious and the trivial approximates to bathos.[22] Here Balwhidder describes his visit to Nanse Banks just prior to her death: "She was sitting in the window-nook, reading THE WORD to herself, when I entered, but she closed the book, and put her spectacles in for a mark when she saw me" (Ch. 8, p 43). The report of the fear which the arrival of the first recruiting party occasioned in the minister is punctuated by the recollection that "Mrs Balwhidder (was) throng with the lasses looking out a washing"; and he notes that, after seeing the soldiers, Mr Dozendale and he "had a sober tumbler of toddy together, marvelling exceedingly where these fearful portents and changes would stop, both of us being of opinion, that the end of the world was drawing nearer and nearer" (Ch. 36, pp 149-50).

Mr Balwhidder's "innocent self-importance"[23] betrays his limitations. It manifests itself in his acute awareness of his rôle as intermediary between community and God, leading at times to telling juxtaposition, the irony of which eludes him: for instance, he writes that the first Mrs Balwhidder "was removed from mine to Abraham's bosom on Christmas day" (Ch. 4, p 24). From the secure vantage-point of the elect he promises his congregation: ". . . it will be my duty to testify, in that place where I hope we are all one day to meet again, that I found you a docile and a tractable flock, far more than at first I could have expected" (Introduction, p 2). In his accounts of local crises he relishes his own place in the vanguard: (on seeing Breadland ablaze) "I said to Mr Pettigrew that, in the strength of the Lord, I would go and see what could be done" (Ch. 7, p 35); (on hearing the reports of what later proves to be a toad contained within a stone) "The man came to me like a demented creature, and the whole clachan gathered out, young and old, and I went at their head, to see what the miracle could be, for the man said it was a fiery dragon, spuing smoke and flames" (Ch. 10, p 51).

In the account of his appearance before the Assembly the centripetal tendency of Mr Balwhidder's thought, and the concomitant hyperbolism, are much in evidence:

When the day came, I thought all things in this world were loosened from their hold, and that the sure and steadfast earth itself was grown coggly beneath my feet, as I mounted the pulpit. With what sincerity I prayed for help that day, and never stood man more in need of it, for through all my prayer the congregation was so watchful and still, doubtless to note if my doctrine was orthodox, that the beating of my heart might have been heard to the uttermost corners of the kirk. (Ch. 20, p 97).

It is a measure of the subtle blend of sympathy and judgment which Mr Balwhidder's account evokes—a supreme tribute to Galt, in that this is the art which conceals itself—that, if here the reader feels for the innocent abroad, by the end of the same annal such sympathy is qualified by the minister's equally inflated account of his return:

By the time I got home to the Manse, I had been three whole weeks and five days absent, which was more than all my absences together, from the time of my placing, and my people were glowing with satisfaction, when they saw us driving in a Glasgow chaise through the clachan to the Manse (p 100).

From this passage it is clear that the "satisfaction" is as much his as the community's. Mr Balwhidder's habit of exaggeration finds expression in a readiness to invest his parishioners with the excess of his feelings: he writes that the birth of his son Gilbert was "to the great satisfaction of me, and of my people, who were wonderful lifted up because their minister had a man-child born unto him" (Ch. 8, p 45). This blend of the factual and the impressionistic or interpretative is characteristic of Mr Balwhidder's chronicle.

Perhaps the most comic aspect of the minister's ego-centricity is in the extent to which it colours his logic. The following grudging tribute to Lady Macadam is, in its illogicality, a superb example of innocent self-betrayal:

Though she never liked me, nor could I say there was many things in her demeanour that pleased me, yet she was a free-handed woman to the needful, and when she died she was more missed than it was thought she could have been. (Ch. 22, p 106).

Similarly, he supposes that the benefactions of Mrs Malcolm's daughters to the poor of the parish will cease with his death

(Ch. 40, p 169); and when, after the raising of the volunteers, all sections of the community mingle happily together at the dance, Mr Balwhidder sees in this "unison of spirit" a clear indication that "the Lord . . . had decreed our national preservation," but he keeps this intimation to himself "lest it might have the effect to relax the vigilance of the Kingdom" (Ch. 44, p 182).

Increasingly Galt's annalist reveals a complex personality that encompasses several conflicting elements; and the irony resides in his being unaware that he is doing so. In Balwhidder naivety cohabits with a strong practical sense, innocence mingles with prudence. Practical materialism rather than any spiritual concern informs most of his accounts of the deaths of individuals: the death of Mr Patrick Dilworth "was a great relief to my people, for the heritors could no longer refuse to get a proper schoolmaster" (Ch. 4, p 23); the burning of Breadland House (and with it Miss Girzy Gilchrist) was "a catastrophe that proved advantageous to the parish" (Ch. 7, p 37) in that the estate was farmed thereafter on modern methods by Mr Coulter; and of the death of Miss Sabrina Hookie, the schoolmistress, he writes:

. . . we could now better spare her than we did her predecessor; for at Cayenneville there was a broken manufacturer's wife, an excellent teacher, and a genteel and modernized woman, who took the better order of children (Ch. 41, pp 170-1).

Proof of the minister's practical sense is his capacity to relate the life of the individual to that of the community. When Thomas Wilson, by enlisting, leaves behind a wife and children they are described in terms ill befitting a man of the cloth as "an awful cess thrown upon the parish," and he laments that "we were saddled with his family"; but the other recruit is not missed since "he was a ramplor, roving sort of creature, and, upon the whole, it was thought he did well for the parish when he went to serve the King" (Ch. 17, p 81) (not least, as Mr Balwhidder makes plain without ever saying as much, because he leaves none to make demands upon the parish's charity). Equally, Mr Balwhidder attempts to assess the effects of events on the lives of individuals, the most ironic exemplification of this being his belief that the loss of twelve stone of lint in the burning of the mill in effect killed his first wife (Ch. 4, p 24).

Micah Balwhidder's account of his means of choosing her successor is an unwitting eloquent testimony to his canny practicality:

> Soon after this, the time was drawing near for my second marriage. I had placed my affections, with due consideration, on Miss Lizy Kibbock, the well-brought-up daughter of Mr Joseph Kibbock, of the Gorbyholm, who was the first that made a speculation in the farming way in Ayrshire (Ch. 6, pp 31-2).

Affections have been relegated; the marriage is approached as a business enterprise. He has carefully weighed pros and cons, but despite "due consideration" he is unable to foresee that marriage to that "engine of industry," the second Mrs Balwhidder, will consign him to isolation within his own household for an important part of his life. While on occasion he regrets his wife's obsessive productivity (*e.g.* Ch. 6, p 33), he is too strong a materialist to set happiness before the prosperity which her industry brings, and there is nothing to suggest that he recognises the irony of his situation, wherein his practical sense, by his own choice, meets much more than its match.[24]

The relative naivety of Mr Balwhidder is well demonstrated through the contrast with the subtle energy of his second wife and her father, Mr Kibbock. Galt's depiction of the manipulation of the minister by his wife and father-in-law is masterly, a model of penetrative yet economic portrayal. Above all else Mr Balwhidder values peace—in the home, in the parish, and in the nation. In the battle over the manse the opposed armies are the heritors and the Kibbocks, and Mr Balwhidder is clay in the hands of the latter, as the account for 1786 makes plain (Ch. 27, pp 119-122). Faced with her husband's willingness to pay for the renovation rather than approach the heritors, Mrs Balwhidder shrewdly couches her objection in the minister's own terms:

> She was excessively angry, and told me, that all the painting and whitewashing in the world would avail nothing, for

that the house was as a sepulchre full of rottenness; and she sent for Mr Kibbock, her father, to confer with him on the way of getting the matter put to rights.

Deftly and suggestively Galt says much about relations in the manse through the account of this one incident; and the irony is doubled by the fact that it is the innocent himself who is unconsciously revealing his own innocence.

A further indication of Mr Balwhidder's limitation is his superstitiousness. His faith in the ominous is ardent, though generally he imputes the superstition to a sage but unnamed authority:

> It was clear to me that the wars were not to be soon over, for I noticed, in the course of this year, that there was a greater christening of lad bairns, than had ever been in any year during my incumbency; and grave and wise persons, observant of the signs of the times, said, that it had been long held as a sure prognostication of war, when the births of male children outnumbered that of females. (Ch. 19, p 91).

However he is quite explicit in expressing his belief in the operations of Providence.

Often a comic edge to the incident adduced demonstrates the distance between Mr Balwhidder and John Galt: Lord Eglesham is pitched into a midden, a new road is the outcome, and for the minister this is

> clear proof how improvements came about, as it were, by the immediate instigation of Providence, which should make the heart of man humble, and change his eyes of pride and haughtiness into a lowly demeanour (Ch. 8, p 43).

The hand of Providence is always present and in its actions there is ever a lesson: a "chastising Providence" (Ch. 13, p 64), in afflicting Mr Balwhidder with toothache, brings to light the guilt of Mr Heckletext. The superstitiousness and the belief in Providence correlate to the limited experience of the man. They also run counter to the minister's practical materialism.

The satirising, albeit not entirely unsympathetically, of Balwhidder's belief in his prophetic talents is further indication of Galt's divorcing himself from the views of his annalist. Here again there is a comic aspect to most of the examples of Mr Balwhidder's divination (and the naming of him after one of the "Minor Prophets" points the irony): in his innocence he believes it an omen of war when he sees "the soldier and the sailor" (Captain Macadam and Robert Malcolm) from the pulpit (Ch. 10, p 54); news of Thomas Wilson's regiment makes his family fear for him, and when his death is reported it confirms for Mr Balwhidder that "there is a far-seeing discernment in the spirit, that reaches beyond the scope of our incarnate senses" (Ch. 18, p 88); and his prediction of the downfall of Louis XVI in the great city of "Public Opinion" (Ch. 34, p 143) is so contrived, so heavily orchestrated, as to be manifestly comic in intention (on the part of Galt, though not, of course, Balwhidder). That Galt has Balwhidder, late in life, renounce his claims ("I had only lived longer than most of those around me, and had been all my days a close observer of the signs of the times" (Ch. 41, p 170)) is perhaps indicative of the fact that, for Galt, the wider world of the nineteenth century must inevitably force even such a recalcitrant to acknowledge its existence.

Balwhidder, with his manifest contradictions and complexities, may well represent the double vision of Scottish Presbyterianism with its conflicting emphases on predetermination and individual practical energy. In particular Balwhidder would seem to exemplify the plight of a retrospective and entrenched dogmatism in a steadily modernising and more liberal world. There is undeniably some satire at the expense of the closed and militant Presbyterianism which Mr Balwhidder typifies (*e.g.* his recurrent dismissal of Episcopalians). Galt's first intention was to have as annalist the village schoolmaster.[25] Possibly the reason for opting for the minister was the potential which his self-portrait afforded for a fuller exemplification of the tensions within Scottish Presbyterianism.[26]

In the last third of the *Annals* the pace of social and intellectual change increases steadily, and it is accompanied by the ironic contrast between Mr Balwhidder's attitude and the norm. Mr Balwhidder can recognise that "there was an erect and out-looking spirit abroad that was not to be satisfied with the taciturn regularity of ancient affairs," yet he regrets what he regards as the concomitant "signs of decay in the wonted simplicity of our country ways" (Ch. 29, p 128). Mr Cayenne, the embodiment of commercial enterprise, evokes an ambivalent response: he disrupts the minister's conservative love of peace and quiet and he offends even to his death-bed his rigorous Christian scruples; yet there is a grudging admiration for the man's achievements (he can even clear the minister's own clouds of depression) and his independent spirit—Mr Cayenne "was a man that would take his own way, and do what he thought was right, heedless alike of blame or approbation" (Ch. 40, p 168)—which is in marked contrast to the restraint and conventionality of Mr Balwhidder that is epitomised in his advice to the newly-wed, "to ca' canny, and join trembling with their mirth" (Ch. 48, p 196).

Galt realises vividly the internal tension between ingrained conviction and a somewhat guilty and self-conscious sense of wonder. Here is Mr Balwhidder on the subject of the new bookseller's shop:

Upon conversing with the man, for I was enchanted to go into this phenomenon, for as no less could I regard it, he told me that he had a correspondence with London, and could get me down any book published there within the same month in which it came out, and he shewed me divers of the newest come out, of which I did not read even in the Scots Magazine, till more than three months after, although I had till then always considered that work as most interesting for its early intelligence (Ch. 31, p 133).

This conveys admirably the sudden widening of horizons before a mind severely circumscribed: "enchanted" and "phenomenon" express exactly the naive curiosity, and "even in the Scots Magazine . . .ff." reflects the slightly resentful incredulity that accompanies the discovery that a corner-stone of life has been removed.

The threat to Mr Balwhidder's peace of mind comes from change in its intellectual, rather than its economic, aspect. He misses the irony of the situation whereby it is Mr Cayenne, thought for long "a serpent plague" but latterly regarded as "one of our greatest benefactors" (Ch. 29, p 127), who is instrumental in bringing to the parish the weavers of revolutionary sympathies. Balwhidder is threatened more by ideas than by wealth and its attendant corruption. His perspective is incapable of widening to accommodate new situations or experiences. Unwittingly he makes this plain in his account of his reaction to "the new spirit" as expressed by the weavers:

> . . . they confounded me with their objections, and used my arguments, which were the old and orthodox proven opinions of the Divinity Hall, as if they had been the light sayings of a vain man. So that I was troubled, fearing that some change would ensue to my people, who had hitherto lived amidst the boughs and branches of the gospel unmolested by the fowler's snare, and I set myself to watch narrowly, and with a vigilant eye, what would come to pass" (Ch. 29, p 129).

A combination of character and conditioning wrought by experience ensures that Mr Balwhidder has no choice but to "watch narrowly."[27]

It is significant that his practical sense is impotent in the face of intellectual and religious developments; rather, he seeks refuge in faith:

> . . . I could mark a visible darkness of infidelity spreading in the corner of the vineyard committed to my keeping, and a falling away of the vines from their wonted props and confidence in the truths of Revelation. But I said nothing. I knew that the faith could not be lost, and that it would be found purer and purer the more it was tried (Ch. 31, p 135).

In such instances the scriptural rhetoric serves to underline the antiquity of the sentiments. At times Mr Balwhidder retreats from the prospect of the wider world and blesses rural isolation in that it offers less strenuous challenges to faith. After a visit to Glasgow he rejoices to his wife: "we live, as it were, within the narrow circle of ignorance, we are spared from the pain of knowing many an evil; and, surely, in much knowledge, there is sadness of heart" (Ch. 32, p 137). Such sentiments are at variance with, and render suspect, his account of his occasional "bit jaunt" in a hired chaise with his third wife, where he seems to congratulate himself upon a certain liberalism: he records that they visit

> divers places and curiosities in the country, that I had not seen before, by which our ideas were greatly enlarged; indeed, I have always had a partiality for travelling, as one of the best means of opening the faculty of the mind and giving clear and correct notions of men and things (Ch. 43, p 178).

In contrast with this claim his own record is that of a reactionary in an age of increasingly liberal attitudes. The splendidly ironic sequence of Balwhidder's thought in the annal for 1804 (Ch. 45, pp 183-187) reveals him as very much the diehard. Having recorded that the church session has agreed to replace church censures with fines, the minister notes that this "was not done without compunction of spirit" on his part, for he "was of opinion, that the principle of Presbyterian integrity should have been maintained to the uttermost." From the intellectual battle, which he is plainly losing, his attention turns to a turtle, the first seen in the parish, and served at a feast to which Mr Cayenne has invited the minister. His simplistic response, in which he relates bodily discomfort to immorality, epitomises his guilt and fear of decadence:

> . . . it is a sort of food that I should not like to fare long upon. I was not right the next day; and I have heard it said, that when eaten too often, it has a tendency to harden the heart, and make it crave for greater luxuries.

As if in an unconscious attempt to atone for his self-indulgence he then mounts an attack against "the Mass . . . with all its mummeries and abominations," brought to the parish by an Irish priest "who was confessor to some of the poor deluded Irish labourers about the new houses and the cotton-mill." While Mr Balwhidder favours an offensive against "the old dragon of Popery," to his surprise "the elders recommended no step to be taken, but only a zealous endeavour to greater Christian excellence on our part." The minister does not think this "the wisest counsel" and favours "attacking the enemy in his camp," but "they prudently observed, that the days of religious persecution were past, and it was a comfort to see mankind cherishing any sense of religion at all, after the vehement infidelity that had been sent abroad by the French Republicans."

The ever-widening gulf between the views of minister and those of the elders is but one indication of how much the former lives in the past. He claims here that by the end of his life he was a convert to their moderation, yet his account immediately undermines this: Father O'Grady has moved on to Glasgow where "he has since met with all the encouragement that might be expected from the ignorant and idolatrous inhabitants of that great city"; the next threat comes from "another interloper (who) came to teach the flagrant heresy of Universal Redemption." Mr Balwhidder acknowledges that for his understanding of such doctrines he relies upon a penetrative elder, for, as he says in a moment of self-delusion, "I have not, at my advanced age, such a mind for the kittle crudities of polemical investigation that I had in my younger years, especially when I was a student in the Divinity Hall of Glasgow." This annal proves that he does not have such a mind at the time of writing, and the record of his earlier years suggests that he never had it.[28]

His subsequent behaviour demonstrates his ineffectuality in dealing with the new thinking. His sermon against the revolutionary doctrines has an effect quite the reverse of that which he intends: the weavers decide to build a meeting-house, and the petulance of his response in taking this personally is a reflection of his myopia (Ch. 47, p 193). His incapacity is emphasised further in his reaction to the failure of the local mill: redundant workers line the streets and he confesses: "For my part, I could not bear the sight, but hid myself in my closet, and prayed to the Lord to mitigate a calamity, which seemed to me past the capacity of man to remedy" (Ch. 49, p 198). By the evening he had recovered sufficiently to trust that "he who sends the night, would bring the day in his good and gracious time"; and to this simple faith he is later able to add the practical exhortation to the workers "to lay up something for a reverse," from which advice, he believes, there has sprung the savings bank. Again, when he finds that the opening of the meeting-house has reduced greatly his own congregation he regards it as a personal trial ("Satan that day had power given to him to buffet me as he did Job of old" (Ch. 50, pp 201-202)). His pulpit outburst (which he later regrets in suitably Old Testament terms) against "the hobble-show at Cayenneville" effectively clinches the question of his retiring. His defence of his ability in preaching ("I found myself growing better at it, as I was enabled to hold forth, in an easy manner, often a whole half hour longer than I could do a dozen years before" (p 200)) and his references to his wife's part in encouraging his retiral are typical of Galt's ironic portrayal of self-delusion.

Balwhidder's final expression of his wonder at the rapid spread of progress is probably the finest instance of his capacity for unwitting self-contradiction and the clearest indication of the entrenchment of his values. He is presented (appropriately) with a silver salver and a tribute "written by a weaver lad that works for his daily bread"; his account continues:

Such a thing would have been a prodigy at the beginning of my ministry, but the progress of book learning and education has been wonderful since, and with it has come a spirit of greater liberality than the world knew before, bringing men of adverse principles and doctrines, into a more humane communion with each other, shewing, that it's by the mollifying influence of knowledge, the time will come to pass, when the tiger of papistry shall lie down with the lamb of reformation, and the vultures of prelacy be as harmless as the presbyterian doves; when the independent, the anabaptist, and every other order and denomination of Christians, not forgetting even these poor wee wrens of the Lord, the burghers and anti-burghers, who will pick from the hand of patronage, and dread no snare (Ch. 51, pp 204-205).

Enlightenment has by-passed Mr Balwhidder: while recognising the new liberal spirit, his own eyes are still fixed on the religious wars of earlier centuries.[29] His own example contradicts his claim for the educative value of experience

(Ch. 43, pp 175-178), a point which is underlined by the fact that in his final sermon he alludes to the opposition which greeted his appointment without a hint of recognition that his parishioners might be justified in so reacting to such an authoritarian procedure (Introduction, p 2).

It is particularly appropriate to Galt's irony that the *Annals* concludes thus on a personal, and amusing, note:

> I am thankful, however, that I have been spared with a sound mind to write this book to the end; but it is my last task, and, indeed, really I have no more to say, saving only to wish a blessing on all people from on high, where I soon hope to be, and to meet there all the old and long-departed sheep of my flock, especially the first and second Mrs Balwhidders (Ch. 51, p 205).

If he is well-meaning, he is nonetheless self-bound and his perspective is narrow to the last. It is also important that the *Annals* ends in this highly particular manner in that it re-affirms the paradox of the "chronicle" which, in achievement, is a highly personalised record. The conclusion, then, serves (if such a reminder is needed) to emphasise that Balwhidder is no mere mouthpiece of his creator but a clearly individualised characterisation; and the subtle irony which informs his self-revelation is warning against identifying his views with those of Galt.[30]

Galt's *Annals* is replete with irony of various kinds. At times Balwhidder is the victim of situational irony, or the irony of fate, where his or others' well-intentioned actions rebound to his detriment, or where he is ignorant of what is predestined (on such occasions his belief in Providence is invariably voiced). Also it might be argued that the some-times-contradictory elements in Balwhidder's response to change encourage one to regard him as an unwitting exponent of an ambivalent attitude to a complex and paradox-ridden world, thus locating Galt's work in the tradition of what has come to be known as "general irony." (This view is certainly preferred to that which regards the increasing ambivalence of Balwhidder's response, especially latterly, as evidence of the intrusion of Galt's own views).[31]

The particular triumph of the novel, however, is in Galt's mastery of the irony which informs Mr Balwhidder's self-revelation. This expresses itself in discrepancies of various kinds: between appearance and reality; between subject and object, or self and world; between innocence and self-consciousness, or self and rôle; between commentary and material; and in the juxtaposing of natural idiom and scriptural rhetoric. The ultimate tribute to Galt's art in the *Annals* is that he carefully controls his readers without their being aware of it, and elicits from them a complex response to his narrator which is a compound of sympathy and judgment. Perhaps this is the especial appeal of the *Annals* to a century which has felt the full force of the shift from absolutism to relativism: we recognise in Balwhidder a man betraying his own limitation, and we both judge and identify. Galt, sublimely detached, invites us to join him in amused observation of his *ingénu*.

Yet the final effect, though plainly reductive, is not destructive. The reader is drawn close to Mr Balwhidder and kept there, with the result that straightforward condemnation of his weaknesses is impossible (the situation is comparable to that in Jane Austen's *Emma* where, as Wayne Booth has shown, prolonged intimacy with the principal character influences the reader's judgment of her).[32] While savouring the ironic self-betrayal we have been carefully manipulated by Galt into the situation where we recognise general human weaknesses and sympathise with their exemplar. Balwhidder's egocentricity is no more than an instance (slightly heightened for comic purposes) of what Jose Ortega y Gasset called "a tendency resident in human nature that prompts us to assume that reality is what we think of it and thus to confound reality and idea by taking in good faith the latter for the thing itself."[33] And surrounding his self-delusion there is a defiant individualism which is curiously moving. After the personal disaster of the appearance at the General Assembly has been faithfully recorded Mr Balwhidder returns doggedly to his own naive faith in Providence, assuring us (and himself):

There is nothing in all the world that doth not advance the cause of goodness: no, not even the sins of the wicked, though through the dim casement of her mortal taber-nacle, the soul of man cannot discern the method thereof (Ch. 20, p 101).

Annals is an amusing and compassionate study. If it is, as I have been arguing, an ironic novel of a very high order, it seems unlikely that Galt could have failed to be aware of the nature of his achievement. What, then, is the explanation of his insistence that his book be regarded as something other than a novel? Any answer must be largely conjectural, but the explanation may be a composite of these: fearful of failure, he was wary of advancing claims as a novelist; he recognised the pre-eminence of Scott as the Scottish novelist of the age; he wished to capitalise on the growing interest in social history which was both reflected in, and further generated by, *The Statistical Account of Scotland* (1791-9); and (perhaps most of all) he genuinely believed that the historian was of greater use to society than the imaginative writer.

REFERENCES

1. *The Literary Life, and Miscellanies of John Galt* (Edinburgh and London, 1834), I, p 156.
2. *Literary Life*, I, p 226.
3. *The Autobiography of John Galt* (Edinburgh, 1833), II, p 220.
4. *Literary Life*, I, p 229.
5. *Literary Life*, I, p 157.
6. Mrs Oliphant, while characteristically condescending, was among the the first to grant this of Galt. She wrote:

   The miracle is . . . that the very same people are intolerable bores and vulgar nuisances in the real story of his life, whom here in fiction he makes the most amusing companions. Nothing more flat and vulgar than the autobiography, nothing more genuine, humorous, and original than the stories. In this way Galt is a greater wonder than Scott himself (*The Literary History of England in the end of the Eighteenth and beginning of the Nineteenth Century* (London, 1882), III, p 196).

7. In this respect there is a similarity between Galt and Jane Austen. *Emma* (1816) is a sustained study of the tension between self-delusion and truth, but Jane Austen's method of narration is more complex and indirect, with the irony pointed by the fluctuation of the narrative between external dramatisation and the subjective view-point of the heroine.
8. "A Scottish Documentary," *The Living Novel* (London, 1966), p 39.
9. All references give chapter and page in *Annals of the Parish,* edited with an introduction by James Kinsley (London, 1967).
10. Galt to Blackwood, 27 February 1821; in *Annals,* ed. Kinsley, p 206.

11. *See* also Ch. 47, p 193:

> . . . in the course of this current Ann. Dom. it pleased Heaven to visit me with a severe trial; the nature of which I will here record at length—the upshot I will make known hereafter.

12. *Lectures on Dramatic Art and Literature* (1808), translated by John Black (London, 1861), p 369.
    For a further comparable example see Ch. 14, pp 67-9, where Balwhidder's account of the decision to build the new school reveals that his active encouragement springs as much from fear that the church may be employed as a school as from concern for the children.
13. Ch. 10, p 53; Ch. 15, p 73; Ch. 17, pp 83-4; Ch. 22, p 106; Ch. 23, p 109; Ch. 40, pp 166-7.
14. Balwhidder writes:

> . . . when I thought of him, the spirited laddie, coming home from Jamaica, with his parrot on his shoulder, and his limes for me, my heart filled full, and I was obliged to sit down in the pulpit, and drop a tear (Ch. 23, p 110).

In the evocation of particular detail the lines recall Sterne. Significantly, it was Galt's intention—from which he was deflected by Blackwood—to dedicate *Annals* to Henry Mackenzie.

15. Unwittingly Balwhidder discloses that his feelings may not be fully reciprocated: Mrs Malcolm is called "unreasonable" (Ch. 19, p 94) for rejecting his offer to seek from Captain Macadam financial help towards Willie's training for the church, and this rare censure is proof of Balwhidder's hurt pride. Similarly, the reader comes to suspect that at least one reason for the enduring acquaintanceship—in which Balwhidder takes such pride—with Lord Eglesham is that the latter finds the minister's gaucherie entertaining.
16. There are recurrent indications in *Annals* of a conflict between Balwhidder's nature and his function, a dichotomy of man and clergyman. Erik Frykman has adduced various instances of the minister's inclinations triumphing over his doctrine (*John Galt's Scottish Stories 1820-1823* (Uppsala, 1959), pp 118-9).
17. *Literary Life*, I, pp 152-3.
18. Macskipnish—a caricature worthy of Smollett—instructs in the dances of the French court (Ch. 2, p 15); on the repeal of the Popish Bill, Jenny and Meg Gaffaw, the parish idiots, bring to Dalmailing a travesty of the national celebrations (Ch. 21, pp 102-3).
19. See also the claims made on behalf of Kibbock's policy of hilltop afforestation (Ch. 6, p 34).
20. Common to their fiction is detailed representation of life in the small community. There are biographical similarities too in that both tried to combine commercial and literary careers. Balzac, younger than Galt by twenty years, spent the period 1819-25 experimenting in fiction; and from 1825-8 he was involved in various ill-fated business ventures.

89

Balwhidder's fusion of world events with those of the parish is splendidly comic and unconsciously self-reductive. See further the first sentences of the accounts of 1762 and 1763 (Ch. 3 and 4, pp 16 and 21).

21. A. J. Ashley, "Coleridge on Galt," *Times Literary Supplement,* 25 September 1930, p 757; cited Ian A. Gordon, *John Galt: The Life of a Writer* (Edinburgh, 1972), p 51.

22. Often this effect is achieved by Galt's skilful juxtaposing of distinct kinds of language (see, for instance: "It pleased however Him, from whom cometh every good and perfect gift, to send at this time among us a Miss Sabrina Hookie . . . ff." (Ch. 9, pp 48-9).). The technique whereby orotundity is undermined by comic detail is reminiscent of Fielding's comic-epic mode.

23. The phrase is used by Jennie W. Aberdein, *John Galt* (London, 1936), p 102, and by Erik Frykman, *John Galt's Scottish Stories,* p 103.

24. Similarly, the connection with Lord Eglesham has a habit of producing effects that are not entirely to Balwhidder's advantage (most conspicuously in the visit to the Assembly).

25. *Literary Life,* I, p 153.

26. Arguably, some of the tensions are within the Scottish character. The attitude in Ch. 5 to which James Kinsley objects as "romantic posturing" (*Annals,* p xv) is not unknown in other Scottish writers (most obviously, Burns). Jeffrey discerned in Galt's novels

> representations of the characters and manners of the middling and lower orders in Scotland, intermingled with traits of sly and sarcastic sagacity, and occasionally softened and relieved by touches of unexpected tenderness and simple pathos, all harmonized by the same truth to nature and fine sense of national peculiarity. (*Edinburgh Review,* XXXIX, Oct. 1823, p 160).

27. James Kinsley has pointed out (*Annals,* p xi, n. 1) that Balwhidder is only half-way through his ministry when he regards the sermon of William Malcolm with misgivings on account of the loss of the "sober presbyterian simplicity (of) the plain auld Kirk of Scotland" (Ch. 30, p 132).

28. See also his response from the pulpit to the rising democratic sentiment: he writes that he "perceived that it would be of no effect to handle much the mysteries of the faith" (Ch. 35, p 147), and thus he had recourse to practical analogy. Elsewhere he has demonstrated and acknowledged his limitations in the exposition of "the mysteries of the faith," yet here he has deluded himself into the belief that it offered a genuinely alternative option.

29. George Kitchin, in a perceptive essay, related "the powerful jargon in which (Galt's) Scottish fiction excelled" to the covenanting heritage with its taste for "the exciting and mystical language of the Old Testament" ("John Galt," *Edinburgh Essays on Scots Literature,* with a preface by H. J. C. Grierson (Edinburgh, 1933), p 116).

John MacQueen has suggested that Balwhidder's language "clearly stems from education in a Scottish university at a period before the Enlightenment and the rise of polite letters" ("John Galt and the Analysis of Social History," *Scott Bicentenary Essays,* edited by Alan Bell (Edinburgh and London, 1973), p 334). Presumably Galt intends the reader to believe that Balwhidder was educated at Glasgow University in the seventeen-fifties. Alexander Carlyle of Inveresk attests to the liberalising influence exerted upon studies there two decades earlier by Francis Hutcheson and Dr Leechman (Alexander Carlyle, *Anecdotes and Characters of the Times,* edited with an introduction by James Kinsley (London, 1973), pp 43-4). Galt's point is that Balwhidder is impervious to all such influence.

30. Keith Costain, while recognising "a deft irony reminiscent of Jane Austen," proceeds, in relating Galt's view of "theoretical history" to the Scottish Realists, to identify Balwhidder's utterances with Galt (and hence to discount the irony) ("Theoretical History and the Novel: the Scottish Fiction of John Galt," *ELH,* XLIII, pp 342-65). The pervasive irony apart, it is unlikely that Galt, after almost two decades of commerce and travel, could endorse Balwhidder's views on progress. John MacQueen, in contrast, and in my view correctly, has argued that Galt and Balwhidder must be clearly differentiated ("John Galt and the Analysis of Social History").

31. *E.g.* Frykman, *John Galt's Scottish Stories,* p 120; Ian Jack, "John Galt," *English Literature 1815-1832* (Oxford, 1963), p 229.

32. *The Rhetoric of Fiction* (Chicago, 1961), pp 243-66.

33. *The Dehumanization of Art* (New York, 1956), p 35.

TOWN AND COUNTRY :
THE AYRSHIRE LEGATEES

IAN CAMPBELL

One of the more interesting products of the recent revival of interest in Galt has been the rescue, and partial republication by Elizabeth Waterston in Guelph, of the emigrant novel *Bogle Corbet*. Guelph was of course a product of Galt's organising zeal in 1824, and his memory is properly guarded in the excellent library facilities in its University—even if neighbouring Galt has been rather incomprehensibly renamed "Cambridge." Bogle Corbet founds and leads a Canadian colony very obviously based on Galt's own, and at the end of the third volume (the one chosen for re-publication) he philosophises:

> . . . Let me not be misunderstood; I have no cause to regret my emigration; I have only been too late. The man must indeed be strangely constituted, who above fifty emigrates for life, with the habits and notions of the old country rivetted upon him, and yet expects to meet with aught much better than discomfort. Emigration should be undertaken at that period when youths are commonly sent to trades and professions: the hardships are too heavy an apprenticeship for manhood, and to riper years penalty and privation.[1]

We can safely ascribe a good deal of this speech to its author's feelings, for Professor Waterston emphasises[2] the realism of this novel, as well as its autumnal atmosphere. *Bogle Corbet* appeared in 1831 when Galt's idealism had been sorely tried, and his travels too had been unsettling and unfulfilling.

Yet this point about the difficulty of adjustment to human nature is one which runs through his work, even when it does not find the pointed expression given it here in the embittered emigrant. Galt's novels are full of change, change affecting ministers and provosts, parliamentary members and members of the local aristocracy. And all change, while it makes for interesting reading, makes for adjustment and readjustment, for the overcoming of prejudice and perhaps for the tacit or explicit admission that there is a time for change, and a time of life when change may be very difficult or impossible.

Criticism of Galt has seen a welcome sharpening of focus on this matter. There was a time when readers pointed, quite rightly, to the way in which Galt captures the atmosphere of small-town Scotland in a relaxing way which gives some taste of its unchanging and trivial mood. Thus S. R. Crockett can write that ". . . there are no books in our national litera-ture which convey so melodious and continuous an impression of peace,"[3] and J. H. Millar of *The Provost* as without rival ". . . as a picture of everyday burghal life in Scotland, the life of which the external aspects are displayed in the columns of the provincial press."[4] Christopher North is much too intent on looking at Galt's social status *vis-à-vis* Lord Byron's, to do more than conventional justice to Galt as observer of the Scottish scene,[5] and even Francis Jeffrey's survey of Galt is hasty, praising *The Ayrshire Legatees* as perhaps unoriginal in conception, although ". . . the execution and details must be allowed to be original; and, along with a good deal of *twaddle,* and too much vulgarity," exhibiting strong powers of "humour, invention, and acute observation."[6]

The Ayrshire Legatees has attracted recent critical interest—including the sincerest compliment, that of re-publication[7]—which illustrates neatly the critical revaluation of Galt in full progress. No longer are we treated to eulogies on small-town observation in the novels, but the sharpness of Galt's vision is seen against the wider context of a time of change. Characters live out their local small-town existences, but the wider world seethes outside, threatening their com-fortable parish and sometimes overturning their happiness altogether. The Gudetown burghers who were pressed to the King's Navy will have felt this interruption keenly, as did the contending families in *The Entail,* balancing local contest with wider market values. People intrude into the abstract calcu-lations of change and progress. Like Scott, Galt has the ability to bring the abstract down to local level, to show how it affects people too localised, too poor, or too inflexible to cope with it. To borrow a phrase from John MacQueen, Balwhidder's failures as a person and a pastor in *Annals of the Parish* do not inhibit the success of the book:

> The very inadequacy of his responses defines the shape of events more penetratingly than investigations apparently more subtle.[8]

"The very inadequacy of his responses": implicit in this is a point which becomes very telling when we turn our critical attention on *The Ayrshire Legatees*. If Bogle Corbet found himself too old to adjust to Canada fully enough to enjoy happiness and freedom from strain, he still adjusted—inadequately. This is what emigration is all about, the uneasy coming to terms with the unfamiliar and the threatening. Emigrant Scotland has produced a whole literature from this feeling, the work of Scottish-Canadian novelists such as Robertson Knowles describing second- and third-generation settlers in Upper Canada unwillingly letting go of their Scottishness and forming new associations, new values, new estimates of which was not only right, but practicable.[9]

Bogle Corbet is a late novel, and only a partially successful one; as Maurice Lindsay reminds us, Galt's abiding concern in the literature of his successful period, like Scott's, was not with heroic pre-Jacobite Scotland, but with "the manners and modes of speech of small-town life which resisted the invasion of Anglifying influences longer than the cities."[10] Here, too, people struggled to control their responses to change, and to come to terms with the unfamiliarity of the new. Small-town Scotland may not contain the surprises of climate and wildlife that Upper Canada could offer, but *The Ayrshire Legatees* offers a few surprises of its own. Some are obvious: the comic devices which prolong the plot such as the over-righteous Mr Craig's fall from grace. Some are a little more subtle, like Rachel's changing loyalties from the long-standing friendships of Garnock to the "officer" whose increasing mention prepares us for the emotional engagement and eventual marriage to Captain Sabre. Least obvious, and critically much the most interesting, is the vivid characterisation of the letters the Ayrshire Legatees send home from London to

Garnock. Here lies the central difference between this novel and the more famous *Annals*: where Micah Balwhidder's character is sole filter of the events described there, and his responses (adequate and inadequate alike) are the vehicles by which change is seen and estimated, and our estimate of his character reflexively formed, here we have more than one character experiencing the change, and more than one character receiving and responding to their best estimate.

The Ayrshire Legatees may look like a slim book but it is an extraordinarily rich one. It passes experience from level to level, and comments on it throughout.

On one level, we have the Pringle family, wrenched from their familiar situation in the Manse of Garnock where "the Doctor" has been the respected minister for years. His managing but clumsy wife, his pert son Andrew whose ambitions plainly go beyond the parish boundaries of Garnock, his affectedly sentimental daughter Rachel go to make up a gallery of fairly predictable characters, and the debt to Smollet's *Humphry Clinker* has been often pointed out. As an episodic novel describing their adventures en route to London, awaiting details of the inheritance (which turns out to be enormous), enjoying metropolitan life with various amusing incidents, and returning to a rejoicing Garnock, *The Ayrshire Legatees* would merit our applause as a slight and successful piece to put alongside, say, *The Gathering of the West*.

On a second level, we have the sharply-depicted local life of Garnock, seen through the medium of those receiving, reading and listening to the letters from London. Already *The Ayrshire Legatees* is elevated to a higher plane than *The Gathering of the West* by this single device. Although the Garnock characters are relegated to a kind of secondary existence by the irrepressible Galt habit of the typecasting name — Mr Micklewham, Miss Eydent — their vitality triumphantly rescues them from "mere" typecasting. Captain Sabre, for all we hear of him from Rachel, suffers the same indignity—and he has far less impact on this book than the small-town gossips of Garnock.

This second level is suppressed during the reading of letters, and then emerges at once in Galt's typecasting responses which follow without break. The metropolitan world is always at second-hand *via* letters, the Garnock world at first-hand *via* personal responses (and usually unconsidered ones). Thus the two levels are counterpointed continuously not only in geographical setting, but in tone and intensity of response.

Galt's ingenuity in *The Ayrshire Legatees* does not stop at the creation of this two-level world. Behind them, shadowy but vitally important to the success of the book, stands a third. And we can best see it by returning to that "inadequacy of response" Galt gave to Balwhidder in *Annals of the Parish*. How, after all, do we recognise the inadequcy of his intellectual equipment, if Balwhidder is sole witness of the change? The reason, surely, lies in the implied and implanted evidence which Galt liberally strews in the reader's way to enable the reader, too, to join in the process of response and estimation. This is what makes nonsense of the argument that Balwhidder's narrowness makes Galt's view of his society too narrow to be of use.[11] Balwhidder's narrowness is transmitted not by his open admission (for which of us would recognise our true narrowness, let alone admit it?) but by implied weaknesses and failures, features which grow as he becomes older and less flexible. In his youth he resists tea-drinking, but the habit grows on him. In his youth the Churches are full, but his preaching fails to hold the liberated weavers, who defect either to more flexible Churches nearby, or to atheism. To their reasonable doubts and desire for change, Balwhidder can offer only ". . . my arguments, which were the old and orthodox proven opinions of the Divinity Hall,"[12] which of course are quite useless to stem the tide of change which brings bookshops and a widening of information and culture, an enlarging of intellectual horizons at all levels, and an eclipse of the Minister's power, even when paradoxically the patriarch Balwhidder is held in continued respect. When he retires, it is rightly seen as the end of an era, and although he pleasantly takes the marks of respect as being directed personally to himself, the audience sees rather the end of an era. It is not given to Balwhidder to see this kind of global vision, especially in his old age.

> . . . I felt no falling off in my powers of preaching; on the
> contrary, I found myself growing better at it, as I wa

enabled to hold forth, in an easy manner, often a whole
half hour longer than I could do a dozen years before.[13]

But when poor dottled Balwhidder retires to write his memoirs,
his parish is entering the nineteenth century with a vengeance,
and change is everywhere rushing on, leaving the minister to
his tranquil retirement. We know this, not through his
enfeebled writing (though Galt overlooks this detail in making
the actual *writing* of the supposed memoirs of good quality
throughout, showing no signs of intellectual decay) but
through the half-understood observations Balwhidder has been
passing on to us for fifty years. Roads, factories, fragmentation
of a unitary class-structure in a village, newspapers, universal
literacy, revolutionary ideas—they are observed passively by
the minister, only to be taken into account actively by the
reader, in a kind of unspoken conspiracy between Galt and
his reader—bypassing the inadequate responses of Balwhidder
altogether. It does not matter that he cannot see it when he
falls short of his duty, or when others make fun of him. What
matters is that the reader accepts his character as consistent,
including its shortcomings, and then feels free to estimate
Balwhidder for himself, making allowances for shortcomings.
This process occurs throughout *Annals of the Parish,* as it
does throughout *The Provost,* and does much to explain not
only the popularity of these books, but their enduring popularity when the changes they depict have sunk into the
commonplaces of history. The reader moves from a passive to
an active rôle: a third element is introduced. The character
of the narrator unfolds itself to the reader only slowly, and the
picture is complete only at the end. As each retires to a
continuing existence beyond the end of his annals, Minister
and Provost elude even the final summing-up the reader would
normally expect. Pawkie, certainly, shows more signs of life
than Balwhidder, and may live to interfere a good many
years yet in the affairs of Gudetown. Yet even old Balwhidder
has it in him to write the *Annals* in his enfeeblement—maybe
he was overdoing the picture of his infirmities a little?

The reader can no more escape involvement in this third
level of activity in *The Ayrshire Legatees* than he can in the
other two works. Slowly piecing together his picture of the
major protagonists, while picking up the thread of the local

plots in Garnock, he constantly revises and updates his estimates of the characters. In switching from London to Ayrshire, he cannot relax his faculties. Brought up short by unexpected and ludicrous contrasts, he sits up and takes notice. And if he relaxes, he can be the butt of fun much more subtle than the mere typecasting names which are sometimes so ludicrous as to be an open joke. Dr Pringle's first letter home is an outstanding case. They have reached Greenock

> . . . where we were obligated, by reason of no conveyance, to stop the Sabbath, but not without edification; for we went to hear Dr Drystour in the forenoon, who had a most weighty sermon on the tenth chapter of Nehemiah. He is surely a great orthodox divine, but rather costive in his delivery. In the afternoon, we heard a correct moral lecture on good works, in another Church, from Dr Eastlight—a plain man, with a genteel congregation. The same night we took supper with a wealthy family, where we had much pleasant communion together, although the bringing in of the toddy-bowl after supper, is a fashion that has a tendency to lengthen the sederunt to unseasonable hours (p 170).[14]

The satire is very rich here. Scottish readers may recognise in it satire of Greenock and its small-town pretensions to having more than one large church, with inter-church rivalry a prominent feature of town life. Students of ecclesiastical history will recognise the dig at the Auld Licht Dr Drystour with his all-too-typecasting name, versus the equally predictable New Light congregation of genteel new-thinking people. Even their preaching style is keyed to their theological position, faith versus works, though with a name like Zachariah, Dr Pringle's preference obviously is tilted in the direction of the Auld Kirk. The satire goes a good deal deeper, when we recognise Dr Pringle straying from strict sabbath observation when he is away from home, and absent-mindedly betraying himself to the congregation by his moral censure of toddy-bowls. Dr Pringle himself, we suspect from his letters, might well abstain from censure of others, particularly the preaching delivery of Dr Drystour. The Garnock readers will chuckle over his sharp observation of their richer neighbours, and the

Scottish reader will chuckle over Galt's witty parody of the Scottish theological scene at local level. But all readers will be taken in, unless they are careful, by the unobtrusive detail of Drystour's text, which is one of these uninviting chapters of the Old Testament which lists appalling genealogies of fathers begetting sons unto the tenth and twentieth generations. It would make a heart-stopping text for a sermon and Galt has slipped in the joke all but unobserved. The reader, too, is being laughed at, and does well to keep on his toes.

Where *The Ayrshire Legatees* gains in potential richness compared even with *Annals of the Parish* is in the complexity of the games Galt can play with his readers and his characters. He has two complete sets of characters to play off obliquely with his readers. The games are played according to quite complicated rules, and it is a fair generalisation to say that Galt's intention throughout is to create tensions, the resolution of which can seem to occur naturally as episode succeeds episode.

Some of these tensions are fairly obvious on the surface. Mr Craig is naturally unpopular among his fellow-parishioners for his extreme apparent rectitude: he must be brought down a peg or two by the end of the novel. Young Andrew Pringle too is unpopular, and even his verbally dull mother sees this and (in the author's preface to the first letter) administers what is for her an uncharacteristically acute dig:

"We see what you could be at, Andrew; ye're just wanting to come with us, and on this occasion I'm no for making step-bairns; so we'll a' gang thegither" (p 165).

A pushy young man, Andrew obviously clashes with his father, though their increasing wordliness (compared with his mother's country simplicity) makes the conflict more oblique. Andrew's references to his father as "the Doctor," and his father's to "Andrew Pringle, my son" indicate the truce that each strong character has declared with the other. It is not disharmony, so much as changing attitudes and ambitions, which make their worlds so different. Andrew's confidences are not to his mother, but to Snodgrass, like himself a young man educated beyond the limitations of Garnock. Significantly, even pallid Rachel needs a more worldly (though not more acute) hearer than her own parents. A wedge has been driven in this family by outside influence, by reading and social pressure, before they venture on the voyage to London. The epistolary form of the novel merely emphasises the extent to which the process has advanced. Rachel and Andrew are on the way out from Garnock values to more metropolitan values as surely as the educated weaver-lads in Cayenneville were moving away from Balwhidder's simple black-and-white world in Dalmailing. Like Rachel and Andrew the weavers had no need to travel to do so; the newly available books and newspapers, the improved attitudes and certitudes, were enough to set the process in motion.

And yet does this polarise the characters into "sympathetic" and "unsympathetic"? Hardly. Here Galt shows the surer touch of a considerable artist, when compared to Mrs Hamilton's immensely popular *The Cottagers of Glenburnie*. The slovenly McClarty family there, who "could na be fashed," are brainwashed throughout the novel by an interfering Mrs Mason (an English visitor) to new standards of dress and hygiene, and Mrs Mason has the satisfaction that when she retires, in old age, she witnesses a village on the way to modern standards in dress, behaviour and prosperity. But it is significant who has wrought the change. It has been a mixture of outside interference, and the triumph of the younger generation over the inflexibility of their parents' attitudes. It took time, of course, but Mrs Mason persevered.

> The habits acquired by such beings were not easily to be changed; for nothing is so intractable as stupidity. But Mrs Mason having discovered the root of the disease, judiciously applied the proper remedies.

She went straight for the children, and trained them to fill their leisure with spinning and weaving work. Her reward was to see the girls improve in "neatness and good-breeding";[15] and only Mrs McClarty stands out against the improvements to neatness, cleanliness and prosperity brought about by Mrs Mason. Throughout the closing chapters, Mrs Hamilton writes about schools, young men and women, the influence they have on their elders. Even though Mrs McClarty received the influence "too late to be of any use,"[16] the next generation obviously will be absorbed into the normality of a developing Britain. She grumbles at change to the end of the book; alone typifying the worst of the past, she is still unsympathetic to the end, so that passes with her.

Galt is much too subtle to indulge in this black-and-white view of change in society. If Rachel and Andrew are changing fast away from their parents' values, they are not changing into paradigms of all that is pleasant. On the contrary, Galt is careful to make a tension in the novel between their liberal, wider values and their narrow characters and unpleasant epistolary style. It is to the old Doctor and his wife that we turn for entertainment, and the village rightly sees the insecurity of Andrew's developing feelings, even if overstating the case in dismissing his letter as "a peesemeal of clishma-clavers" (p 205). Rachel's affected sentimental style deliberately repels us from too easy an identification with her character, and her attempts to conceal her growing emotional attachment to Sabre are pathetically weak. Significantly, Garnock people estimate the letters very shrewdly. Though Snodgrass is Andrew's confidant, like Andrew *in* Garnock but not *of* it, he feels able to communicate Andrew's confidences to the public eye, and the public eye is not deceived, any more than it is by the Doctor's sabbath-breaking, nor Mrs Pringle's open avarice and petty-mindedness. Yet how much more sympathetic observers the older generation are; we may smile in embarrassment when they attempt to remove the cab-driver's plate in order to "take his number" (p 177) or at the *naïveté* of their descriptions of Episcopalian worship (p 191), but in general they are just in their peasant shrewdness, and of course they have the quarter of a million inheritance to shelter them, and help them gain admittance whatever they want. They are not altogether representative provincials in the big city, but the *entrée* they have through their money, offsets the limitations of their observational powers. Like their children, the Pringles give the reader a jumbled mass of half-assimilated impression. The reader, armed with his increasing familiary with the Pringle family character, completes the observations himself.

Estimates certainly are made. "Andrew Pringle, my son" loses no time in cutting himself off from Garnock, joining in with Argent the lawyer's son (again the name is significant) and indeed eventually marrying Argent's daughter, and becoming an M.P. by the same route—money, not worth. Argent is what brings him through the process of adjusting from old Scottish to new British values. Similarly Rachel protests more loudly, but cuts herself off from her old values just as expeditiously. Captain Sabre brings social position, and she brings wealth—and again they are cut off from Garnock. Given the means by money and travel, these representative Young Scots prove themselves more than willing to become Young Britons—which is to say, to leave their early Scottish background and begin a new life in the South. Aware that he might have made his case too clear for artistic comfort, Galt plainly tries in the novel to correct the faults of the younger generation, and to make Andrew and Rachel more sympathetic as they, too, learn from their mistakes in London and even feel some regret for the life they are leaving behind. But on balance they show their response to change in a decisive cutting-off from Scotland. Galt, who had had to cut himself off from a lot of his familiar scenes in his youth, and would continue to do so through the force of necessity, must have written these characters with some personal feeling.[17]

The parents, on the other hand, make some adjustments. They learn through experience. Mrs Pringle, always canny, tries to spread her wings a little, and finds she is not at home in the freer, free-spending air of London. Too set in her ways, she cannot make a total transformation, and is plainly glad to be home, though equally glad to make use of her money to embark on a more comfortable lifestyle, so long as it is in the familiar scenery of Garnock. Like Boswell, she has felt the derision of the London crowd against a Scottish voice (p 207), and has come across the dishonesty of the London landlady lining her pockets at the expense of the ignorant provincial (p 198). London Sabbaths plainly grated on the nerves of both the older Pringles—though Galt slips in the scene where Mr Micklewham surprises Mr Snodgrass (Pringle's successor at Garnock Kirk) reading *Ivanhoe* on a Sunday morning (p 216) as an indication that change is inevitable.

Dr Pringle too has to learn by experience how far he can change and adjust to the new scenes of prosperity. He finds St Paul's disgusting, and he is as quickly exploited by the Saints (p 221) as his wife was by the milliners. Andrew Pringle has learned that ". . . man in London is not quite so good a creature as he is out of it" (p 241), and his father learns the same lesson, more slowly, and more expensively. Both the older people learn something provoking.

> The Englishers are sae obstinate in their own way, that I can get them to do nothing like Christians; and, what is most provoking of all, their ways are very good when you know them; but they have no instink to teach a body how to learn them (p 232).

Mrs Pringle is no fool.

And so the older ones go back to Garnock, a Garnock which has followed their rise to fame and fortune with sharp attention, and significantly welcomes them unstintingly. Garnock is no Glenburnie, frozen in the middle ages waiting for a reformer, but more and more like Dalmailing, in full flood of change.

> As the carriage drove along, the old men on the dikes stood up and reverently took off their hats and bonnets. The weaver lads gazed with a melancholy smile; the lassies on the carts clapped their hands with joy; the women on both sides of the street acknowledged the recognising nods; while all the village dogs, surprised by the sound of chariot wheels, came baying and barking forth, . . . (p 279).

Not frozen for the admiring eye but in the full flux of change, Garnock contains as easily the weaver looms (who will not be in Pringle's congregation, but who welcome his return and tolerate him as they did Balwhidder), as it does the older men to whom Pringle's status is unquestioned. The lasses do not envy a lifestyle they still have no hope of emulating. The carriage is an evident novelty, and the dogs still pester the street as they have done for centuries.

Into this, the novelist intrudes the new wealth to end the plot. Pringle can buy an adjacent manorhouse, and retire with his wife, opening the way for Mr Snodgrass. A few convenient marriages, and the Garnock sub-plot is neatly wound up. Andrew and Rachel are already forgotten in London. Garnock *wants* Dr Pringle back, as surely as Cross-Meikle wanted back Adam Blair, even in his disgrace. Galt, like Lockhart (and Scott) sees the indispensability of the minister to the total parish unit on which Scottish life still depended. Yet he introduces, as did Lockhart, an equivocal note into the status of the minister in his parish. Is Mr Snodgrass, with his furtive reading of *Ivanhoe,* not more likely to have a flexible outlook to deal with the weaver lads than Dr Pringle ever could? Surely yes, but then Dr Pringle now has the money to retire, and open the way for Mr Snodgrass. And he has the good sense to do so, too, for like Balwhidder he probably sees the writing on the wall, without fully appreciating its meaning. Pringle wears his wealth lightly, as he did his first name; James Moffatt sensibly saw, many years ago, that Galt knew how to handle Biblical subjects, being "too natural to drag them in."[18] Pringle makes little sacrifices, little concessions, in dress, in behaviour, in affectation, and of course he is humbled by his failure with the "Saints." Perhaps it is going a little too far to say, as one recent critic has, that "His provinciality is his character; his impervious innocence triumphs over the menacing depersonalization of the metropolis."[19] Certainly it does in London, but in Garnock the Pringle who is welcomed back so sincerely, and who is so transparently glad to be back, is not the Pringle who left. His dress and manners are different, and so—significantly—is the underlying intelligence which sees that he must vacate the Manse at once, for a younger and more flexible man. It took an absence from Garnock, an immersion in the wider world, to see this. That Galt happened to give him immense wealth is not really an easy way out, for no wealth could have given Dr Pringle the acuteness to get out when he did.

Bogle Corbet, writing his lonely diary in Guelph, reflected Galt's autumnal dissatisfaction with a life of change and travel. If fifty is too late an age to haul up roots and start a new style of living, it does not deny happiness—only settled contentment. But then Bogle did not have a quarter of a million pounds. With that help, the Pringles might have settled back happily to their pastoral ways in Garnock.

The argument here has been that Galt has pushed the discussion of Scottish contemporary affairs far beyond that easy conclusion, and far again beyond the simple reformation which Mrs Mason wrought on Glenburnie by importing foreign ideas. Garnock is changing despite Dr Pringle, and the change goes on, we surmise, right through his absence in London. The young change their ways, and the weavers come to outnumber the old farmers, by inexorable social change. The Church as Pringle knew it will have to change, or fossilise. The internal strife the change brought about is hinted at in distant Greenock, but no such division (foretaste of the 1843 Disruption) threatens Garnock, when Dr Pringle has the good sense, and the new vision, to see what he must do, and step down to live up to his wealth.

Is this typical? Of course not. Very few ministers have Dr Pringle's thousands. But through and around their little affairs, the Pringle family demonstrate a change overhanging the whole country in 1821. The defecting of the younger generation to London, the adjustment of Garnock to internal change, the graceful acceptance of change within limits by the old, the continuing harmony at parish level to cope with the enormously divisive effects of change, these are points made at local level, for universal consumption. By sharply setting up multiple layers of plot, and poking fun at everyone through his writing, Galt holds the reader's attention most skilfully while making his social points. But then it was Galt himself who made the famous observation that "Fables are often a better way of illustrating philosophical truths than abstract reasoning" (p 291), and in *The Ayrshire Legatees* he triumphantly demonstrated the truth of his own maxim.

NOTES

1. John Galt, *Bogle Corbet*, ed. E. Waterston (New Canadian Library no. 135) (Toronto, 1977), p 198.
2. Pp 4-7.
3. Quoted from D. Storrar Meldrum's edition of Galt, with introduction by Crockett: the *Annals* were bound in with *The Ayrshire Legatees* (Edinburgh and London, 1895), p xvii.
4. J. H. Millar, *A Literary History of Scotland* (London, 1903), p 557.
5. In the *Noctes Ambrosianae* for November 1830.
6. F. Jeffrey, *Contributions to "The Edinburgh Review"* (second edition, London, 1846), III, p 116.
7. By James Thin in The Mercat Press (Edinburgh, 1978), in facsimile of an 1895 MacMillan edition.
8. John MacQueen, "John Galt and the Analysis of Social History," *Scott Bicentenary Essays*, ed. Alan Bell (Edinburgh and London, 1973), pp 332-42: quotation from p 334.

9. An example would be Knowles' *St Cuthbert's,* the episodic account of an *émigré* Scot minister in Canada.
10. Maurice Lindsay, *History of Scottish Literature* (London, 1977), p 320.
11. For the most cogent statement of this argument see David Craig, *Scottish Literature and the Scottish People* (London, 1961), p 158.
12. John Galt, *Annals of the Parish,* ed. J. Kinsley (London, 1967), p 129.
13. *Annals,* p 202.
14. Although it is out of print, the text here used is of the Everyman edition of the *Annals, The Ayrshire Legatees* and selections of the *Literary Life* (London, 1910, 1937), with page references in parentheses after each quotation.
15. Elizabeth Hamilton, *The Cottagers of Glenburnie* (Edinburgh, 1808), p 392.
16. *Cottagers of Glenburnie,* p 394.
17. The best account of Galt's life at this time is in I. A. Gordon, John Galt, *The Life of a Writer* (Edinburgh and Toronto, 1972), pp 27-32,
18. James Moffatt, *The Bible in Scots Literature* (London, n.d.), p 226.
19. Francis R. Hart, *The Scottish Novel, A Critical Survey* (London, 1978), p 34.

RINGAN GILHAIZE
AND PARTICULAR PROVIDENCE

JOHN MACQUEEN

The social and economic developments analysed in *Annals of the Parish,*[1] *The Provost* and *The Entail* have their roots in the period of the Reformation. R. H. Tawney's account of Puritanism and the rise of English capitalism is very relevant:

"The capitalist spirit" is as old as history, and was not, as has sometimes been said, the offspring of Puritanism. But it found in certain aspects of later Puritanism a tonic which braced its energies and fortified its already vigorous temper. At first sight, no contrast could be more violent than that between the iron collectivism, the almost military discipline, the remorseless and violent rigours practised in Calvin's Geneva, and preached elsewhere, if in a milder form, by his disciples, and the impatient rejection of all traditional restrictions on economic enterprise which was the temper of the English business world after the Civil War. In reality, the same ingredients were present throughout, but they were mixed in changing proportions, and exposed to different temperatures at different times. Like traits of individual character which are suppressed till the approach of maturity releases them, the tendencies in Puritanism, which were to make it later a potent ally of the movement against the control of economic relations in the name either of social morality or of the public interest, did not reveal themselves till political and economic changes had prepared a congenial environment for their growth. Nor, once those conditions were created, was it only England which witnessed the transformation. In all countries alike, in Holland, in America, in Scotland, in Geneva itself, the social theory of Calvinism went through the same process of development. It had begun by being the very soul of authoritarian regimentation. It ended by being the vehicle of an almost Utilitarian individualism. While social reformers in the sixteenth century could praise Calvin for his economic rigour, their successors in Restoration England, if of one persuasion, denounced him as the parent of economic licence, if of another, applauded Calvinist communities for their commercial enterprise, and for their freedom from antiquated prejudices on the subject of economic morality. So little do those who shoot the arrows of the spirit know where they will light.

> (*Religion and the Rise of Capitalism,*
> London, 1926, 4, ii; Penguin edition,
> pp 225-26).

Scottish developments differed significantly from those in England, but even so small an example from fiction as Davie Deans's admonition to his daughter in *The Heart of Midlothian*—"If you neglect your warldly duties in the day of affliction, what confidence have I that ye mind the greater matters that concern salvation?"—shows that they had something in common.

Galt himself remained a Calvinist to the end of his days, a Calvinist whose theological presuppositions had in some degree been modified by Newtonian physical science. In Calvin's theology, predestination and providence were central and related doctrines; sometimes at least, predestination was regarded as a special application of the divine providence. Providence, in turn, operated in three ways, through the order of nature, by special external acts; and by the interior operation of the Holy Spirit.

> The world is governed by God, not only in that he maintains the course of the world in being such as he established it all at once; but in that he has a particular care for each creature. . . . It is a perversity to want to hide and obscure . . . the special providence of God, which is so well and plainly shown to us by clear and certain testimonies of scripture that it is a wonder how anyone can doubt it.

> (*Institutes* I. 16. 4., quoted in F. Wendel,
> *Calvin,* translated by Philip Mairet,
> London, 1965, p 180).

In this tradition, Galt saw himself as a consistent predestinarian who, when he analysed the hypotheses to which he gave willing intellectual assent, was forced to deny the doctrine of a particular providence. His verses include such extended philosophical pieces as *The Demon of Destiny* (1839). "I proclaim myself openly a predestinarian," he proclaimed in a chapter of *The Literary Life and Miscellanies* (1834), a chapter entitled "Fatalism, and Particular Providence," in which he continued:

In the order of things and the succession of events, the providence of God is constantly seen; and such is the harmony of the universe, that the smallest occurrence affects its whole frame and system.

The simplest form in which we can contemplate providence, is by considering the whole universe as one machine. It consists of parts, each an entire thing of itself, endowed with distinct qualities, and placed in such a situation with respect to others, that it is constantly acted upon by them, and reacts upon them at the same time. Every part is subject to the principles or laws of its own particular organisation, as well as to those of the universe, and every part is essential to the accomplishment of the object for which the whole was formed.

The tact of human sense is not sufficiently fine to discover the principle of motion, we only know of its existence by effects; but there is no fact in existence of which the mind is more assured, than that every thing hath both an individual and a universal motion. The individual motion consists of augmentation or diminution of growth or of decay; and the universal motion consists of the revolutions which the thing as a part of the universe performs, in connexion with the other parts.

If, therefore, the universe consists of things in motion, arranged according to a plan, it must also be allowed that the action of one thing upon another will produce an effect previously determined. This is the law of necessity, philosophical fatality, religious predestinarianism; but it is not according to the doctrine of a particular Providence.

(I, 287-8)

In *Annals of the Parish* especially Galt is concerned with the smallest occurrences in relation to the general body of world events. The relationship is established, not in terms of the principle of motion, but in terms of effects—how small occurrences affect, and still more how they are affected by, the whole frame and system of society. That is why the novels of a widely travelled man, who spent much of his life outside Scotland, concern themselves so markedly with Scottish local affairs, and the local affairs of Scotsmen overseas. Galt recognised the significance of small events in the destinal scheme.

Annals of the Parish commences at a period when the 1690 settlement and the conditions of the later seventeenth century had suffered the minimum of disturbance—when in Ayrshire at least religion had scarcely begun the transformation to capitalism. Galt makes it very clear that Scotland in general, and the parish in particular, were prepared by the prevailing Calvinism for the changes which overtook them during Balwhidder's ministry. Calvinism itself is a factor which Galt does not over-emphasise, but which is certainly, even universally, present. Covenanting stubbornness and individualism go far to explain the success of such people as Mr Kibbock, Mr Cayenne, and the second Mrs Balwhidder. In *Annals of the Parish* however Galt more assumes than analyses these qualities.

In 1823 Galt published his three-volume *Ringan Gilhaize*, with its subtitle "The Times of the Covenanters," the novel in which he extended his historical scope to analyse the Calvinistic character, and some of its effects on Scotland. The distinctive technique developed in *Annals of the Parish* assumed further importance. In *Annals of the Parish,* Galt as ultimate narrator almost invariably operated on a level quite distinct from that of Balwhidder, the assumed narrator, and so enabled the reader to gain the minister's perspective, as well as that of Galt, on the emergence of more enlightened times from what in Scotland was still the last stage of Reformation conflicts. This double perspective is the chief source of irony. A similar technique recurs throughout the series of fictitious autobiographies—*The Provost,* for instance, *Lawrie Todd, The Member* and *The Radical*—which Galt produced in the twenties and thirties of the nineteenth century. In *Ringan Gilhaize* it received its most symphonic development—again, in a novel which deals with a revolutionary change in social structure and intellectual history, the transformation of the hierarchical Catholic Scotland of the earlier sixteenth century, to the impoverished, obsessed, egalitarian middle class Calvinistic society of the late seventeenth century, the society which fifty years later had prepared itself to be again transformed by the Agricultural and Industrial revolutions. The period covered—from the 1550s to 1690—is beyond the reach of any single human memory, and in the first part of the book Galt adopts not a double but a triple perspective, relating in the person of the seventeenth century Covenanter and Cameronian, Ringan Gilhaize, the events of the mid-sixteenth century, of which he had gained knowledge by conversations in boyhood with his grandfather, Michael Gilhaize, who died, he relates, at the advanced age of ninety-one years, seven months and four days, at a time when he was himself eight years old.

In the first part of the book, Galt tells the story of Michael Gilhaize by the mouth of Ringan; in the second, Ringan describes his own experiences. In the earlier section the reader remains conscious of Ringan as intermediary, but Galt successfully distinguishes between the style of grandfather and grandson. "It is a thing past all contesting," Ringan begins, "that, in the Reformation, there was a spirit of far greater carnality among the champions of the cause, than among those who in later times so courageously, under the Lord, upheld the unspotted banners of the Covenant" (I.i.1), and the presence or absence of carnality in itself sufficiently distinguishes the two parts. At the beginning, for instance, there are virtually no biblical quotations; the second part abounds with precise biblical references. "My father chose the lxxvi psalm, and when it was sung, he opened the Scriptures in second Kings, and read aloud, with a strong voice, the xxiii chapter, and every one likened Josiah to the old King, and Jehoahaz to his son Charles, by whose disregard of the Covenant the spirit of the land was then in such tribulation" (II.xii.119). The most notable series of references occurs in the third volume, where Ringan, at least partially recovered from the madness which followed the murder by dragoons of his wife and daughters, and the destruction of his home at Quharist, consults the Word on his first personal encounter with the outlawed Cameronians. The son to whom he refers, Joseph, his only surviving child:

But though my spirit clove to theirs, and was in unison with their intent, I could not but doubt of so poor a handful of forlorn men, though it be written, that the race is not to the swift nor the battle to the strong, and I called to my son to bring me the Book, that I might be instructed from the Word what I ought at that time to do, and when he had done so I opened it, and the twenty-second chapter of Genesis met my eye, and I was awed and trembled, and my heart was melted with sadness and an agonising grief. For the command to Abraham to sacrifice Isaac his only son, whom he so loved, on the mountains in the land of Moriah, required me to part with my son, and to send him with the Cameronians; and I prayed with a weeping spirit and the imploring silence of a parent's heart, that the Lord would be pleased not to put my faith to so great a trial.

I took the Book again, and I opened it a second time, and the command of the sacred oracle was presented to me in the fifth verse of the fifth chapter of Ecclesiastes—

"Better is it that thou shouldst not vow, than that thou shouldst vow and not pay."

But still the man and the father were powerful with my soul; and the weakness of disease was in me, and I called my son towards me, and I bowed my head upon his hands as he stood before me, and wept very bitterly and pressed him to my bosom, and was loath to send him away.

He knew not what caused the struggle wherewith he saw me moved, and he became touched with fear lest my reason was again going from me. But I dried my eyes, and told him it was not so, and that maybe I would be better if I could compose myself to read a chapter. So I again opened the volume, and the third command was in the twenty-sixth verse of the eighth chapter of St Matthew:

"Why are ye fearful, O ye of little faith?"

(III.xix, 175-7)

The direct consequence of Ringan's adherence to his own particular providence, as he interprets it, is the death of Joseph and the mutilation of his body. Ringan hears of it when he is imprisoned with other Presbyterians in the Edinburgh tolbooth:

At that moment a shriek of horror rose from all then looking out, and every one recoiled from the window. In the same instant a bloody head on a halbert was held up to us.—I looked—I saw the ghastly features, and I would have kissed those lifeless lips; for, O! they were my son's.
(III.xx, 195).

Galt is fully capable of tackling the savageries of seventeenth century history, and indeed, for a modern reader, one of the most convincing aspects of the book is the depiction of the way in which a totalitarian society affects its adherents and, still more, its opponents. It was this realism, presumably, which denied the book any popularity with Galt's contemporaries, and ensured its neglect by the Victorian and Edwardian reading public. But although the twentieth century has become more accustomed to cruelty, in life as in literature, there is still little sign of new interest. It is obsession however, rather than cruelty, which gives point to the first passage quoted. Galt, as has been mentioned, was a predestinarian within the Newtonian system of mechanics. Ringan is a predestinarian of more theological ancestry, who believes to obsession that he is singled out by a particular providence to play the rôle which he completes with the assassination of Claverhouse after the victory of Killiecrankie. The entire course of his life—when he listened to his grandfather's stories of the Reformation, when he took part in the Pentland raid, when he was wounded by Claverhouse at Drumclog, when the members of his family one by one were destroyed—is directed, he believes, to a single end, the destruction of the prelatical House of Stewart, and its most dedicated upholder, Claverhouse.

The process began long before Ringan's birth in the struggle waged by John Knox and the Lords of the Congregation against the Queen Regent and her daughter, Queen Mary, but the completion is delayed for more than a century and Ringan Gilhaize is reserved to strike the final blow:

I took off my bonnet, and kneeling with the gun in my hand, cried, "Lord, remember David and all his afflictions;" and having so prayed, I took aim as I knelt, and Claverhouse raising his arm in command, I fired. In the same moment I looked up, and there was a vision in the air as if all the angels of brightness, and the martyrs in their vestments of glory, were assembled on the walls and battlements of heaven to witness the event,—and I started up and cried, "I have delivered my native land!" But in the same instant I remembered to whom the glory was due, and falling again on my knees, I raised my hands and bowed my head as I said, "Not mine, O Lord, but thine is the victory."

(III.xxxiii, 308).

Gilhaize's belief is of course central to the Calvinism which gained control over Scotland, not so much in the time of John Knox as in that of his spiritual heir, Andrew Melville (1545-1622). Melville spent much of his early life in Geneva, and his *Second Book of Discipline* (1587) was the effectual instrument by which the church in Scotland became Calvinist rather than merely Protestant. Biblical oracles were regarded by men like Gilhaize as the means by which God communicated his purposes to the elect; these texts, chosen apparently at random, were central to the predestinal scheme as it affected certain individuals, highly-favoured, not in terms of worldly prosperity or happiness, but simply because God has chosen and shaped them to be his particular instruments. God shapes Ringan Gilhaize, partly by the influence of his grandfather, and to a lesser extent his father; still more by the harsh series of events which make up his life, and which, in his own words, turn his spirit into iron and his heart into stone—the flight from Rullion Green, his various imprisonments and exiles, his wound at Drumclog, the destruction of his family. All this is justified, as it were, because it resulted finally in the expulsion of the Stewarts, and in particular because it prepared Ringan to become the assassin of Claverhouse, the only man capable of restoring the Stewart fortunes, a man, too, who in Cameronian eyes had sold himself into the power of Satan. In one sense, the death of Claverhouse is almost like that of Evandale in *Old Mortality,* a cowardly murder; from another, it is the climax of the struggle between the powers of darkness and light. The latter certainly is how Gilhaize himself views it.

In his own eyes, Gilhaize, like his fellow Cameronians,

avoids carnality because he acts in full submission to the will of God, and is prepared to abrogate all claims of the flesh, even when the claims are on behalf of his own youngest, and last surviving, son, appropriately named Joseph.

In his own eyes—but one must bear in mind the double, and even triple, perspective of the novel—Gilhaize sees his task as war with the worshippers of the Beast and his Image, a war to which Galt, as opposed to Gilhaize, owed no allegiance whatsoever. Galt was aware of the extent to which the Calvinist elect were capable of self-deception and even hypocrisy. The reader is not intended, for instance, to take even a passage like the following simply at face value. Gilhaize sees some part of the truth, and he retains the reader's full sympathy, but he certainly exaggerates the importance of his own actions:

> Many a time yet, when I remember that night, do I think with wonder and reverence of our condition. An infirm grey-haired man, with a deranged head and a broken heart, going forth amidst the winter's wind, with a little boy, not passing thirteen years of age, to pull down from his throne the guarded King of three mighty kingdoms, —and we did it,—such was the doom of avenging justice and such the pleasure of Heaven. But let me proceed to rehearse the trials I was required to undergo before the accomplishment of that high predestination.

> (III.xviii, 166-7).

The last word, of course, is particularly significant, but almost equally significant is the reference to the deranged head. Throughout the book, as will have become evident, the suggestion recurs that Gilhaize is not wholly responsible for his actions, that in some degree he is mentally deranged. As a consequence of the discovery that his wife and daughters had been raped and murdered by the dragoons, he becomes for six or eight months clinically mad. Even during his childhood there were such incidents as his over-reaction to his father's account of the reading of the liturgy in Edinburgh—"I . . . was thrilled with an unspeakable fear; and all the dreadful things, which I had heard my grandfather tell of the tribulations of his time, came upon my spirit like visions of the visible

115

scene, and I began to weep with an exceeding sorrow."
(II.x, 98). Later (II.xxviii, 279), there is his equally violent,
if prophetic, reaction to the discovery of the dead child after
Rullion Green, and to his escape, with his wife's help, from
prison (III.iii, 19-23)—a violence showing, I suggest, his own
subconscious urge to the destruction of his family and friends.
Gilhaize combines strong family affection with what might
almost be regarded as a schizophrenic impulse towards
solitariness and destruction, an urge which readily identifies
itself with the "purification" which was central to the protestant
Reformation in its more extreme forms. A significant phrase
which occurs almost at the end of the book, is "The godly
people of Edinburgh . . . rose, as it were with one accord . . .
and purified the chapel, even to desolation" (III.xxviii, 262)
—that is, they reduced it to ruins. Gilhaize purifies his life
in an almost identical way.

Nor is this the only way in which Galt qualifies Gilhaize's
opinion of his own principles and actions. Occasionally his
methods approach caricature, as in the snatch of dialogue
between Nanse Snoddie and Robin Fullarton:

> "What's te prelates, Robin Fullarton?" said auld Nanse
> Snoddie, turning round to John's son, who was standing
> behind his father.
> "They're the red dragons o' unrighteousness," replied
> the sincere laddie with great vehemence.
> "Gude guide us!" cried Nanse with the voice of terror;
> "and has the King daur't to send sic accursed things to
> devour God's people?"
>
> (II.x, 103).

The sheer ignorance of anything but biblical texts which
underlies Nanse's reaction is not without relevance for the
Covenanters as a group. Galt too is at pains to emphasise the
narrow limits, social and geographic as well as intellectual, of
the world within which the Covenanters exist. Michael Gilhaize had moved freely, and as a matter of course, over the
length and breadth of Scotland. He was acquainted with
queens, regents, archbishops and earls, and was equally
familiar with a baillie's family in Crail and the expelled nuns
who established the maidenly character of the Kirkgate in

Irvine. It was Michael nevertheless who chose of set policy to limit the outlook and experience of his descendants when he settled at Quharist in Ayrshire. His intentions were good. The corruption of courtly life was already beginning to affect him when he saw the group of Edinburgh labourers who gave form to his resolution:

> Hitherto he had never noted, or much considered, the complicated cares and trials wherewith the lot of man in every station is chequered and environed; and when he heard these bondmen of hard labour, jocund after sound slumbers and light suppers, laughing contemptuously as they beheld the humiliating sight, which divers gallants and youngsters, courtiers of the court, degraded with debauch, made of themselves as they stumbled homeward, he thought there was surely more bliss in the cup that was earned by the constancy of health and a willing mind, than in all the possets and malvesia that the hoards of ages could procure. So he composed his spirit, and inwardly made a vow to the Lord, that, as soon as the mighty work of the redemption of the Gospel from the perdition of papistry was accomplished, he would retire into the lea of some pleasant green holm, and take, for the purpose of his life, the attainment of that happy simplicity which seeks but the supply of the few wants with which man comes so rich from the hands of his Maker, that all changes in his natural condition of tilling the ground and herding the flocks only serve to make him poorer by increasing.

> (I.xvii, 184-5).

This passage typifies the change from the old pre-Reformation Scotland to the new Israel, and it is not accidental that the paragraph immediately following describes the arrival of John Knox and his servant in Edinburgh. Galt, in the person of Gilhaize, is indicating the extent to which—and the motives for which—post-Reformation Scotland deliberately turned its back on the cosmopolitan sophistication of the pre-Reformation period to become local, introverted and Hebraic. Once again the idea of purification to desolation has some relevance. The seventeenth century world of Ringan Gilhaize is a harsher version of the parochial world in which the Rev. Micah Balwhidder later took up his ministry, and it was by the action of Michael Gilhaize and others like him that the world of *Annals of the Parish* came into being. Quharist, the name of Gilhaize's home, means "Where is it?" and so emphasises the obscurity of the place on which so much of the action of the novel centres. The experience of *Ringan Gilhaize* includes a gradually increasing sense of claustrophobia. The obsessional quality in Ringan himself gains much of its power from this sense.

Not all Scotland is presented as insane or obsessed. The voice of reason is most nearly represented by Deacon Fulton of Paisley, who helped Gilhaize and Esau Wardrop to escape from the council chamber where they had been imprisoned after the Pentland rising:

> "True, true, we are a' Covenanters," replied the deacon, "and Gude forbid that I should e'er forget the vows I took when I was in a manner a bairn; but there's an unco difference between the auld covenanting and this Lanerk New-light. In the auld times, our forebears and our fathers covenanted to show their power, that the king and government might consider what they were doing. And they betook not themselves to the sword, till the quiet warning of almost all the realm united in one league had proved ineffectual; and when at last there was nae help for't, and they were called by their conscience and dangers to gird themselves for battle, they went forth in the might and power of the arm of flesh, as weel as of a righteous cause. But, sirs, this donsie business of the Pentland raid was but a splurt, and the publishing of the Covenant, after the poor folk had made themselves rebels, was, to say the least o't, a weak conceit."

(III.vi, 49-50).

I have already commented that Ringan Gilhaize at no point totally loses the reader's sympathy, and it is noteworthy that here even the unfanatical voice of reason is in favour of action. It is the manner, not the fact, to which the deacon raises objections, and he is prepared to assist the prisoners' escape after their capture. In the context of the book however it becomes clear that the deacon's rationality offers no immedi-

118

ately effective instrument for the restoration of liberty in Scotland. The existence of such men encourages hope for the future; on the other hand, it is by men like Gilhaize that a time is created in which the deacon's commonsense will have scope to flourish, a time such as is analysed in *Annals of the Parish, The Provost* and *The Entail.* Deacon Fulton is a more attractive character than Mr Kibbock, Provost Pawkie or Claud Walkinshaw, but their spiritual kinship is clear. And although Ringan Gilhaize is a half-mad fanatic, the vision of the future which he sees before Rullion Green has a strong element of truth in it: "I yet had a blessed persuasion that the event would prove in the end a link in the chain, or a cog in the wheel, of the hidden enginery with which Providence works good out of evil" (II.xxv, 251). For Galt, the events of the Covenant, and the personalities of the Covenanters, were the necessary prelude to the awakening of the later eighteenth century. Gilhaize was not the chosen instrument of a particular providence, but he was one of the many links by means of which the general destinal forces of the world worked towards their ultimately benevolent conclusions.

[1] See J. MacQueen, "John Galt and the Analysis of Social History" in A. Bell (*ed.*), *Scott Bicentenary Essays* (Edinburgh & London, 1973), pp 332-342.

RINGAN GILHAIZE
A NEGLECTED MASTERPIECE ?

PATRICIA J. WILSON

John Galt thought well of *Ringan Gilhaize: or the Coven-anters* (1823), his first historical novel, and the first novel published for him by Oliver and Boyd, but it has never been among his more popular works. Galt was disappointed at the reception of the work in his own lifetime and consoled himself "that whatever may be the blindness of the present age, thank God there will be a posterity—"[1]

The interest of posterity was at first slow to justify his faith. After the three volume edition of 1823, the novel did not reappear until between 1881 and 1883 when a single volume edition, entitled *Ringan Gilhaize or The Times of the Covenanters,* was printed by the Glasgow printers Dunn and Wright in a short excursion into publishing. The change in the sub-title was not acknowledged, and there was neither introduction nor foreword to indicate that the original novel had been most conscientiously bowdlerised to suit Victorian taste.[2] The first single volume edition of real interest was that of 1899, edited and with an introduction by Sir George Douglas, who, two years earlier had written an appreciative essay[4] on Galt in which he commended *Ringan Gilhaize.* In 1936 came the two volume edition of *Ringan Gilhaize* with an introduction by William Roughead.[5]

Sir George Douglas noting that *Ringan Gilhaize* was Galt's own favourite concludes that for once Galt "knew when he had done his best," and it is he who unhesitatingly gives his introduction to the novel the title "A Neglected Masterpiece." Roughead is extremely sensitive to the skill with which Galt handles his materials. He admires *Ringan Gilhaize* as a tour de force, but ultimately prefers Galt in homelier vein.

Today *Ringan Gilhaize* is being looked at with renewed interest. It forms the obvious third novel in the trilogy of important nineteenth-century Scottish novels dealing with the Covenanters. Sir Walter Scott's *Old Mortality*[6] is available in the Penguin English Library Series. James Hogg's *The*

120

Brownie of Bodsbeck[7] was republished in 1976, edited and with an informative and scholarly introduction by Douglas Mack. *Ringan Gilhaize* is not yet available in a new edition, but already both literary scholars and students of history are giving it serious critical attention, and pronouncing favourably on it. It seems in this bicentenary year appropriate to repeat one of the most laudatory comments so far made.

[*Ringan Gilhaize*] is a fine novel in its own right, and as a criticism of *Old Mortality* it makes it impossible for us to take Scott's presentation of history seriously.[8]

Earlier in his *English Literature 1815-1832,* Ian Jack found "a technical expertise or sophistication about *Ringan Gilhaize* which is seldom to be found in Scott," and more recently Francis Hart, discussing the difference in the mode of characterisation between *Old Mortality* and *Ringan Gilhaize* suggests that "Scott belongs with the older mode of allegorical fable and Galt with the newer romantic one of symbolic naturalism."[9] Galt would have felt his faith in posterity wholly justified.

Writing of his novel, he says

The history of *Ringan Gilhaize* is curious. The book itself was certainly suggested by Sir Walter Scott's *Old Mortality,* in which I thought he treated the members of the Presbyterian Church with too much levity, and not according to my impressions derived from the history of that time. Indeed, to tell the truth I was hugely provoked that he, the descendant of Scott of Harden, who was fined in those days forty thousand pounds Scots for being a Presbyterian, or rather for countenancing his lady for being so, should have been so forgetful of what was due to the spirit of that epoch, as to throw it into what I felt was ridicule.[10]

Nor was this the first of Galt's expressions of disapproval for even before *Ringan* was published he makes a character say that in *Old Mortality* ". . . True Presbyterians conceived that [Scott] had laid an irreverent hand on the ark of our great national cause, the Covenant. . . ."[11]

It was Sir George Douglas in his introduction to *Ringan* who first put his finger on the real difference between Galt's approach and that of Scott:

> . . . Galt laid bare the soul of the Covenanting movement [which] . . . Scott in *Old Mortality* most signally failed to do.

Writing at greater length, Douglas says:

> . . . into the spirit of the particular movement with which he deals, it must be acknowledged that Galt has pene-trated further than Scott. For the true aim of a writer of a novel treating of these times in Scotland was obviously to disregard such a non-essential as sporadic insincerity, to penetrate the outer crust of dourness and intolerance, and whilst maintaining the balance of perfect fairness, to compel the reader to sympathise with the best of the Covenanters, not only in their bitter resentment of cruel wrongs, but in their most earnestly cherished and loftiest ideals. And this, *which Scott did not care to do,* Galt has accomplished . . . [my emphasis][12]

And in this accomplishment lies one of the crucial differ-ences between *Ringan Gilhaize* and *Old Mortality,* for, as Charles Swann rightly says, we cannot from a reading of *Old Mortality* see why anyone might want to be a Covenanter, whereas

> By choosing to tell Ringan's story in the first person Galt is claiming that he can imaginatively repossess the past.[13]

Galt would have appreciated this response. In his *Literary Life* he writes of the mode of narration he used in *Ringan Gilhaize.*

> I have supposed a Covenanter relating the adventures of his grandfather, who lived during the Reformation. It was therefore necessary that I should conceive distinctly what a Covenanter would think of a Reformer in the church, to enable him to relate what such a person would do in the

time of John Knox. There was here, if I may be allowed the expression, a transfusion of character that could only rightly be understood by showing how a Reformer himself acted and felt in the opinion of a Covenanter. To enable the reader to estimate the invention put forth in the work, and to judge of the manner in which the Covenanter performed his task, I made him give his autobiography, in which was kept out of view everything that might recall the separate existence of John Galt. But I cannot have succeeded in my object; not one person has ever evinced an apprehension of the intention which I thought would have attracted consideration, and yet I do not see myself that I have failed in my object.[14]

Blackwood had urgently and on several occasions tried to persuade Galt to write *The Entail,* the novel which immediately preceded *Ringan Gilhaize,* in the first person, which mode he thought was particularly Galt's forte. Galt had resisted the pressure as far as *The Entail* was concerned, but when he moved to Oliver and Boyd, and set about writing his next novel, it is as though he raised to the power two the difficulties of telling a story in the first person, and was disappointed that no one noticed that in the undertaking he had, to continue the metaphor, achieved success squared.

Failed in his object he has not. From the first sentence of the novel Galt makes us aware of the different tone of the two periods. He makes the Covenanting grandson Ringan Gilhaize begin with these words:

It is a thing past all contesting, that, in the Reformation, there was a spirit of far greater carnality among the champions of the cause than among those who in later times so courageously, under the Lord, upheld the unspotted banners of the Covenant.[15]

Ringan is slightly uneasy about the laxity of earlier days but knows it will not become him "to brag of the [Covenanters'] motives and intents as higher and holier than those of the great elder Worthies of 'the Congregation'." (I, p 1) He has nevertheless deduced the fact as he grew up in a different age from that of his grandfather who is the source of his information. The old man also comments on the spirit of greater carnality when he says he had often thought in later life that there had been a woeful immorality in a vintner's wife having been jocose with him on the very day a martyr had been burned in St Andrews:

> . . . but at that time he was not so over straitlaced as to take offence at what she said; indeed, as he used to say, sins were not so heinous in those papistical days as they afterwards became, when men lost faith in penance, and found out the perils of purchased pardons. (I, p 49)

The old man's simple acceptance allows him to accommodate himself to the change he has helped to bring about. Ringan is less comfortable about some of the facts he has to relate.

> . . . on Sunday, the 9th of February, A.D. 1567, [the Queen] parted from [Darnley] to be present at a masking in the palace; for the Reformation had not then so penetrated into the habits and business of men as to hallow the Sabbath in the way it has since done amongst us. (I, p 230)

The great watershed was the Solemn League and Covenant in 1638. After the signing of that there was among the Covenanters a "strictness of walk and conversation . . . which showed how much in sincerity they were indeed regenerated Christians." (I, p 30)

Whatever Ringan's embarrassment, however, about the greater carnality of the period of the Reformation, he venerates his grandfather.

> I am bound to say it was his own exceeding venerable appearance, and the visions of past events which the eloquence of his traditions called up to my young fancy [which] worked deeper and more thoroughly into my nature, than the reasons and motives which guided and governed many of his other disciples. (I, pp 275-276)

So great is Ringan's respect for the old man that the term "my grandfather" is never rejected as cumbersome, and its repetition contributes to the haze of veneration through which Ringan sees not only the old Reformer, but also the whole struggle against Papacy and the "pious worthies" who waged it. Those who meet the grandfather address him as Gilhaize, and not until he is dead do we learn that his Christian name was Michael. It is then the aged Ebenezer Muir who recalls "that sanctified character Michael Gilhaize."

Sir George Douglas comments appreciatively on the mode of narration Galt used. He sees it as an "ingenious and yet perfectly natural and legitimate device"[16] by which the author has contrived to extend his "household memorial" (Galt's own term), so as to make it embrace the 130 years of the religious struggle from its beginning during the regency of Marie of Lorraine to its close with the arrival of William of Orange.

Roughead points out that the ground covered by *Ringan Gilhaize* equals in extent that of *The Monastery, The Abbot* and *Old Mortality.* Ringan has to narrate, as well as his own adventures, those of his father and grandfather. The reader must therefore accept that Ringan, who was eight when his grandfather died, has a prodigious memory, and that Michael Gilhaize lived to a ripe old age. Galt helps the acceptance by fostering the idea that the old man was something of a living legend at Quharist (where is it?) near Irvine, and by making a virtue out of the necessity of his great age ". . . he lived until he was ninety-one years, seven months and four days old," Galt demands that we suspend our disbelief.

Galt has a great tract of time to cover and he is skilful both in what he includes and in what he omits. What a Gilhaize does not see, the reader does not see either. Because, for example, Ringan is wounded at Drumclog, he simply reports briefly on Bothwell Brig and the later sufferings of prisoners taken there. Because the men who murdered Archbishop Sharp were not of Ringan's neighbourhood, we hear only that the "apostate prelate" was killed.[17] To supply the omissions in his tale Ringan refers us more than once "to the histories and chronicles of the time—while I return to the narrative of my grandfather." (I, p 238) On another occasion when he refers us to the annals and chronicles of the time, he warns us that "the truth in them has suffered from the alloy of a base servility." (I, p 294) He decides that to describe the vengeance of his English subjects on Charles I would lead him far from "this household memorial . . . though [the circumstances] have been strangely palliated by the supple spirit of latter times, especially by the sordid courtliness of the crafty Clarendon." (I, p 318)

In this way Galt keeps firmly to his "household memorial," to Ringan's story, and by telling that in the first person he succeeds so well in imaginatively repossessing the past that the reader accepts the Covenanter as "a man of strong affections and his deeds the effects of wrongs that he [has] suffered in the persecution." Galt has indeed succeeded in his object of "engraining the Covenanting dispositions of one who thought himself animated by Heaven in a righteous cause," but during the months that he worked at his "engraining," Galt wrote more than once to his publisher George Boyd indicating the kind of readership he was aiming at. Galt was not setting out to add to the store of bigoted Covenanting literature which would appeal only to those with narrowly partisan views, for he writes

> . . . I shall do all I can to make [the novel] effective . . . the more particularly so, as I address it to the feelings of the presbyterians in particular and the devout in general. (Letter of 13/1/1823)

and again,

> I will endeavour to make the work something which on a Sabbath night, when man's feelings are holiest—such as a Scotchman will more than once be pleased to return to. . . . (Letter of 31/1/1823)

Galt writes again on February 3, proposing that when the first edition is sold, Boyd should bring out

> . . . a cheap edition in one volume—for I mean if possible to make it a Sunday Evening story—like the pilgrim's progress. (Letter of 3/2/1823)[18]

Galt even expresses the hope that the novel will have "the better chance of being popular in England by not being so full of Scotch as some of my other things."

126

The novel was not however widely popular, nor did it succeed in making the intended appeal to "the devout in general." Galt had made Ringan a Covenanter, and readers concluded that Ringan's sentiments were Galt's own. This Galt denied.

The sentiments which it breathes are not mine, nor the austerity that it enforces, nor at all the odour of the piety with which the enthusiasm of the hero is tinged. But in every case where I have seen it noticed, his sentiments have been regarded as mine, which, though perhaps respectable to me as a man, I disclaim, as an author, merely, however, because they are not mine.[19]

Ever since the publication of his first fictional work *The Ayrshire Legatees* Galt was constantly having to deny that the views of his fictional characters were his. He denied, for example, that the political views of young Andrew Pringle in *The Legatees* were his. In the case of *Ringan Gilhaize* it is to Professor Ian Gordon that I am indebted for the information that on the publication of his novel, Galt went so far in disclaiming the Whig and Presbyterian sympathies of his hero as to send, along with a presentation copy of the novel, a letter to Sir Robert Peel in which, Professor Gordon says, he carefully distinguishes between the feeling for the Covenanters "profoundly venerated by my countrymen" and his *own* feelings "faithfully attached to the existing Government."[20] Galt had no wish to have his writings deprive him of the opportunity of public business.[21] Nor, however, did he want his fictions taken as fact, for this denied the artistry of his imaginative creations.

Charles Swann in his article on Galt discerns the artistry and also shows very clearly from internal evidence in *Ringan Gilhaize* that the views of Ringan are not Galt's. He says

The obvious danger of a first-person narrative—and this is especially likely to be true of the historical novel—is that the price of authenticity means that a broad objective view of change is replaced by a purely subjective response to events. But Galt's handling of the fictional autobiography is marked by his ability to make the narrator tell us more about himself or the world that he is describing than he himself can recognise. . . . [In the case of Ringan] Galt so manages to control his story that we do not identify with him, or necessarily approve his sentiments, but understand him in the context of his history—which may not be the same as Ringan's *sense* of his history.[22]

And this is true. We understand how suffering has brought Ringan to the point where, in his own eyes, to kill Claverhouse is to fulfil his vow of vengeance for the murder of his family, to perform the task his grandfather saw in store for him, and to liberate his native land from bondage. Such is Galt's skill that to the end of the novel, we can sympathise with Ringan, but we do not indeed identify with him. Nor do we look on the death of Claverhouse in Ringan's terms. The fact that Ringan sees it as he does is a measure of the degree of alienation which his sufferings have induced or created.

Without destroying the credibility of his novel, or discrediting his hero, Galt manages to make Ringan see the killing of Claverhouse as the step needed to deliver his country from bondage, and at the same time to let the reader see Claverhouse as almost an anachronism and his death as almost irrelevant. This demands considerable artistry and skill and is achieved partly by the way Galt makes us aware throughout the novel of a changing social situation, and partly by the way he traces in the minds of three, in fact four, generations of the Gilhaize family a disparity between the imagined and the real which is at its most acute in Ringan.

Nor does this represent the whole of Galt's artistic achievement. He manages in addition to deal with a period of religious intolerance and even bigotry, a period of oppression and reprisal, and to write about it very much from the Covenanting side, without ever sounding an embittered note. His characters use the abusive epithets typical of the period, but are never blinded by them to the humanity of many on the opposing side. Galt makes us, in fact, aware that in the persistence on both sides of humane feelings and sound sense despite the conflict and treachery that more than a century of civil strife has produced, there is more hope for the future than in the death of Claverhouse. Dealing, as he does, with a period of bitter strife, Galt has to include some horrific happenings, but he handles these with great restraint. He ensures our sympathy with Ringan by showing him at his happiest and most attractive immediately before the worst blow befalls him. When Ringan ultimately expounds on the need for retaliation, he does it powerfully and with dignity, but without the Presbyterian eloquence that the subtitle might have led us to expect. Galt's main speakers do not, in fact, use Presbyterian rhetoric in their most important speeches[23] in the novel. But perhaps enough has been said to suggest that the means Galt uses to achieve these ends are worth a closer study.

To look first at the way Galt presents the changing social situation, we find that Grandfather Gilhaize from the time he joins the Reformed cause and is involved in the religious struggle wears always the literal and metaphorical protection of a livery. He fights against the oppressions of a corrupt Church and State but he does so under the leadership and protection of pious noblemen. When the younger Glencairn proves a less earnest man than his father, Gilhaize can look to the Lord James Stuart as a man eminently worthy of respect. Gilhaize never doubts the Lords of the Congregation, "those high and pious noblemen [who] had nothing more at heart than to worship God according to their conscience, and the doctrines of the Old and New Testaments." (I, p 83) Nor does he doubt that Providence will prosper the cause of the Reformed.

Gilhaize's active service ends with the reward of a small piece of land from Lord Eglinton. When, later in his life, the outlook darkens, Gilhaize can go to Edinburgh, "as to the source and fountain-head," and there seek the hall and don the livery of some nobleman until he learns what is happening. He is involved in two further successful exploits, one in the public field, the taking of Dumbarton Castle, one in the private, the finding in destitution of the now penitent Marion Ruet, sister to his wife and erstwhile lemane of the Archbishop of St Andrews. Nothing happens in the public or the private field to disturb his belief in the Reformed cause or in the special favour of Providence towards it.

On his journeys Gilhaize meets many people who favour Reform but they favour it for social rather than theological reasons. And they often favour it because they hope to do better under the new religion. There are stablers and farriers like Tobit Balmuto who favour Reform because the monks are willing to use their services and skills but less willing to pay for them. There are monks like Dominic Callendar who have taken vows before they knew what it meant to renounce the world. The new religion allows Dominic Callendar to marry Madeline Sauchie who is liberated from an uncongenial convent. James Coom, the smith, who has had to be called in to repair with a metal hoop the timber hip of the Virgin Mary at Kilwinning when it "sklintered aff," thinks the Reformation a "braw thing."

> It used to cost me as muckle siller for the sin o' getting fu', no aboon three or four times in the year as would hae kept ony honest man blithe and ree frae New'ersday to Hogmanae. (I, p 108)

People have many grievances but these have social rather than spiritual roots. The end of Papacy is to cure their manifold ills. Ordinary people tend to look to their superiors to give the lead. We hear more in the first half of general oppression than of individual personal suffering. The mood is hopeful. Even the burning of the old priest Walter Mill is good for the Reformed cause because it rebounds against the Catholic Church and finally loses it the sympathy of many waverers.

To draw attention to the difference in atmosphere and attitudes between the earlier days of the Reformation, and the later Covenanting days, Galt makes skilful use of one item. That item is the Massacre of St Bartholomew's Eve. When news first reaches Edinburgh of that event, John Knox is in failing health but at such a juncture the spirit is rekindled within him and he denounces Charles IX from the pulpit as inhuman, as worse than Herod, for so attacking his Protestant subjects. It is a source of reassurance to all Protestants that the old Reformer is still alive and capable, as it were, of hurling the necessary thunderbolts in the Protestant cause. There is, in other words, a leader on the religious front, as there are statesmen-like figures to be the spokesmen and leaders among the nobles.

When, however, in the second half of *Ringan Gilhaize* the Massacre of St Bartholomew's Eve is recalled it is to liken it to an outrage much nearer home, in fact, to the coming on Ayrshire of the Highland Host, "tempted by their need and greed, and a royal promise of indemnity for whatsoever outrages they might commit." (II, p 155) And Ringan makes the comparison specifically.

> . . . when, since the massacre of the protestants by orders of the French King, on the eve of St Bartholomew, was so black a crime ever perpetrated by a guilty government on its own subjects. (II, p 156)

Oppression and suffering are now felt at an individual and personal level. Men must look to their own defence, there is no mention now of the protection of patrons. Everywhere there is division and treachery, shown not only in the divided and disputed leadership among the Covenanters but in the divided and sometimes outraged homes in which they seek shelter. Nahum Chapelrigg is shot at a house where he seeks shelter. Ringan is concealed by Sawners Paton the miller, lest the miller's wife should see him. Menie Adams shelters some Covenanters only to betray them in the hope of winning favour with her curate fiancé. Ringan tells us that the Laird of Ringlewood's home,

> the mansion of a gentleman much beloved of all his neighbours was allowed to burn to the ground before their eyes, without any one venturing to come to help him, to so great a degree had distrust and the outrages of military riot at that epoch altered the hearts of men. (II, p 138)

The homes in which Ringan shelters show how national, political and religious troubles are now affecting the lives of ordinary people. At a different social level, when Ringan is sheltered, by accident, in the house of the Bishop of Edinburgh and overhears the members of the Privy Council airing their views on the measures taken against the Covenanters he realises that there too men are divided in their opinions. Argyle's ill-fated expedition[24] shows in extreme form lack of clear leadership, the presence of conflicting counsels and ubiquitous treachery. Ringan may conclude from this that "the Lord's time was not yet come for the work to thrive" (II, p 278) but the reader is bound to be aware of a deeply divided society, where even old traditional loyalties cannot

131

be relied on. An old servant shuts his door on the fugitive Argyle. The vulnerable state of the Covenanters is shown again and again in Galt's frequent references to their exposure to severe weather conditions. Nothing can be interposed to shelter them from the elements. And this exposure mirrors the political condition of men whose faith in their King and his government has been eroded by oppression and persecution. Galt makes Ringan specifically link the Covenanting struggle for religious freedom with the earlier struggle for national independence which led to the drawing up of the Declaration of Arbroath, but this time it is not the barons but the ordinary people who are exercising the divine right of resistance against oppression.

The named villains of the second half of the novel are Charles II and Archbishop Sharp. The latter is murdered and the former dies, but their deaths make little difference. James II is harsher to Scotland than his brother had been, and when he has fled, Claverhouse kindles the hills in his cause. Ringan may believe that the death of Claverhouse delivers his native land from bondage, but the reader cannot see the death of Dundee as bearing that significance, and although this is partly due to the advantage of hindsight, it is largely Galt's skilful direction of the novel which has made us aware that the days when Michael Gilhaize worked and fought under an artistocratic patron are long gone. We are now in the more potentially radical and democratic days of his grandson, the Covenanter.

With the arrival of William of Orange the future will lie more with the merchants, like Mr Jaddua Fyfe and others whom Ringan meets in Edinburgh before he goes north to Killiecrankie, and who obviously expect William of Orange to know on which side his bread is buttered. If the Dutchman has been benign when he granted an audience to a Presbyterian minister about to leave Holland for Ayrshire, Mr Jaddua Fyfe thinks that fitting.

Aye, aye, he has nae his ellwand to seek when a customer's afore the counter,—that's in the way o' business. (II, p 294)

When we come to consider Galt's treatment of the four generations of the Gilhaize family, and his way of tracing

132

Ringan's increasing alienation, it is worth recalling that at the end of last century when Sir George Douglas wrote his essay on Galt in *The Blackwood Group* he described Galt as a novelist "in advance of his time" and supported the idea by comparing his writings with those of Zola. Today one is still aware of a modern note in Galt's work. His terminology, when he tells us in *The Literary Life* that whatever merit there is in his sketches will be found to depend on "the metaphysical anatomy of his characters" is quaint to our ear, but his work is a vivid reminder, if any were needed, that acute psychological observation antedated the vocabulary of psychiatric study.

In the span of the novel Galt introduces four generations of the Gilhaize family, and they are all recognisably sons of that house. Galt makes us aware of the characteristics they share and of the effect on them of a darkening situation. There is in all of them a simplicity and lack of guile which takes a different colouring in each generation. Michael Gilhaize has his own wisdom and shrewdness but like the Reverend Micah Balwhidder in *Annals of the Parish* he is something of an innocent.[25] He grows up in a hopeful time. We learn that in the green years of his childhood he passes on to other children at Linlithgow news, or gossip, of quarrels between the Protestant lords and the priesthood so that ". . . it might in a manner be said, all the boys in the town were leagued in spirit with the reformers," and we certainly hear that at a pageant for St Michael fifty of these "thoughtless innocents . . . pelt some of the performers with unsavoury missiles" (I, pp 4-6) but there is obviously a disparity between the imagined situation and the real one, because only two boys leave Linlithgow in 1558 with Gilhaize to join the protestant lords, and even these two quickly fall away from the "holy enterprise" and become ne'er-do-weels. Gilhaize briefly regrets their fall but his own ideals are never disturbed. Nothing happens then or later to make him doubt that Providence is on the side of the Reformed, "those who were chosen to work the great work of the Gospel in Scotland." (I, p 102)

For Michael Gilhaize's simple faith his son Sawners has a godly but rather "stubbornly affection." He has the seriousness but not the wisdom of his father, and where Michael's imagination made things rosier than they were, the son's makes them darker. Ringan tells us that because his father had known of fearful things in the "lowering time of the Spanish Armada" before he could understand what it was, "his imagination was kindled with some dreadful conceit of the armada and he thought it could be nothing less than some awful and horrible creature sent from the shores of perdition to devour the whole land." (I, p 278) He could not sleep for thinking "how this dragon would grind and gnash the bodies of all protestants," so that his parents were concerned for the health of his mind. To soothe his apprehensions, Sawner's mother, the calm and pious Elspa Ruet, took the little boy of six or seven to see with his own eyes the wreck of one of the ships of the Armada, driven by the storm on to the rocks at Pencorse, but Galt adds:

> his mind had ever after a strange habitude of forming wild and wonderful images of every danger, where the scope and nature was not very clearly discerned and which continued with him till the end of his days. (I, p 278)

and Galt shows this in action when Sawners is much older. He is in Edinburgh "anent some matter of a legacy . . . when Charles I was mindit to enact a part in the Kirk of Scotland little short of the papistical domination of the Roman Antichrist." Ringan says this fired his father's blood and spirit with the fierceness of a furnace. Sawners is lodging with Janet Geddes, and as Galt tells the story, she and Gilhaize lament together "all the Saturday afternoon and night, about the woes of idolatry that were darkening again over Scotland . . . [so that] they heated the zeal of one another to a pitch of great fervour." Ringan is sure there was reason and piety in their fears but knowing his father's earnest and simple character he thinks there might be "some lack of the decorum of wisdom in the method of their sorrow." Sawners is accorded the respect due to the son of so revered a father, but the robes he has inherited sit somewhat uneasily upon him.

Sawners's extravagant behaviour continues when he returns home with such sad and altered looks that his wife, concluding he had failed to get the legacy, says comfortingly "they had hitherto fenn't without it, and so might they still do." His only answer is to throw a leathern bag of money on the table, saying, "What care I for this world's trash, when the ark of the Lord is taken from Israel?" The hearts of all are daunted, Sawners speaks of the King bringing in again "the worship of the Beast," and tells of the scenes in St Giles Kirk in Edinburgh.

> I [Ringan], who was the ninth of his ten children, and then not passing nine years old, was thrilled with an unspeakable fear; and all the dreadful things, which I had heard my grandfather tell of the tribulations of his time, came upon my spirit like visions of the visible scene, and I began to weep with an exceeding sorrow, insomuch that my father was amazed and caressed me, and thanked Heaven that one so young in his house felt as a protestant child should feel in an epoch of such calamity. (I, pp 281-282)

Galt handles the extravagance of Sawners's behaviour well. We can be in part amused at it, and can yet feel for the state of mind of the child Ringan as he was "thrilled with an unspeakable fear." As he grows up, Ringan has more of the "decorum of wisdom" than his father, more self-control, but the "stubbornly affection" which Ringan's father felt for the faith of John Knox becomes sheer tenacity in Ringan. A simple faith that Providence will prosper the Covenanting cause is no longer enough. The godly Mr Swinton, denied by the sergeant the use of the horse that was brought to carry him to Irvine, can steadfastly believe that

> Good . . . will come of this, and though for a season we are ordained to tribulation . . . yet a firm footing and a fair green path lies in a peaceful land beyond. (I, p 27)

We see the Presbyterian view of Providence toughening and hardening under adversity and persecution, as Ringan tenaciously maintains his faith against harder and harder odds.

Involved in the Pentland Rising he resolves

> first, Not to falter in our enterprise until we had proved the utmost of the Lord's pleasure on our behalf; and,

135

second, To use the means under Him which, in all human undertakings, are required to bring whatsoever is ordained to pass. (I, p 47)

The expedition fails and he has to accept that "no human helps and means could change what was evidently ordained otherwise." (I, p 49) Their numbers grow, however, and hope rises again so that

had the Lord been pleased with our undertaking, there was no reason to think the human means insufficient for the end. But in the mysteries of the depths of this wisdom he had judged, and for the great purposes of his providence he saw, that it was meet we should yet suffer. (I, p 57)

When Ringan is taken prisoner by soldiers who boast of the slaughter they have done, he says

I inwardly chided the slow anger of the mysterious Heavens for permitting the rage of those agents of the apostate James Sharp and his compeers, whom a man-sworn King had so cruelly dressed with his authority. (I, p 109)

But a seraphic voice whispers to the ears of his understanding that the enormities practised must lead to

a tempering of the hearts of the people, that they might become as swords of steel, to work out the deliverance of the land from the bloody methods of prelatic and arbitrary domination. (I, p 109)

Ringan is buoyed up by such beliefs, and by the thought that his venerable grandfather was convinced there was a great task in store for him. From halfway through the novel Ringan gives indication that in the troubles that fell on his country he ultimately lost everything, his home, his wife, his family, but he sees these sufferings as the heavens' way of marking him as ordained

from the beginning to launch the bolt that was chosen from the quiver in the armory of the Almighty avenger, to

overthrow the oppressor and oppression of my native land.
(1, p 152)

The disparity now between what Ringan's eyes show him
and the interpretation he wishes to put on the facts is so
great that he desperately looks everywhere for signs and seeks
guidance in particular in the Bible. Galt uses several means
to show Ringan's alienated state. After the destruction of his
home[26] he sets out to find the Cameronians because of the
clause, in their declaration published at Sanquhar, in which
they disowned Charles Stuart, but when Robin Brown the
carrier with the voice of reason tries to persuade him that he
is too ill and his boy too young to join with the Cameronians,
Ringan is deaf to common sense.

To reason more or farther concerning aught but of the
means to achieve my purpose, was a thing I could not
abide. (II, pp 224-5)

It is ironic that when Ringan tells Cargill he has consulted the
Bible and been instructed to send his son away with the
Cameronian leader, it is Cargill, the known fanatic, who
demurs and advises him to

apply again, and maybe—maybe, Ringan, ye'll no be put
to so great a trial. (II, p 232)

Ringan, however, imagines himself required to sacrifice his
son and does so. Left in the next months in an invalid state,
Ringan describes his mental condition.

Nor should I suppress, that in my infirmity, there was
often a wildness about my thoughts, by which I was
unfitted at times to hold communion with other men. . . .
[Things around him seemed then] the substanceless
imageries of a dream . . . I contested as it were with the
reality of all that I saw, touched and felt. . . . (II, pp 235-6)

From now on Galt makes us aware of how Ringan
appeared to other people. When he is arrested in Glasgow to
be taken to Edinburgh, the soldiers would have made him

walk but all "who beheld my pale face and emaciated frame cried out against it." (II, p 240) Strangers look at him "with silence and wonder," or answer his "wild interrogation with pity," and a friend looks at him "compassionately."

The full extent of Ringan's alienated state is, however, brought home to us when he goes to address Renwick's followers at Lasswade. Galt describes with great care the natural beauty of the scene. At one time it would have delighted Ringan, but at this juncture, in the full grip of his avenging vow, he can take no pleasure in it; the very trout can only mirror the situation of the persecuted remnant.

> In the clear linn the trouts shuttled from stone and crevice, dreading the persecutions of the angler, who, in the luxury of his pastime, heedeth not what they may in their cool element suffer. (II, p 262)

So out of tune is Ringan that even nature seems at fault.

> I had come with the sternest of intents, and I neither noticed nor spoke to anyone; but going to the brink of the linn I sat myself down in a gloomy nook, and was sullen, that the scene was not better troubled into unison with the resentful mood of my spirit. (II, p 263)

From now on his moments of frenzy are followed by total delusion.

> I felt that I was a chosen instrument: I thought that the ruin which had fallen on me and mine was assuredly some great mystery of Providence: I remembered the prophecy of my grandfather, that a task was in store for me, though I knew not what it was; I forgot my old age and my infirmities; I hastened to my chamber, I put money in my purse; I spoke to no one; I bought a carabine; and I set out alone to reinforce [General] Mackay. (II, p 310)

The knowledge that the victory at Killiecrankie was to Claverhouse makes Ringan cry "aloud the blasphemy of the fool, 'There is no God'."

But scarcely had the dreadful words escaped my profane lips, when I heard, as it were, thunders in the heavens, and the voice of an oracle crying in the ears of my soul, "The victory of this day is given into thy hands," and strange wonder and awe fell upon me, and a mighty spirit entered into mine, and I felt as if I was in that moment clothed with the armour of divine might. (II, p 320)

Ringan is convinced that it was given to him to fire the "bolt of justice that summoned Claverhouse to the audit of his crimes."

Thus [he says] was my avenging vow fulfilled,—and thus was my native land delivered from bondage. (II, p 322)

We can see that the vow is indeed fulfilled, but so skilfully has Galt made us aware of the changed state of things in Scotland, that the second part of Ringan's statement merely indicates the extent of his delusion, the extent of the disparity between what he imagines and what is, but to this state have Ringan's sufferings and beliefs brought him.

Ringan's son Joseph is the first of the Gilhaize sons who is overtaken by real horrors almost before he can know imaginary ones. He has the earnestness and guilelessness which mark all the males of the family. These characteristics make the child give unquestioning obedience to authority in the shape of his father, of the "master," Donald Cargill, and of the Bible. Joseph accepts the Old Testament as literally true as though the sacrifices it relates, the demands it makes, the paradoxes it presents, are no more fearful or strange than the events in the world the child knows. Yet the child's eye views that world with candour. He sees that the five dragoons who pass Ringan on the road avoid his eye, although they have been quartered in the Gilhaize household. Joseph wonders "that they did na speak to me: I thought they had a black look." Ringan, his heart once more thawed into charity with all men by his release from prison, makes excuses for them without looking at the soldiers. But the child persists: "I dinna like them the day, father, they're unco like ill-doers." Events prove the child right.

Joseph can look on the dejected remnant of the

Cameronians and see that they are "a wee waff-like," but can believe that they may deliver the land because the Book says that the race is not to the swift nor the battle to the strong. Galt so convinces us of the guilelessness of the child that when Ringan asks Joseph to read him the twenty-second chapter of Genesis, there is genuine pathos in the answer he gives.

> I ken't, father, it's about Abraham and wee Isaac; but though ye tak me into the land of Moriah, and up to the top of the hill, maybe a ram will be catched by the horns in a whin bush for the burnt offering, and ye'll no hae ony need to kill me. (II, p 231)

We are far indeed from the sunny days of the youth of Grand-father Michael Gilhaize but the child Joseph is recognisably a descendant of the patriarch.

Galt is intent on making us understand his Covenanters. From the opening pages of the novel we are in no doubt where the bias lies as Ringan tells of "the martyrdom of that true saint and gospel preacher Mr George Wishart" and of "the well-earned death of the cruel Cardinal Beaton, his ravenous persecutor." (I, p 5) Very quickly, however, we recognise that the emotive epithets are the labels in current use, but the terminology does not prevent Michael Gilhaize, for all the ardour of his zeal for reform, from recognising that in Leonard Meldrum, who is the Roman Catholic seneschal in the castle of the Archbishop of St Andrews, "there was more of the leaven of a sanctified nature, than in the disposition of many zealous and professing Christians." (I, p 30) And it is Meldrum who is made to perceive with regret that the Church's treatment of heretics was more likely "to shock men's minds into schism and rebellion, than to allure them back into worship and reverence, and to a repentance of their heresies." (I, pp 26-27)

All through the novel there are instances of Christian kindness between people of opposing views. It is Gideon Kemp who states very explicitly the idea that a suffering man cannot be treated as an enemy. He is leaving Ringan Gilhaize, a fugitive from the defeat at Rullion Green, in the care of Johnnie Jamison who was "of a farm, inclined to the prelatic side." Despite Jamison's assurance that he wouldn't betray either friend or acquaintance, Gideon spells out his views strongly.

When the sword, Johnnie, is in the hand, it's an honourable thing to deal strongly with the foe; but when forlorn and dejectit, and more houseless than the beasts of the field, he's no longer an adversary, but a man that we're bound by the laws of God and nature to help.[27] (II, p 99)

Even very late in the novel Ringan's basic fair-mindedness makes him admit, when he overhears Patterson, the Bishop of Edinburgh, speak ". . . take him all in all for a prelate, he was, in truth, not void of the charities of human nature." (II, p 254)

Earlier the soldiers of the Reformed cause who escort the captive Archbishop Hamilton from Dumbarton to Stirling are so impressed by his gallant bearing that "it was thought by many that, though both papist and traitor, they might have been worked on to set him free" (I, p 251) and Bailie Kilspinnie, whose wife the Archbishop had wiled away, "all his days never ceased to wonder how so wicked a man could die so well." (I, p 252) Charity survives and Galt's view of the period includes it.

When he has acts of violence to deal with, he treats them with economy and restraint. He does not, for example, deal with the actual attack on Ringan's brother's home, but reports on it and on Bell, his daughter, who survived many months the outrage done on her, her mind gone. Bell never speaks ". . . where she was led, she went; where she was left, she stood." In the end it is only an unusual stillness that shows that "her sorrows are over." Particularly in scenes of pathos it is the inclusion of realistic detail which lends them conviction. When Michael Gilhaize and his wife Elspa find Elspa's sister, the now destitute Marion, in the rags of her earlier finery, a shopkeeper Ursie Firikins invites them in off the street where the contrast between the douce couple and the ragged outcast is drawing attention. Indoors it is Michael Gilhaize who goes to prepare a drink of meal and water for Marion who is near to starvation, while Elspa nurses her fainting sister.

The incidents which deserve particular mention, however, are the ones which lead up to Ringan's vow of vengeance. These are a real test of Galt's art. It is essential that we see Ringan as the earnest and upright man he is, and as basically gentle and kindly. The wrongs he so resents are very real. Ringan says quite explicitly at his trial before Lord Kelbourne that he cannot be backward in his testimony because the questions put to him are propounded as tests. He is fined, bonds are required for the payment, but once these are given he is to be set free because of ill-health. It takes a day to arrange the bonds, but the next morning at break of day Ringan and his son leave Ayr for Quharist, their hearts lifted up with hope. Galt excels himself here in describing the setting, as though he were breathing life into the waves and the leaves so that every moving thing seems vibrant with life. The beauty and freshness of the morning after Ringan's trial and confinement, the peacefulness of the sleeping town, which he sees as both trusting and vulnerable in its sleep, make him say: "I felt my heart thaw again into charity with all men, and I was thankful for the delight." (II, p 203)

In this benign state of mind, discoursing to his little boy on the divine origin of charity, Ringan goes forward to find his home desolated. No one ever tells him, and he never asks, what actually happened to his dead wife and daughters.

> All is phantasma that I recollect of the day of my coming home. . . . When I left Ayr the leaves were green, and the fields gay, and the waters glad; and when the yellow leaf rustled on the ground, and the waters were drumly, and the river roaring, I was somehow, I know not by what means, in the kirkyard, and a film fell from the eyes of my reason, and I looked around, and my little boy had hold of me by the hand, and I said to him, Joseph, what's yon sae big and green in our lair? and he gazed in my face, and the tears came into his eyes, and he replied—
> "Father, they are a' in the same grave."
>
> (II, p 205)

The constant use of "and" in the above passage recaptures the way the accumulating facts penetrate, one after the other, into the awakening consciousness. The mind is loath to accept what the sight reveals. The child's answer leaves no possibility of doubt. That Ringan should then kneel at the grave and vow enmity against Charles Stuart and all his line, is eminently understandable.

Ringan becomes more and more a man apart, a man lost in the grip of his obsession with his vow of vengeance. His state of alienation is presented well and carries conviction[28]

We can believe him when he says he was sullen and resentful as he sat apart at Lasswade waiting to address Renwick's followers, but Galt brings Ringan swiftly and recognisably to life when he leaps to his feet to speak. The tone of his speech is not embittered, nor does he resort to the excesses of Presbyterian eloquence. What Galt seems to have had in mind when he wrote the last page and a half of Ringan's powerful speech is a vivid memory of Mark Antony's speech in the market place over the body of Caesar. Echoes of it are strong. Like Antony, Ringan is successful in swaying his listeners, despite Renwick's hope that the door to possible reconciliation might be kept open. "The meeting with one accord agreed [with Ringan]."

Galt does use the language of the saints but not the coarseness and extravagance often associated with much Presbyterian eloquence of Covenanting times. For instance, in response to the news from Edinburgh that the King is trying to force the prayer book on the Presbyterian Kirk, it is not inappropriate that neighbours should collect at the hearth of Sawners Gilhaize, and that the aged Ebenezer Muir should preface his remarks by recalling that he had "often partaken of the sweet repast of the conversations of that sanctified character Michael Gilhaize." This is recognisable, but not distasteful, Presbyterian eloquence. The body of the old man's speech is dignified. The language is plain but powerful. It convinces us that the old man and his listeners are sincere both in recognising and regretting the need to resist in matters of conscience. After the speech Psalm 140 is sung "with the melodious energy of holiness."[29]

Galt deals very differently with the warlike and extravagant Nahum Chapelrig. To Nahum, papistry has "its roots of rankness in the midden-head of Arminianism" but despite more "lair" than commonly falls to the lot of country folk, Nahum goes on "which, in a sense, is a greater Antichrist than Antichrist himself even where he sits on his throne of thraldom in the Roman vaticano." Ringan tells us that, for his years, Nahum was looked up to "among all his acquaintance notwithstanding a small spicin of conceit that he was in with himself." (I, p 284) Galt is an adept at this kind of fun.

And he makes short shrift of another example of extravagance. Ringan has advised an ill-prepared and dejected "army" of Covenanters to evade Dalziel's advancing forces and seek safety in flight. Those with irrelevant notions of military honour think this unsoldier-like and Ringan says

> there were also divers heated and fanatical spirits whom, because our undertaking had been for religious ends, nothing could persuade that Providence would not interfere in some signal manner for their deliverance, yea, even to the overthrow of the enemy; . . . one of these . . . began to preach of the mighty things that the Lord did for the children of Israel in the valley of Aijalon, where He not only threw down great stones from the heavens, but enabled Joshua to command the sun and moon to stand still—which to any composed mind was melancholious to hear. (II, p 64)

The nature of Galt's theme in *Ringan Gilhaize* does not allow much scope for humour. Galt does introduce two comic incidents which in the context of the tale he tells are too farcical not to be a little incongruous. One is the arrival earlier than expected of Mary Queen of Scots at Leith. The farcical events that ensue among the town dignitaries belong in tone to *The Gathering of the West,* the piece of fictitious reporting that Galt had done for Blackwood, in the autumn of 1822, on the visit of George IV to Edinburgh after his coronation. The events at Leith are pure Galt, and the tree of municipal muddle that grew in his pages must have sprung from the mustard seed of fact that fog at sea made the time of the Queen's arrival uncertain.

The other broadly comic episode is the Hallowe'en plot against Lieutenant Swaby, the English soldier, which leads to his being locked in with "Zachariah Smylie's black ram, a condumacious and outstropolous beast," rather than the girl he had hoped for. The incident is funny, but too farcically so for the tone of the novel, although it has to be admitted that there are one or two touches that show Galt in his best vein. We are told of the unsuspecting ram

> the auld toop was breathing thickly, mumbling and crunching the kail-blades in a state of as great sensual delight as any beast could well be. (II, p 38)

Since the ram does more damage to Swaby than Swaby to the ram, Ringan concludes

> Verily Providence might be said, with reverence, to have had a hand in the mirth of his punishment. (II, p 39)

Where Galt's skill in *Ringan Gilhaize* is unerring is in his handling of dialogue. Because of the number of characters, we have inevitably fewer passages of extensive dialogue here than in the earlier novels, but that given in the scene between Elspa Ruet and her erring sister Marion is unforgettable in its rightness.

The Archbishop's lemane has made an assignation with, she thinks, Michael Gilhaize. At the house of the Widow Dingwall, however, she finds not the young man she expected but her sister Elspa. Disconcerted, Marion puts on "a bad boldness of look" and informs her sister

> "It was na to see the like of you I cam' here," said she, with a scornful toss of her head.
> "I ken that, Marion," replied Elspa, mournfully.
> "And what business then hae ye to come to snool me?"
> Elspa for a little while made no answer to this, but, drying her eyes, she went to her seat composedly, and then said,—"Cause ye're my sister, and brought shame and disgrace on a' your family. —O Marion, I'm wae to say this! —but ye're owre brave in your sin."
> "Do ye think I'll e'er gae back to that havering, daunering cuif o' a creature, the Crail bailie?"
> "He's a man o' mair worth and conduct, Marion," replied her sister, firmly, "than to put that in your power —even, woman, if ye were penitent, and besought him for charity."

"Weel, weel, no to clishmaclaver about him, how's a'
wi' the bairns?"

"Are ye no frighted, Marion, to speer sic a question,
when ye think how ye left them, and what for ye did sae?"

"Am na I their mither, have na I a right to speer?"

"No," said Elspa; "when ye forgot that ye were their
father's wife, they lost their mother."

"Ye need na be sae snell wi' your taunts," exclaimed
Marion, evidently endeavouring to reserve the arrogance
she had assumed; "ye need na be sae snell; I'm far better
off, and happier than e'er I was in James Kilspinnie's
aught." (I, pp 173-4)

Elspa warns her that the Archbishop might quickly put her
out if he knew of her clandestine meetings with other men.
In an attempt to reach her better nature Elspa reminds
Marion of the past when they were "twa wee playing lassies."
Marion asks again after her children, and would obviously
like to see them, but not if it means going back to Crail.
Briefly Elspa softens her into tearfulness, but Marion is
adamant that she will not return a penitent to Crail. She
would rather make away with herself than go back there.

"Dinna say that," replied her sister: "O, Marion, if
ye felt within the humiliation of a true penitent, ye would
na speak that way, but would come and hide your face in
your poor mother's bosom; often, often, Marion, did she
warn you no to be ta'en up wi' the pride and bravery of a
fine outside."

"Ye may gang hame yoursel'," exclaimed the unpeni-
tent woman, starting from her seat; "I'll no gang wi' you
to be looket down on by every one. If I should hae had a
misfortune, nane's the sufferer but mysel'; and what would
I hae to live on wi' my mother? She's pinched enough for
her ain support. No; since I hae't in my power, I'll tak
my pleasure o't. Ony body can repent when they like, and
it's no convenient yet for me. Since I hae slippit the tether,
I may as well tak a canter o'er the knowes. I won'er how
I could be sae silly as to sit sae lang willy-waing wi' you
about that blethering bodie, James Kilspinnie. He could
talk o' naething but the town-council, the cost o' plaiding,

146

and the price o' woo'. No, Eppie, I'll no gang wi' you, but I'll be glad if ye'll gang o'er the gait and tak your bed wi' me. I hae a braw bower—and, let me tell you, this is no a house of the best repute."

"Is your's ony better," replied Elspa, fervently. (I, pp 177-8)

Marion's recovery from tearfulness proceeds apace throughout this last speech leading to her brazen invitation to Eppie to join her, and then to the triumphant attempt to put the shoe on the other foot as she cautions Eppie about the doubtful reputation of the Widow Dingwall's house. Even Galt's good women characters are not, however, mim-mouthed and Elspa is stung to a fervent and splendid retort.

Galt shows the same degree of rightness in the names he gives to his characters, and numerous as these are in *Ringan Gilhaize,* they are all distinguished by a name. Early in his manuscript Galt talks of a noted stabler at the foot of Leith Wynd, but immediately inserts the character's name so that he becomes "Habby Bridle, the noted stabler at the foot of Leith Wynd." Of Tobit Balmuto, a horse-setter in Kirkcaldy we get so many details, as he toasts "an oaten bannock on a pair of tormentors," that Galt seems to be working from a present, or remembered, painting. Although we are never to meet Tobit with his "blue puddock-stool bonnet" again after he hires Spunkie to Gilhaize so that he can overtake Sir David Hamilton on his mare, Skelp-the dub, we are given the further detail that he was thought to be "an off-get of the Boswells of Balmuto."

One name however gave Galt trouble for two-thirds of the first volume and that was the name to be given to Marion Ruet. Marion was the wife of the worthy bailie of Crail, a plaiding merchant, a slightly timorous man but not really a foolish one. From the bailie and their children, Marion was wiled away by the Archbishop of St Andrews. Galt tried the title Mistress Merrywill but Merrywill is every time deleted. Obviously it is not a happy choice for the bailie. Then for some pages Merrywill is as usual deleted and Flisk substituted. This is even worse, and briefly Galt tried Fergus or Ferguson for the bailie, and then the name Kilspinnie is written in boldly, and there is no further hesitation. It suits both husband and wife, until Marion is found abandoned and destitute. She is then referred to again by her maiden name of Marion Ruet which suits her now penitent state.

The debate about the merits of *Ringan Gilhaize* is worth pursuing. It is an interesting attempt at an historical novel —and a fascinating one to have been written in 1823. How good it is as a novel is debatable, but well worth debating, because it shows Galt doing with skill and artistry things he had not done before. His use, for example, of weather and landscape, and of certain views as they appear at memorable moments,[30] is worth an article on its own. Whether we retain the title of "masterpiece" when we mention *Ringan* is not important: what we should aim to remove is the epithet "neglected."

NOTES

1. *The Literary Life* and *Miscellanies of John Galt,* 3 vols., Edinburgh and London, 1834, I, p 258.
2. Whoever edited the novel must have known the Glasgow area because he silently corrects an error of direction when Michael Gilhaize has crossed the Clyde at Glasgow and decides to make for Paisley instead of Kilmarnock.
3. John Galt, *Ringan Gilhaize,* ed. Sir George Douglas, London, 1889; reissued 1902.
4. Sir George Douglas, *The Blackwood Group,* Famous Scots Series, Edinburgh, 1897.
5. John Galt, *Ringan Gilhaize,* ed. D. S. Meldrum and William Roughead, Edinburgh, 1936, vols. 7 & 8 in *The Works of John Galt.* All three editions (1881-1883), 1899, 1936, follow the text of the first edition which Galt himself read and corrected in proof.
6. Sir Walter Scott, *Old Mortality,* Penguin English Library, ed. Angus Calder.
7. James Hogg, *The Brownie of Bodsbeck,* ed. Douglas S. Mack. Scottish Academic Press, 1976.
8. Charles Swann, "Past into Present: Scott, Galt and the Historical Novel," *Literature and History,* No. 3, March 1976.
9. Francis R. Hart, *The Scottish Novel: A Critical Survey,* London, 1978, p 50.
10. John Galt, *The Literary Life,* Vol. I, Ch. 39.
11. John Galt, *The Steamboat,* Ch. 14, "The Covenanter," Edinburgh, 1822.
12. Sir George Douglas, *The Blackwood Group,* Famous Scots Series, Edinburgh, 1897, p 73.
13. Charles Swann, "Past and Present: Scott, Galt and the Historical Novel," *Literature and History,* March, 1976.

14. John Galt, *The Literary Life*, Vol. I, pp 250-251.
15. John Galt, *Ringan Gilhaize*, edited Meldrum and Roughead, Edinburgh, 1936. Vol. I, p 1. (All references are to this edition).
16. John Galt, *Ringan Gilhaize*, ed. Sir George Douglas, 1899, Introduction, p xii.
17. Further use is, however, made of both points when Ringan is "tested" on them at his trial before Lord Kelbourne. As a Covenanter, Ringan will not call those who fought at Bothwell Brig "rebels" or the death of Sharp "murder."
    Galt handles the trial scene well, basing it partly on the account of a hearing of Mr Archibald Riddel before the committee of public affairs under the Earl of Linlithgow, published in Robert Wodrow, *The History of the Sufferings of the Church of Scotland*, Glasgow, 1829, Vol. III, Chap. IV, but adding his own conclusion. Galt makes Ringan repeat of Sharp's death the stanza Sir David Lindsay wrote of Cardinal Beaton's, concluding: "Although the loon be well away,/The fact was foully done."
18. Unpublished letters from John Galt to George Boyd, held in the National Library of Scotland.
19. John Galt, *The Literary Life*, Vol. I, p 253.
20. Letter from Professor Ian Gordon, March 3, 1975.
21. In the December after the publication of *Ringan*, we find Galt asking George Boyd to have his name brought forward as little as possible in getting a new book, *The Spaewife*, mentioned in the journals. He tells Boyd:

> You know my parliamentary concerns, and some folk are apt to think business may be neglected by and for the vanities of authorship and one need not (rouse? cause?) senseless jealousy.

Unpublished letter from John Galt to George Boyd, 14/12/1823, held in the National Library of Scotland.
22. Charles Swann, "Past into Present: Scott, Galt and the Historical Novel."
23. See the speech of Ebenezer Muir, Vol. I, pp 286-287.
24. Galt does a splendid job here in clarifying and reducing to manageable proportions the account of Argyle's expedition given in Wodrow, Vol. III, ch. 9.
25. When Gilhaize was very young, Glencairn sent him on a mission to St Andrews. In recounting all that had there befallen him, Gilhaize does not keep back the tale of the amorous advances made to him by the Archbishop's mistress. Glencairn is amused. He had not thought his agent old enough to be the target of seduction. Ringan tells us further that in the midst of temptation his grandfather thought of the husband and five babies the siren had abandoned and "it was a chaste spell and a restraining grace." (I, p 53)
    On one occasion when Gilhaize travels in the company of John Knox, it happens that the Reformer spoke . . . "of things of indifferent import; but nevertheless there was a flavour of holiness in all he said, and my grandfather treasured many of his sweet

149

sentences as pearls of great prise." (I, p 221) (This is very skilful on Galt's part: the character is perfectly satisfied with virtually nothing, and Galt need not invent or seek out dialogue for Knox.)

26. Ringan may be only 54 at this time but alone in the cold and the dark with his little boy, his only remaining child, Ringan is very like Lear in the storm with only his Fool beside him:

> An infirm, grey-haired man, with a deranged head and a broken heart, going forth amidst the winter's wind with a little boy not passing thirteen years of age, to pull down from his throne, the guarded king of three mighty kingdoms. (II, p 222)

He pleads that God will not require him to send away his son, "I am a poor, infirm, desolate, and destitute man." (II, p 230)

27. In *The Brownie of Bodsbeck* Wat of Chapelhope is equally vehement when his daughter fears she has offended him in nursing Covenanters whose civil and religious principles were the opposite of his, and adverse to those of the government.

> "Deil care what side they war on, Kate . . . ye hae taen the side o' human nature. . . ."

James Hogg, *The Brownie of Bodsbeck*, ed. Douglas Mack, Scottish Academic Press, 1976, p 163.

28. Galt has made us believe so completely in Ringan's alienation that when he makes Ringan say, when William and Mary were proclaimed King and Queen, that "in Scotland the chief agents in the work of deliverance were the outlawed Cameronians, as instructed by me" (II, p 307) we frankly cannot believe it, whether the plot really demanded it or not.

29. It is a measure of how the climate of opinion has changed that by the time Ringan and the other prisoners in the tolbooth of Edinburgh sing the thirty-one verses of Psalm 109, they sing it as a deliberate curse on Charles and James Stuart. Ringan is aware here that they have made themselves wroth with a recital of their wrongs.

30. Michael Gilhaize, having wakened from a nightmare on the night of Darnley's murder at Kirk o' Field, looks out from his window to see by the stars how far the night had passed. The night is quiet, the stars reflected in the still dark waters of the North Loch but his continuing unease is shown in his view of "the swelling bank on the northern side [which] was like the awful corpse of some mighty thing prepared for interment." (I, p 233)

THE MEMBER
AND PARLIAMENTARY REFORM

JOHN T. WARD

John Galt's delightful novel *The Member: An Autobiography*, appeared in 1832, during the gathering political crises provoked by the proposals of Earl Grey's Whig Government to reform the House of Commons. It was thus remarkably well-timed as an amusing commentary on the traditional practices of the old Parliamentary system. And at 40 Galt was well qualified to write such a work, as an experienced lobbyist at Westminster on behalf of both Scottish and Canadian interests: he knew how the system worked.

The book's dedication (dated January 1, 1832) was naughtily made (by "Archibald Jobbry," the anti-hero "autobiographer") to William Holmes,[1] an energetic Tory whip on the anti-Reform side. In sardonic vein Galt (via Jobbry) praised Holmes's

> own far more brilliant and distinguished career as a patriotic senator [which was] probably, also drawing to a conclusion . . .

and his

> talents, zeal and genius, in what, though not generally so considered by the unthinking mass, I have long esteemed nearly the most important situation which any British subject can fill; but which, alas! is perhaps destined to pass away and be forgotten, amidst this general convulsion so fatal to the established institutions of a once happy and contented country. If, indeed, my dear and worthy friend, the present horrid measure be carried into full effect, it is but too plain that the axe will have been laid to the root of the British Oak . . .

. . . and so on. In this splendid piece of "mickey-taking" all the allegations ascribed by "reformers" to "anti-reformers"

151

were listed—"a melancholy vista" of a ruined Church, a destroyed peerage, a "well-meaning" Monarch "probably packed off to Hanover," dividends reduced, property taxation introduced and "parliamentary grants and pensions of every description no longer held sacred! " All this is comparable to George Macdonald Fraser's deadpan footnotes to the memoirs of Lord Flashman, V.C.

"Black Billy" Holmes of Grafton Street in London was no landed grandee or vastly wealthy plutocrat, as Tories were imagined to be in contemporary (and, still more, subsequent) radical demonology. As Jobbry forecast, his fame did not survive for long. He sat for such tiny boroughs as Bishop's Castle, whose sixty burgesses favoured "London barristers, merchants and bankers" and who (from 1761) made the little town "the one notoriously corrupt borough in Shropshire" until the Earl of Powis took control,[2] and Haslemere (in 1830-1832) whose 130 electors were controlled by the Tory Earl of Lonsdale.[3]

"Bill," however, was "a most skilful dispenser of patronage"[4] and consequently a man of consequence, entrenched among the Government organisers by 1811.[5] Perhaps from habit, Jobbry's dedicatory letter was accompanied by

4 brace moorfowl, 2 ditto B. cocks, item 3 hares, one side of a roe, and one gallon whisky (*véritable antique*). . . .

Certainly, Holmes seems to have known and been known by every politician of importance—which led to his *niche* among footnotes to biographies of the high and mighty.

Holmes certainly worked hard to perpetuate the dominance of the followers and successors of William Pitt against Whig landed dynasties and Liberal industrialist *nouveaux-riches* alike (to whom were now added some "workers" and some "intellectuals" calling themselves Radicals). But when the crunch came he (perhaps inevitably) disastrously lost out.

On September 15, 1830, High Society excitedly attended the opening of the Liverpool and Manchester Railway, and Holmes sought to heal the rift between the prime minister, the Duke of Wellington, and the estranged William Huskisson. The consequence was the tragic death of Huskisson, run over by another train, headed by *The Rocket*. Holmes narrowly avoided a similar fate, by holding on to the ducal coach. But his hopes for a Tory *rapprochement* were inevitably dashed just as the crucial period opened.[6]

Holmes made sure that his men in the Commons were "ready for anything" during the exciting days of 1831, and he went on to organise opposition to "Reform" in the House of Lords.[7] Having grown up politically in the rather lax days of Lord Liverpool, when neither he nor Charles Arbuthnot, the patronage secretary at the Treasury,[8] were over-burdened with work (Liverpool only required "a generally favourable disposition" among his followers), Holmes was unaccustomed to major responsibility.[9] As Secretary to the Master-General of the Ordnance (Lord Beresford) he shared with his over-staffed office the verbal lashing of Sir James Graham in 1830.[10] But the debates on Reform proved too much.

By March 5, 1831, the enthusiastic Whig Thomas Creevey told Miss Elizabeth Ord that the Reform battle was won: [11]

> Poor Billy Holmes! Both he and Croker will have but a slender chance of being M.P.s again under our restored constitution. In short, Bessy, there is no end to the fun and confusion that this measure scatters far and near into by far the most corrupt, insolent, shameless, profligate gang that this country contains. They are all dead men by this Bill, never to rise again, and their occupation is dead also. . . .

Such prejudiced forecasts were, of course, absurdly exaggerated. John Wilson Croker[12] long remained a politician and propagandist with an influential mouthpiece in the *Quarterly Review.* But "poor Billy" was replaced as Tory organiser by the more dynamic Francis Bonham.[13] In 1837 Lonsdale employed him as agent in East Cumberland for their old enemy Graham, who was now moving towards Conservatism. They lost.[14]

This, then, was the great Holmes to whom *The Member* was jokingly dedicated. He was less of a fool than Jobbry implied; but he was on the losing side in a seminal and traumatic battle, and an impoverished author like Galt (himself a Tory of sorts) had to use every ounce of humour to earn much-needed royalties. The comic intent would be appreciated by contemporaries.

II

It would be inappropriate here to attempt some sort of literary criticism of *The Member*. The task has already been expertly performed.[15] It may suffice to observe that this curiously-arranged collection of "autobiographical" jottings remains immensely entertaining. But the historian has to ask further questions. As a *genre,* how far does the "political" novel—by a Disraeli, a Trollope or a Galt—really present historical "evidence"? Does the political novelist take sufficient care over the accuracy of his background? Certainly Disraeli took care (whatever one may think of his background explanations) and his *dramatis personae* are recognisable.[16] Trollope's Barsetshire, under the Whig Duke of Omnium and the Tory squires and churchmen "rings true," despite the author's disastrous electoral experience as "an advanced conservative liberal" at corrupt Beverley in 1868.[17] And Galt's service as a Parliamentary agent stood him in good stead.[18]

The author of *The Ayrshire Legatees* (1820), *Annals of the Parish* (1821), *The Provost* (1822), *The Entail* (1823) and *The Last of the Lairds* (1826) had fallen on evil days. Careers as a lobbyist, businessman, journalist and hack-writer had failed, but the situation would hopefully be remedied by appointment as superintendent of Upper Canada in 1826. Unlike Jobbry he made no fortune in the Empire and within three years the Canada Company sent him back to London, to face his creditors and a term in a debtors' prison. He continued to write for the Tory *Blackwood's Magazine* and *Fraser's Magazine* but was reduced to churning out three-volume novels for the new libraries, in order to make ends meet and pay off his debts. In 1831 Galt's financial straits were much improved by his appointment as secretary of the British American Land Company. An assured income allowed him to free himself from the shameful commissions of Messrs. Colburn and Bentley and to return to his (less remunerative but more satisfying) concern with short "autobiographical" novels (like *Sir Andrew Wylie of that Ilk*—despite its two volumes), based on close observation of the current scene and allowing full rein to Galt's ironic sense of humour. It must have been a relief to move away from such stuff as *Ringan Gilhaize, or The Covenanters* (1823), the intriguingly-titled

154

The Bachelor's Wife: a Selection of Curious and Interesting Extracts . . . (1824), *The Painter: A Sicilian Tale* (1841), *The Fatal Whisper* (1841) and *Haddad-Ben-Ahab or The Traveller, A Tale of Stamboul* (1831) and their like to the quality of *The Entail, or The Lords of Grippy*. Galt wrote *The Member* in 1831 and had it published by his old patron James Fraser of *Fraser's Magazine* in January 1832, on the eve of the final Reform debates.

The Scotland in which Galt wrote was politically "backward," easily manipulated since the Union by Whiggish Campbells and latterly by the Pittite Henry Dundas[19]—"Harry the Ninth"—and his family. Dundas's task, wrote his Whig nephew Henry Cockburn, "consisted in laying forty-five Scotch members at the feet of the government."[20] Even Dundas never quite succeeded in this aim of controlling Edinburgh and the fourteen "districts of burghs" (whose Members were elected by delegates of the self-perpetuating councils) and the thirty county seats (whose M.P.s were chosen by handfuls of freeholders, whose voting rights were often "fictitiously" created by the land-owners). "From 1707 to 1832," explains Professor Gash, "Scotland resembled one vast rotten borough."[21] In 1788 county voters allegedly totalled 2662 but in fact were fewer, "Parchment barons" who had no *dominium utile* but who had retained or bought the *dominium directum* in some parcel of land. The total reported electorate of 4239 in 1820 rose to 65,000 under the Reform Act of 1832, but Dr Ferguson has clearly demonstrated that the Scottish Act—"the worst drafted of all the acts which deal with the representation of Scotland"—"introduced as many evils as it cured."[22]

Galt—and Jobbry—knew all this. When Jobbry, afflicted with a sudden desire to serve the public weal and an urgent desire to evade a voracious "nestful of cousins' children," first "began to clok on the idea of getting [himself] made a Member of Parliament" he found that "we in Scotland are not so clever in the way of getting into Parliament, without family connections, as they are in England." As he told the equally sly Mr Curry,[23]

in our country in Scotland, the pedigree family "bear the bell" in all electioneerings; for my Lord Entail, their cousin, has made as many freeholders on the list as the valuation of his estate allows, and three of the district-boroughs are under his thumb; so by that means they have all the rule and power of the shire.

Now Galt was always unsympathetic and often unfair to the lairds. Ancient lineage "cut no ice" with him. "Some of the ancient families, in their turreted houses, were not pleased" with the development of industry, he maintained in the *Annals,*

> especially when they saw the handsome dwellings that were built for the weavers of the [cotton] mills, and the unstinted hand that supplied the wealth required for the carrying on of the business. It sank their pride into insignificance, and many of them would almost rather have wanted the rise that took place in the value of their lands, than have seen this incoming of what they called o'er-sea speculation.

He added, of some local heritors[24]

> who were in general straitened in their circumstances, partly with upsetting, and partly by the eating rust of family pride, which hurt the edge of many a clever fellow among them, that would have done well in the way of trade, but sunk into divors for the sake of their gentility.

Jobbry shared Galt's feelings about[25]

> several old lairds, that counted their descent from Adam's elder brother, who, when they heard that I was minded to go into Parliament, snorted east and west, and thought it a most upsetting audacity. But I had not been risking my health for five-and-twenty years in the climate of Bengal to pleasure them. . . .

Galt's own (unsuccessful) mercantile career led him to support Glaswegian *bourgeois* hostility to the Corn Law of 1815.

Ayrshire landowners did not in fact live down to Galt's estimation of them. They constituted (under a generally Whiggish grand aristocracy and generally smaller Tory lairds)

156

a remarkable group of proprietors who adjusted to the opportunities provided by the Industrial Revolution. To my mind[27]

Farmers, politicians, mineral developers, transport pioneers, patrons, businessmen, harbour builders, socialites, scholars, sportsmen, merchants and military men [they] present a rich panorama [which] deserve[s] much further examination.

Rather than re-present an array of evidence, one example may suffice. The Blairs of Blair were able to trace the sort of medieval lineage at which Galt scoffed. They owned (in 1883) 7280 Ayrshire acres around Dalry, with a gross annual value of £5828.[28] Colonel William Blair was the last Tory M.P. for the county before the Reform and therefore precisely the sort of man whom Galt lambasted. But he was also a major agricultural improver, a director of the Glasgow and Ayrshire Railway Company of 1837 and a mineral developer; his successor, Captain William, became an expert on iron and coal workings.[29]

Of course, Ayrshire's Parliamentary representation had long been dominated—at Edinburgh and, since 1708, at Westminster—by members of the dynastic families: Montgomeries, Dalrymples, Cathcarts, Brisbanes, Campbells, Kennedys, Fergussons, McDowalls, Fullartons and Boyles all took their turn.[30] Blair was disastrously defeated in 1832. Precisely which candidate Jobbry (or, indeed, Galt) might have preferred is a matter for conjecture. Having made his creature, Jobbry, decide to contest an English seat, Galt evades the issue, which is a pity, as an informed caricature of a Scottish election would have provided additional delight and insight. But perhaps this is to ask too much. Political satire was a dangerous game in early nineteenth-century Ayrshire. One Tory laird and M.P., Sir Alexander Boswell of Auchinleck, son of Johnson's biographer, had published an attack on the awful Whig James Stuart of Dunearn in 1822, was "called-out" and was killed in the duel with the future most inefficient Factory Inspector.[31] Galt was wise (one imagines) to send the dreadful Jobbry down to England to seek his seat in Parliament! This may be a too cynical interpretation of Galt's motives. But what was (presumably) the last Scottish political

duel was fought in the University of Glasgow as late as 1899
—though without any deadly consequence.[32]

III

Jobbry was not the first Scot to make a fortune ("a decent competency," as he put it) in India and—as a glance at *Burke's Landed Gentry*[33] amply confirms—to invest part of it in a landed estate. India had long attracted Scots, from the days when Dundas ran the Board of Control and actively promoted Scots to East India Company posts.[34] And English seats attracted Scottish (particularly Tory) candidates for many years.

Pre-Reform England had a wide variety of franchises. The counties returned 82 M.P.s (elected by 40s. freeholders), the universities 4 (elected by M.A.s) and the boroughs 403. Mr Michael Brock identifies six types of borough distinguished by often-ancient electoral qualifications: "Scot and lot" (38), "Potwalloper" (14), "Burgage" (35), "Corporation" (29), "Freeman" (80) and "Freeholder" (6). The first group enfranchised men paying poor rates: the second, men resident for six months and not in receipt of Poor Law aid; the third, owners of particular old properties; the fourth the (generally self-perpetuating) corporations; the fifth, those men who held their "freedom" under local regulations; and the sixth, the freeholders.[35] The extent of domination by single patrons or interest groups varied considerably, as did the direct or indirect expenditure required of candidates.

Rascally Jobbry selected one of the five single-Member boroughs. These were Abingdon, Banbury, Bewdley, Higham Ferrers and Monmouth. If "Frailtown" in "Vamptonshire" (a geographical detail only discovered by Mr Jobbry, M.P., in chapter vii) really was a "corporation" borough, Abington (a "scot and lot" borough) and Monmouth (a "freeman" constituency) cannot have been the model. Nor did Higham Ferrers qualify, under Mr Brock's definition, as another "freeman" borough. But Professor Gordon, on evidence scattered about by Jobbry, identifies (to my mind, pretty conclusively) "Frailtown" with Higham Ferrers, "Beverington" with Bedford and "Physickspring" with Wellingborough. So perhaps Jobbry's memory failed him, or Galt exercised the freedom necessarily allowed to novelists. And perhaps we are inclined to be a bit too pernickety about sorting out the actual locations. Surely, we learn something about what contemporaries thought from

> some account of Eatanswill; of the state of parties therein; and of the election of a Member to serve in Parliament for that ancient, loyal, and patriotic borough.

or from such "reports" as those on "Darlford" and "Barchester."[37]

However, if Higham Ferrers (in Northamptonshire) was indeed the model for "Frailtown," it merits a note. It had returned a Member since 1557; its earliest charter was granted in 1251; its electors in 1831 consisted of the corporation (mayor, recorder, deputy recorder, seven aldermen and thirteen capital burgesses) and freemen—thirty-three voters in all, from a borough population of 965 living in 169 houses;[38] the patron was Earl Fitzwilliam.[39] The last fact again makes one wonder whether Galt really did intend to portray Higham Ferrers in any meaningful way, for the borough's elections bore little resemblance to those of "Frailtown." Fitzwilliam was a Whiggish territorial magnate in Yorkshire, Northamptonshire and Ireland who returned his relatives, the Hon. Frederick Ponsonby and Viscount Howick, his son (Viscount Milton), his friend C. C. Pepys (Lord Cottenham) and his relative the Hon. J. G. Ponsonby in the years before 1832.[40] This was all splendidly Whiggish, but very different from the experiences of "Frailtown." Perhaps Jobbry's geography erred; perhaps Galt further exercised literary licence (as he did by reducing the electorate to six—five fewer than the notorious Old Sarum). The precise location of Jobbry's jaunts into politics scarcely matters.

IV

Jobbry had to break the law by actually buying his seat (albeit at a knock-down price, because only two Parliamentary sessions remained, and by careful blackmail). Next he had to consider which party to support:

159

between Whigs and Tories I can make no distinction,—a Tory is but a Whig in office, and a Whig but a Tory in opposition, which makes it not difficult for a conscientious man to support the government[42]

—"to help his kith and kin by a judicious assistance to Government." And then, to advance himself and the interests of those "voracious larks" of relatives, he had to ingratiate himself among the mighty and distribute (taxpayers') *largesse* among the humble. But the "independent member" is no hack. He is concerned about an elector's plight; he supports Roman Catholic Relief; he "looked on [the ultra-Tories] as the pillars of the state; but [he] was not himself one of them"; he learns (unpleasantly) of magisterial hostility to "the complaints of the people"; and finally is "vext" at being unable to sell his now condemned seat. By the Reform Act, Jobbry complains,

the power of representing two-and-twenty millions was proposed to be given to no less than the half of one million . . . I saw that the die was cast, . . . well aware that the one-and-twenty millions and a half will not be long content with such a fractional representation as it is proposed to give them; for what is reform intended to do, unless it be to work out the abolition of rents and tithes, ...

There is a melancholy ("moderate Tory") conclusion to the novel, when Jobbry writes in his last paragraph that

It is true that Lord Dilldam wished me to stand again, upon the high Tory interest; but my moderation would not listen to the suggestion: indeed, his lordship shewed himself not very wise in this, for how could I expect to be well received in a town where my temperate politics were going out of fashion, the obstinate side? All was over; and to struggle I saw would be of no avail, so I determined at the dissolution, to close my career, which I have accordingly done; and now, as a simple spectator, I look a far off for the coming on of what is ordained to take place.

Such was the attitude of many despondent Tories in 1832—including Croker (Disraeli's "Rigby"), though he carried on

160

Eglinton Castle, Irvine

The seat of Galt's "Lord Eglesham." The bridge was
constructed in 1839, the year of Galt's death.

The centre of Irvine in the nineteenth century

a brave fight. When Haslemere's representation was abolished in 1832 Bill Holmes was also cast adrift—though he fought Ipswich in June 1835, sat for Berwick in 1837-1841 and contested Sheffield in 1841.[44] But many, like Jobbry, simply left public life, as a *bourgeois* electorate took over.

Galt was (too briefly) and is admired as a realistic novelist,[45] albeit writing under the shadow of the (much higher) Tory Scott. His portrayal of a Scottish "nabob"-politician in *The Member* is both witty and a convincing (however exaggerated) example of his "theoretical histories." Why the book disappeared from view—reappearing after a few months, bound with *The Radical,* as *The Reform* (1832)[46]—is a mystery. Thereafter, all was silent in this area of Scottish literature for many a year. Perhaps the rediscovery of the author of more than just the *Annals* by universities and colleges will rehabilitate one of Scotland's most amusing and most observant novelists.

NOTES

1. William Holmes (*c.* 1778-1851) MP. 1808-32, Treasurer of the Ordnance.
2. Sir Lewis Namier, *The Structure of Politics at the Accession of George III* (1973 repr.) pp 162, 245-8, 286 *et seq.;* T. H. B. Oldfield, *The Representative History of Great Britain and Ireland* (6 vols. 1816), iv, p 405; J. Holladay Philbin, *Parliamentary Representation, 1832. England and Wales* (New Haven, Conn. 1965), p 156.
3. Oldfield, *op cit.,* iv, pp 599-602; Philbin, *op. cit.,* p 184. Holmes sat for Grampound (1808-12), Tregony (1812-18) and Totnes (1819-20).
4. *Dictionary of National Biography* (1908), ix, pp 1093-4, vii, 828-32.
5. Denis Gray, *Spencer Perceval. The Evangelical Prime Minister, 1762-1812* (Manchester, 1963), p 426.
6. C. R. Fay, *Huskisson and His Age* (1951), p 8; Lady Longford, *Wellington, Pillar of State* (1972), pp 220-1; John Gore (ed.), *Creevey* (1949 repr.), p 317; J. T. Ward, *Sir James Graham* (1967), pp 89-92.
7. Michael Brock, *The Great Reform Act* (1973), pp 190, 241-2.
8. Charles Arbuthnot (1768-1850). Francis Bamford and Duke of Wellington (eds.), *The Journal of Mrs Arbuthnot* (2 vols. 1950).
9. W. R. Brock, *Lord Liverpool and Liberal Toryism* (1941), p 101; Asa Briggs, *The Age of Improvement* (1969 impr.), p 188.
10. Sir Spencer Walpole, *A History of England from the Conclusion of the Great War in 1815* (1903 impr.), ii, p 440.
11. Gore, *op. cit.,* p 323.

L   161

12. J. W. Croker (1780-1857), M. F. Brightfield, *J. W. Croker* (1940).
13. F. R. Bonham (1785-1863). Norman Gash, "F. R. Bonham: Conservative Political Secretary," 1832-47, *English Hist. Rev.* (1948). Lady Longford, *op. cit.,* p 283, states that Bonham "was socially a cut above . . . Holmes" for some reason.
14. Ward, *op. cit.,* pp 160-1.
15. I. A. Gordon, *John Galt, The Life of a Writer* (1972), intro. to *The Member* (Edinburgh, 1975 edn.).
16. M. E. Speare, *The Political Novel. Its Development in England and in America* (New York, 1924); R. E. George, "The Novels of Disraeli," *Nineteenth Century,* xcvi (1924); M. Masefield, *Peacocks and Primroses* (1953); S. M. Smith, "Willenhall and Woodgate: Disraeli's Use of Blue Book Evidence," *Review of English Studies* ns, xiii (1962); Robert Blake, "Disraeli's Political Novels," *History Today,* xvi (1966).
17. Anthony Trollope, *An Autobiography* (1883; 1962 edn.), ch. 16.
18. Gordon, *op. cit.* and *loc. cit.;* John Galt, *Autobiography* (2 vols., 1833).
19. Henry, 1st Viscount Melville (1742-1811) laird; Sol. Gen. Scot. 1766, Lord Advoc. 1775, Treasurer Navy 1782, Pres. Board of Control 1784, Home Sec. 1791, War Sec., 1st Ld. Admiralty 1804, impeached 1805. H. Furber, *Henry Dundas 1st Viscount Melville* (1931).
20. *Cf.* Henry Cockburn, *Life of Lord Jeffrey* (Edinburgh, 2 vols., 1852), i, p 77; Karl Miller, *Cockburn's Millennium* (1975), *passim.*
21. N. Gash, *Politics in the Age of Peel* (1953), p 36.
22. W. Ferguson, *Scotland, 1689 to the Present* (Edinburgh, 1968) *passim,* "The Reform Act (Scotland) of 1832: Intention and Effect," *Scottish Hist. Rev.,* xlv (1966); J. T. Ward, "A Footnote on the First Reform Act," *ibid.,* xlvi (1967); J. Wilson, *Political State of Scotland* (1833), R. S. Tait, *The Parliaments of Scotland* (Glasgow, 1924), John Cay, *An Analysis of the Scottish Reform Act . . .* (Edinburgh 1850).
23. John Galt, *The Member* (Edinburgh 1975 edn.), pp 4, 6.
24. John Galt, *Annals of the Parish, or The Chronicle of Dalmailing . . .* (Edinburgh, 1821; 1911 edn.), pp 178, 181.
25. John Galt, *The Member* (1975 edn.), p 4.
26. John Galt, "Hints to the Country Gentlemen," *Blackwood's Magazine* (1822).
27. J. T. Ward, "Ayrshire Landed Estates in the Nineteenth Century," *Ayrshire Arch. & Nat. Hist. Soc. Collections,* 2s, viii (1967-9), pp 93-145; *cf.* J. T. Ward and R. G. Wilson (eds.), *Land and Industry* (Newton Abbot, 1971) *passim.*
28. John Bateman, *The Great Landowners of Great Britain and Ireland* (1883 edn.; Leicester, 1971 repr., intro. David Spring), p 43, (1879), p 41; *Parliamentary Papers* 1874, lxxii, "Scotland. Owners of Land and Heritages," p 18.
29. William (*d.* 1841), William Fordyce Blair (1805-88). Blair of Blair Muniments (Scottish Record Office, Edinburgh), GD. 167/4E etc. and further references in Ward "Ayrshire Landed Estates."

30. A list will be given in my forthcoming history of the Scottish Tory Party; see *Glasgow Herald, 5* Apr. 1939.
31. Sir A. Boswell, 1st bt. (1775-1822), landowner, sportsman, antiquarian, poet, publisher.
32. *Glasgow University Magazine, 8* Mar. 1899. I am indebted to Mr Gerald Warner and Dr Francis Lambert for this reference.
33. The most useful edition is that of 1898 (2 vols.).
34. Janet R. Glover, *The Story of Scotland* (1977 edn.), pp 290-2; C. H. Philips, *The East India Company* (1940) *passim.*
35. Brock, *op. cit.,* ch. 1, includes a fascinating analysis. *Cf.* Oldfield, *passim;* E. Porritt, *The Unreformed House of Commons* (2 vols., 1903: repr. 1963), *passim;* Philbin, *passim.*
36. Brock, *op. cit.,* pp 20, 21; Gordon, intro., p ix.
37. Charles Dickens, *The Pickwick Papers* (1836-37), ch. 13; Benjamin Disraeli, *Coningsby* (1844), bk. 5, ch. 4; Anthony Trollope, *Dr Thorne* (1858), ch. 16.
38. Philbin, *op. cit.,* pp 138-9, 332-3; Oldfield, *op. cit.,* ii, pp 292-5.
39. William, 4th Earl Fitzwilliam (1748-1833), landowner; Lord Lieut. Ireland, 1795. J. T. Ward, "The Earls Fitzwilliam and the Wentworth Woodhouse Estate in the Nineteenth Century," *Yorkshire Bulletin of Economic and Social Research,* xii (1960).
40. Philbin, *op. cit.,* pp 138-9.
41. Porritt, *op. cit.,* p 346 seq.
42. *Cf.* Disraeli, *Coningsby,* bk. 2, ch. 6: "'A sound Conservative government,' said Taper, musingly. 'I understand: Tory men and Whig measures'." Taper (*ibid.,* bk. 1, ch. 1) "under the old system had sneaked into the Treasury Board." He resembled Holmes.
43. L. J. Jennings (ed.), *Correspondence and Diaries of John Wilson Croker* (3 vols., 1884), p ii. As Walter Allen pointed out (intro. to *Coningsby,* 1948 edn., pp 15-16) Disraeli's "Rigby" was unfair to Croker, while his "Monmouth" was rather better than the appalling Marquess of Hertford (Thackeray's "Steyne").
44. F. W .S. Craig (ed.), *British Parliamentary Election Results, 1832-1885* (1977), pp 41, 162, 282.
45. Christopher Harvie, *Scotland and Nationalism. Scottish Society and Politics, 1707-1977* (1977), pp 71, 134, 143-4.
46. Gordon, intro, p xiii, n. 5.

MIND-FORG'D MANACLES :
JOHN GALT'S *THE ENTAIL* AS ROMANTIC
TRAGICOMEDY

KEITH M. COSTAIN

John Galt thought *The Entail* different in character from any
of his previous fictions. He wrote excitedly of it to his publisher, Blackwood, on June 23, 1822, to say that

> I may be mistaken in my anticipation, but I think it will
> be out of all comparison the most vigorous and lively
> work I have yet attempted. . . . It has taken full possession
> of my fancy & I always know that when I am myself
> interested I do not fail in the effort.[1]

Hitherto he had written compact comic narratives that could
be accommodated in "the single post octavo" volume,[2] with
the exception of *Sir Andrew Wylie* (1822), a novel Galt judged
had been spoiled by Blackwood's insistence that a story conceived on a smaller scale be expanded to fill three volumes.
The Entail, however, was more ambitiously conceived both
in scope and depth so that it required the latter format, as
Galt advised Blackwood in a letter on June 8, 1822, in which
he wrote that "during the summer I intend to devote myself
exclusively to 'The Entail' which I foresee will extend to
three volumes."[3]

In spite of the fact that Galt generally found a traditional
plot a "comparatively galling harness"[4] he submitted to the
discipline of forward planning which the scale of the work he
had in mind required. His imagination fired from the start,
he worked quickly and in his letter of June 23 informed
Blackwood "I have constructed the whole fable of my Entail,
determined the characters and most of the incidents."[5] The
novel was composed with the rapidity with which it was
planned. The first volume was largely written by September 3,
1822, and sent to Blackwood on October 11, when Galt
announced "I have also a considerable portion of Vol II

164

ready."⁶ The book was finished, printed, and distributed to the booksellers by early December, a date that seems to have surprised his publisher since the novel was printed with the date "1823" on its title-page.

This novel, written with such rapidity, was an immediate success. Scott, who described Galt's plays as "the worst tragedies ever seen,"⁷ and Byron who, in December 1813, had irritably confided to his journal that "Galt is almost the last person on whom anyone would commit literary larceny"⁸ were both enthusiastic. In his *Life of Byron* (1830) Galt recalls with relish that Byron "sent me word, by the Earl of Blesinton [*sic*], that he had read my novel of *The Entail* three times. . . . This was the more agreeable, as I had heard within the same week, that Sir Walter Scott had done and said nearly the same thing."⁹ Lady Blessington records Byron singling out *The Entail* for special notice in saying of Galt:

> There is a quaint humour and observance of character in his novels that interests me very much, and when he chooses to be pathetic he fools one to his bent, for I assure you "The Entail" beguiled me of some portion of watery humours, yclept tears, "albeit unused to the melting mood."¹⁰

Scott and Byron were not alone in their appreciation of *The Entail*. Initially referring to *The Provost* (1822) Coleridge noted in his copy of that work: "This and 'the Entail' would alone suffice to place Galt in the first rank of contemporary Novellists [*sic*]—and second only to Sir W. Scot [*sic*] in technique."¹¹ When Francis Jeffrey declared *The Entail* "a work undoubtedly of no ordinary merit"¹² he understated the opinion of other discerning contemporary reviewers and readers.

Despite its flaws *The Entail* is Galt's masterpiece and, as Francis Russell Hart has recently observed, "Galt's most admired work."¹³ It stands out in its emotional and imaginative power from Galt's skilfully written but ironically distanced comic fictions which, perhaps, is why such initially unsympathetic critics of Galt's writing as Scott and Byron found this work especially attractive. Various explanations have been offered of the source of the novel's power, none entirely satisfactory since each tends to treat the tragedy and the comedy in the novel as separate entities. This essay will argue, by contrast, that the fusion of tragic with comic elements is the basic structural principle of the novel and that its power derives from the union of a tragic with a comic vision at a time when the "tragic spirit" sought an outlet in fiction.[14]

At the centre of *The Entail* stands Claud Walkinshaw, a complex figure in whose nature and fate the elements of tragedy and comedy are inextricably entwined. If one is to judge by the evidence of the text he it was who took "full possession" of Galt's "fancy." While he occupies the centre of the stage the power of the novel is undisputed, but critics have rightly noted a diminution of power when he is removed from the drama long before the novel ends. It will be argued here that the original force of *The Entail* is diminished because Galt did not sustain the tragicomic vision with which he began, for it depends upon the protagonist he removed from the action. This, however, does not alter the fact that the tragicomic vision of *The Entail* is something new in the novel,[15] is in itself impressively dramatised, and was to be developed by later writers of the nineteenth century.

II

The case which this essay makes relies upon two bases: a certain view of tragicomedy and, despite his reputation as a comic writer, the fact that Galt was also disposed to write of the tragic in human experience. It is necessary, therefore, before *The Entail* is examined in detail, to offer a preliminary definition of the term "tragicomedy" as it is used in the ensuing discussion. It is also necessary, since Galt is generally thought of as a comic writer, to show how Romantic poetry, drama and fiction stimulated a fundamental element in his character that induced him to contemplate and to write of the tragic element in man.

To begin with a working definition of tragicomedy, that which most closely corresponds to what one finds in *The Entail,* it seems to me, is expounded by Karl S. Guthke in his book *Modern Tragicomedy.* Modern tragicomedy, he argues, is a "synthetic union of [the elements of tragedy and comedy] which creates a virtual identity of both, where the comic is the tragic and the tragic the comic."[16] The synthesis is possible because both tragedy and comedy express the dual nature of man from which contradictoriness of motive and conduct springs. Both genres demonstrate man's ability to conceive the ideal and his inability to attain it; both acknowledge man's capacity for aspiration and self-sacrifice while pointing to his propensity to pride and greed. The two genres differ, of course, in their manner of expressing their common awareness of human contradiction: in Kierkegaard's formulation of the distinction between them "the tragic is the suffering contradiction, the comical the painless contradiction."[17] However, since awareness of human contradiction is at the root of both genres a basis exists for synthesis. Such a synthesis has been attempted by a variety of writers who, as Guthke indicates, have recognised "the *identity* of tragic fear and comic laughter."[18] It is these writers, John Galt among them, who have helped to develop the genre known (not always happily) as "tragicomedy."

The Romantics thought that by itself comedy was incapable of adequately expressing their view of the world. They thought tragicomedy more suitable for the purpose since, as Guthke observes, they considered it "the most truthful and intimate expression of the mentality of the moderns because this mentality was no longer characterised by harmony and confidence in the healing powers of life, but by contrast and unrest, tensions and disharmonies of all kinds."[19] The awareness of the tragic manifested in Romantic literature encouraged Galt to portray the tragic element in human life, as is suggested by what he writes in his *Literary Life* of his reaction to Mrs Radcliffe's novel, *The Italian*:

I can recollect no work by which I have been more affected. It set me to the composition of a tragedy, which I called The Confessor, and in which were several scenes taken from incidents in the romance that I thought impressive.[20]

Galt's Romantic reading included Scott and Byron in particular, but he also read a variety of other writers who can be classified (sometimes roughly, as in the case of Mrs Radcliffe) as Romantic. His list encompasses Southey, Campbell,

Shelley and Wordsworth. He responded eagerly to Goethe's *Werther,* declared Schiller's *Robbers* "a work of genius," and offered guarded approval of the poet Bürger.[21] It was Alfieri's tragic dramas that moved Galt, in 1812, to produce his own volumes of *Tragedies*[22] (the volume privately derided by Scott), each of the plays in it, he notes, "formed in a great measure on Alfieri's plan."[23] Galt's plays sufficiently resembled the works of his Romantic contemporaries for Henry Crabb Robinson to describe "The Witness" (not included in the above-mentioned volume) as "a short tragedy, ill-conceived as a tragedy or dramatic poem, but containing fine passages, and evidently the work of a man of genius of the School of Coleridge."[24]

Galt's dramas make for heavy reading today but in "Maddalen," one of those included in the Alfieri-inspired volume of 1812, lie the seeds of *The Entail.* The novel is an infinitely more successful working out of the idea behind the play, which Galt explains as an undertaking

> . . . to try whether such a person as the Duchess, a character of meaner energies than the generality of those on whom the interest of the solemn drama is supposed essentially to depend, might be rendered capable of exciting a tragical degree of pathetic sympathy.[25]

Galt was experimenting to see whether ordinary life could be tragically depicted for the Duchess in the play, in spite of her title, is more bourgeois than noble. He seems to have been acting on his belief, later enunciated in a discussion of tragedy in his *Literary Life,* that "the affections in private life are quite as likely, if we look well about us, to furnish topics of distress as those of the blood royal in any age or country."[26]

Some of the central dramatic elements in "Maddalen" resemble significant features of *The Entail,* a novel Galt wrote, in part at least, with a dramatic model in mind.[27] In both works the tragic focus is set upon sacrifice. In "Maddalen" the Duke brings his daughter as a sacrifice "to the altar of the golden Moloch,"[28] while in *The Entail* Claud Walkinshaw sacrifices his eldest son "beguiled," as he eventually confesses, "by the Moloch o' pride and ambition."[29] The Duchess in "Maddalen" is a forerunner of Claud Walkinshaw's wife, the Leddy Grippy of *The Entail,* employing a comic turn of phrase amid tragic circumstances. But it is Claud Walkinshaw, the Laird of Grippy, whose "meaner energies" are so dramatised as to excite "a tragical degree of pathetic sympathy." Prefigured in "Maddalen" by the Duke, he pursues as ultimately worthless an objective, casting a shadow across the world of *The Entail* like Heathcliffe's over the world of *Wuthering Heights.*[30]

What actually induced Galt to turn an early drama into an extensive novel is a matter of speculation. Perhaps he was persuaded to do so by the recent success of *The Provost,* which was developed from an early sketch.[31] Perhaps he was influenced to write a novel in which the tragic is equated with the comic rather than, as in his earlier works, subordinated to it, by his reaction to *Adam Blair,* Lockhart's novel of passion. Lockhart's work was published early in the year in which Galt wrote *The Entail* and he was enthusiastic about it. In March 1822 Galt wrote to Blackwood in terms not unlike those he was later to use to characterise his own embryonic novel to say that *Adam Blair* is "without question a work that displays the author to be possessed of extraordinary power. . . . It belongs to no age or country, but to general human nature."[32] As members of Blackwood's circle Galt and Lockhart were personally acquainted, and it is possible that Galt sought to equal or surpass Lockhart's achievement in writing a novel which displays the destructive influence of passion, and which belongs "to no age or country, but to general human nature."

Whether this supposition is correct or not *The Entail* is a more powerful novel than *Adam Blair.* Adam is not permitted to reach the level of the tragic though later, in *The Scarlet Letter,* Hawthorne was to show how tragically a plight such as Adam's could be rendered. Galt was tougher-minded than Lockhart, following the logic of his protagonist's situation to its bitter end so that Claud Walkinshaw suffers tragically in an essentially comic world.

Claud's tragic status is underscored by the association of his course of life with the story of Faust, that tragic figure of central importance to the Romantics. It was not, however, to Goethe's version of the story that Galt was indebted for that, he writes, ". . . gave me no pleasure, though its glaiks of

169

nature were often most impressive."[33] Instead, he was deeply moved by Byron's version of the Faust story as it appears in his *Manfred*. Galt's judgment of *Manfred* is extravagant:

> The delineation of that Promethean fortitude which defied conscience, as he [Byron] has shown it in Manfred, is his greatest achievement. The terrific fables of Marlowe, and of Goethe, in their respective versions of the legend of Faustus, had disclosed the utmost writhings which remorse, in the fiercest of its torments, can express; but what are these Laocoon agonies to the sublime serenity of Manfred. In the power, the originality, and the genius combined, of that unexampled performance, Lord Byron has placed himself on an equality with Milton.[34]

In writing his story of a man who "defied conscience" with something approaching "Promethean fortitude" Galt seems to have adapted elements of Byron's version of the Faust story to the realities of bourgeois life in a mercantilist society.

In his discussion of *Manfred* in his *Life of Byron* Galt indicates that family sacrifice is its central tragic motif, as it is also of his own early play "Maddalen" and of *The Entail*. In Galt's reading of Byron's poetic drama Manfred permits his sister literally to make a sacrifice of herself in order that he may satisfy his desire for forbidden knowledge. The "primary spring of Byron's tragedy," as Galt conceives it, is that this human sacrifice which is "among the initiate propitiations of the demons" is carried out in vain for it does not produce "that happiness which the votary expected would be found in the knowledge and power purchased at such a price." Manfred's challenge to the supernatural order is punished by the needless loss of "the dearest object to himself, and to whom he also was dearest."[35] Similarly, in *The Entail* Claud Walkinshaw defies the supernatural, in the form of Providence, in order to satisfy desires as prideful as Manfred's only to lose his best-loved son as needlessly as Manfred had lost his beloved sister, and as much in consequence of his own conduct. Both suffer similarly: Manfred's conduct, in Galt's view, "severs him from hope, as everlastingly as the apostacy of the angels has done Satan"[36] and Claud exclaims sorrowfully to his minister "I fear, I fear Dr Denholm . . . that I

170

can hae no hope" (p 149). For his "apostacy" Claud is ultimately as "manacled with guilt"[37] as Manfred, confessing "I sold my soul to the Evil One in my childhood that I might recover the inheritance of my forebears" (p 149).

The world of *Manfred* is, however, symbolic, and Manfred is a symbolic figure who, to use Galt's words, "despises sympathy, and almost glories in his perdition."[38] With superhuman fortitude Manfred transcends the tragic whereas Claud Walkinshaw, a creature of flesh and blood living in an actual society, is reduced to despair at the thought of eternal damnation. Instead of enduring his fate, like Manfred, in proud solitude, he confesses to sin, seeks to atone and to enter the comic world of Christian charity from which he has long been alienated.

III

In his book *Letters from the Levant,* published the year after his *Tragedies,* Galt writes:

> It is generally thought that the development of passion forms the proper theme of Tragedy, and the effect of manners that of Comedy. I am not sure that this is correct. Passions and manners appear to me common to both provinces of the drama; and the circumstances with which they are connected, constitute all the difference between a tragedy and a comedy. It is impossible to conceive men in any state without passions, and it is no less so to discriminate characters without manners.[39]

It remains to be shown how, in *The Entail,* Galt so orders "circumstances" that they operate upon "passions" and upon "manners" to produce a complex interfusion of the tragic with the comic. It is important, first, to consider the rôle of the narrator whose "attitude and perspective," as Karl Guthke observes, are primarily responsible in the novel for "the realization of the tragi-comic."[40]

The narrator of any novel defines its "world," the objective order of its "reality." In a tragicomic novel the narrator draws the reader's attention to the contradiction, which is both tragic and comic, between the protagonist's desires,

171

motives, and conduct and what the narrator knows to be the unchangeable order of existence. This is what happens in *The Entail*.

The primary characteristic of the order of existence presented in *The Entail,* even more emphatically than in Galt's earlier novels, is benevolence. A benevolent Providence governs events by inscrutable laws ordained to ensure the general good. The individual must live within the limits prescribed by those laws in order to live peacefully and harmoniously with himself and with others. The benevolent man, whose world is the world of comedy, recognises this necessity whereas the foolish and tragic man challenges, like Claud Walkinshaw, the eternal order of things on which the general good depends. Such a man must be reminded, through repeated failure, that there is a naturally just relationship between his character, conduct and fate. It is only after the frustration of his dearest plans that Claud begins to understand reality more clearly. "He began to think," the narrator explains, that

> . . . there was something in the current of human affairs over which he could acquire no control, and that, although in pursuing so steadily the single purpose of recovering the family inheritance, his endeavours had, till this period, proved eminently successful, yet he saw with dismay, that from the moment other interests came to be blended with those he considered so peculiarly his own, other causes also came into operation, and turned, in spite of all his hedging and prudence, the whole issue of his labours awry. He perceived that human power was set at nought by the natural course of things. . . . (p 115).

Claud's blindness to the "natural course of things," his ignorance of the fact that the interaction of "interests" is unforeseeable, lead him to the absurdity of defying an omnipotent Providence and attempting to re-shape an immutable order of metaphysical reality. But if his conduct is absurd it is also tragic for it calls out the best as well as the worst elements in his strong character. He endures suffering of an intensity that could not be borne by those among whom he lives.

Claud is " a character fit for tragedy" who finds himself in "a world that distinctly belongs to the realm of comedy," as is the case with other tragicomic figures.[41] There is a contradiction between Claud and his world because he will not assent to its benevolent reality, not only because he is blind to the "natural course of things," which brings about the general good, but also because he opposes the values of his world, which themselves are based on benevolence. The world Claud inhabits is peopled largely (though by no means entirely) by those who are good-humoured and accepting. As characters in a comic world generally are, they are prepared "to forgive the weaknesses, the treachery, the downright depravity which, in spite of man's best intentions, are inherent in his behaviour."[42] Not until the end of his life is Claud prepared to forgive. Instead of assimilating those moral qualities which, in his world, make for community, he remains the sour embodiment of self-interest.

The moral contradiction between Claud and his world is especially evident when the narrator draws attention to the conflicting attitudes to Nature held by the protagonist and his fellow-men. Those who truly belong to the comic world of *The Entail* feel at one with Nature. Mr Keelevin, Claud's lawyer, is an illustrative example. Unlike the stereotyped lawyers of satirical drama and fiction (some of whom put in an appearance later in the novel) self-interest is not his principal motive. He regards as an act of injustice Claud's disinheritance of his eldest son, Charles, and his settlement of all his landed property on Walter, his second son, in order to regain and (he hopes) retain intact the family estate of Kittlestonheugh which his grandfather lost by a rash speculation. Thus, when Charles dies as a result of his father's betrayal of him, Keelevin rides to Claud's house to persuade the old man to provide for Charles's family. On the way he pauses to admire a pastoral scene, and the narrator observes that he looked

. . . on the beautiful tranquillity of the landscape before him, with a sensation of freshness and pleasure, that restored him to confidence in the charity of his intentions. The waters of the river were glancing to the cloudless morning sun,—a clear bright cheerfulness dwelt on the

173

foreheads of the distant hills,—the verdure of the nearer fields seemed to be gladdened by the presence of spring,— and a band of little school-boys, in their Sunday clothes, playing with a large dog on the opposite bank of the river, was in unison with the general benevolence that smiled and breathed around, but was liveliest in his own heart (p 143).

Such scenes, in which the benevolence of the observer is confirmed and strengthened by intimations of a general benevolence making itself felt through natural beauty and harmony define the moral character of a world from which Claud Walkinshaw holds himself aloof.

When Claud surveys a landscape his pleasure in the view, we are told, arises not from rapt admiration of its beauty nor from experience of its harmony but from pride and self-congratulation. After he has regained the family estate the narrator remarks of Claud that

> . . . his only enjoyment seemed to be a sort of doating delight in contemplating, from a rude bench which he had constructed on a rising ground . . . the surrounding fields of his forefathers (p 112).

But "doating delight" gives way to "the nausea of moral disgust" when Keelevin brings him the news of Charles' death. Then he "seated himself with his back towards the view which had afforded him so much pleasure" (pp 147-8). This ludicrous posture emphasises the absurdity of one who tried to alter the reality and who rejected the benevolent values of the world in which he lived to suit his own unregulated desires, and who suffered for it, tragically.

Thus, by obliging the reader to recognise the contradictions in the relationship of Claud Walkinshaw to his world the narrator shows how inextricably mingled are the elements of tragedy and comedy as long as Claud dominates *The Entail*. In his analysis of Claud's character he also insists upon the inseparability of the tragic and the comic. Claud engages in absurd, self-defeating activities the comic aspect of which is clearly seen but the narrator does not permit the reader to

174

make easy judgments. Despite his folly Claud has the moral stature of a tragic hero; laughably ineffectual though many of his schemes may be they involve the perverse exercise of moral qualities which in themselves are worthy of the highest praise.

The narrator informs us that once Claud had bought back part of his family's estate coldly and deliberately "he resolved to marry, and beget children, and entail the property, that none of his descendants might ever have it in their power to commit the imprudence which had brought his grandfather to a morsel, and thrown himself on the world" (p 12). No matter how foolish such a policy may be and no matter how many ludicrous circumstances to which it gives rise, it nevertheless takes considerable courage to sustain. Claud must constantly fight against his own conscience, the more "natural" expectations of his family and of the people among whom he lives, and what he believes to be Divine displeasure at his motives and conduct. The narrator maintains that whatever else one may think of Claud,

> . . . there was undoubtedly something sublime in the forti-
> tude with which he endured the gnawings of remorse.—It
> may be impossible to consider the course of his sordid
> ambition without indignation; but the strength of character
> which enabled him to contend at once with his paternal
> partiality, and stand firm in his injustice before what he
> awfully deemed the frowns and menaces of Heaven, forms
> a spectacle of moral bravery that cannot be contemplated
> without emotions of wonder mingled with dread (p 140).

Claud lacks neither courage nor "the milk of human kindness" —or, as the narrator phrases it, "the leaven of original virtue." He may act harshly to get and to "grip" the family estate but, the narrator explains, there is a "vast abyss of sensi- bility which lay hidden and unknown within the impenetrable granite of the old man's pride and avarice" (p 146). This sensibility is especially aroused by his eldest son from whom, he tells Mr Keelevin, "I first kent the blessing of what it is to hae something to be kind to" (pp 145-6). Yet this is the son he betrays in an act of tragic folly underscored by the narrator as such when he notes that Claud felt

. . . a sentiment of sorrow, in strong affinity with remorse, [which] embittered his meditations, when he thought of the precipitancy with which he had executed the irrevocable entail, to the exclusion of Charles; to whom, prior to that unjust transaction, he had been more attached than to any other human being (p 106).

Once having "irrevocably" betrayed him it would have been psychologically easier for Claud to allow his love for his son to turn to hatred but, the narrator points out, "there was so much of the leaven of original virtue in the composition of his paternal affection, and in the general frame of his character, that this disagreeable feeling never took the decided nature of enmity. He did not hate because he had injured . . . (p 107). Neither, on the other hand, does Claud try to undo the entail (which is not quite "irrevocable") for his consciousness of having committed wrong "causes his feelings to recoil inward" so that, as with others in his predicament, "instead of prompting atonement" they "irritate us to repeat and to persevere in our injustice" (p 113).

The narrator reveals Claud to be as self-contradictory as he shows him to be in contradiction with his world, and the contradictions of Claud's character, like those between himself and his world, would be laughable were they not also tragic. In order to preserve the family "name" he destroys the son he loves better than anyone. For the greater glory of the Walkinshaws he bestows his lands upon Walter, a semi-idiot. One must ask why Claud's mind forges such manacles for him, and the answer to this question would seem to lie in Claud's irrational willingness to deceive himself as to the proper ideal to which he should devote his life.

Claud grew up in a society strongly affected by the beliefs of the Covenanters. He understands that his society expects him to obey the Divine Will, lead a life of strict religious devotion, and respect his fellow-men. But Claud's society is as contradictory as any other and also cherishes a feudal reverence of "name" and "family" and the landed property required to support these intangible attributes. Faced with mutually incompatible feudal and religious ideals, living in an age becoming steadily more secular than that of his covenanting forebears, and urged by an old family servant to think

Bronze relief sculpture of John Galt by Robert Bryden, 1904
In the possession of Kyle and Carrick Museums, Ayr.

Galt's birthplace, High Street, Irvine

His parents occupied the top flat (*left*). The building
is now demolished.

his family superior and to regain the lost ancestral estate of Kittlestonheugh Claud chooses the worldly feudal ideal over the religious ideal as one to which his life might worthily be devoted. He then pursues this false ideal *as if* it were that higher ideal which his repressed but by no means defunct religious sensibility never allows him to forget. Charles's wife judges Claud "one of the most sordid of men," but her assessment is too simple. She fails to understand the man the narrator reveals. She does not comprehend that with Claud even avarice "was but an agent in the pursuit of that ancestral phantom which he worshipped as the chief, almost the only good in life" (p 76). Before Charles's death shocks him into a recognition of reality Claud is incapable of acknowledging that his "worship" is idolatrous. For him it is as personally exacting and all-consuming as the Covenanter's devotion to God, as the narrator suggests when he remarks that

. . . as all he did and thought of in life was with a view to the restoration of the Walkinshaws of Kittlestonheugh, we might be justified, for the honour of human nature, to believe, that he actually contemplated the sacrifice which he was making of his first-born to the Moloch of ancestral pride, with reluctance, nay, even with sorrow (pp 69-70).

Claud destroys his son, his own peace of mind—even his hope of salvation—in the service of an ideal, but of a false ideal. What could be more laughable, or more tragic?

A final point should be made before turning to the dramatisation of character from the narrator's commentary and analysis. In the synthesis of tragic and comic elements that is tragicomedy the narrator makes the reader aware that if the tragic is also comic the comic can be tragic. If Claud is a tragic extremist whose extremism makes him comic as well as tragic his son Charles is a comic extremist whose turn of mind helps to bring about his tragic fate. He suffers from the tutelary influence of his grandmother, whose values are those of the comic world of the novel and thus are the opposite of Claud's, just as Claud suffers from the indoctrination of Maudge Dobbie, the Walkinshaw "bairnswoman" who exalts his family and exhorts him to regain its lands. Mrs Hypel, the grandmother, encourages Charles "to value love as the first of earthly blessings and of human enjoyments." Under her influence "his natural sensibility was exalted and refined," and he is persuaded to dissociate himself from the ways of a world concerned with "getting and spending." The narrator comments that

> . . . these romantic lessons were ill calculated to fit him to perform that wary part in the world which could alone have enabled him to master the malice of his fortune, and to overcome the consequences of that disinheritance which his father had never for a moment ceased to meditate, but only waited for an appropriate opportunity to carry into effect (p 41).

It is not that the narrator opposes the values of the heart, which Charles is taught to regard as of the highest importance —the entire novel advocates the superiority of such values over those of the designing head—but the narrator recognises, as Charles does not, that the grandmother's romantic idealism is held with too much intensity and single-mindedness owing to her own sorrowful experience of life. In rejecting self-interest she also rejects common prudence, encouraging her grandson to do the same, to his detriment. Thus Charles gives his father an excuse to disinherit him by making a love-match, which Claud opposes, with the daughter of a penniless laird. Then, when Claud, "afflicted by the discordant cheerfulness of Charles's voice in the outer room, joking with the clerks" (p 73), has brought his eldest and second sons to the law office to sign the entail Charles does as he is asked without inspecting the document. He thus ironically signs away his own birthright in large measure owing to his grandmother's early training, which emphasised love and trust, whereas Walter, mentally weak but put on his guard by a worldly mother, must be bribed to sign a paper that will make him heir to Kittlestonheugh. The grandmother's nurturing of Charles's sensibility also proves misguided in its excess. When, at last, he learns of his disinheritance the "heart-withering communication" (p 125) induces in Charles a "vehemence of feeling" which, coupled with the effects of a storm in which he lingers despairingly, causes him to succumb to a "rapid and raging fever" (p 126), leaving his family to suffer in straightened circumstances for many years to follow.

IV

The synthesis of the tragic and the comic is discernible not only in the commentary of the narrator, who "conditions" the reader to recognise the interfusion of tragedy and comedy in ordinary human life, but it is manifested also both in the manner in which the protagonist reveals his inner self, and in the types of relationship he has with other significant characters.

Despite his driving purpose Claud Walkinshaw dramatically discloses that he feels the scheme of disinheritance, essential for its success, is sinful. Claud believes in salvation, desires it, but comically and tragically bends all his energies to gall his sensitive conscience and, as he thinks, to damn himself. The unquiet nature of Claud's conscience is dramatically exposed in various tragicomic scenes. For example, soon after Charles's marriage and much to everyone's surprise he orders family worship offering his wife as an explanation of this uncharacteristic action the rationalisation that "when we're in a way to be made ancestors . . . we should be thinking of what's to come o' our sinful souls hereafter" (p 61). The comedy of the scene lies in the reader's knowledge and the Leddy Grippy's ironic ignorance of the fact that Claud has just given orders for the drawing up of the new entail and is fearful of his moral position. The comedy broadens when, after solemnly assembling family and servants, Claud opens the Bible at random and is confronted with the story of Esau and Isaac, a text he interprets as a divine admonition against his proposed course of legal action.[43] If, however, the contrast between Claud's soberly rationalised purpose in gathering family and servants together for worship and his rushing from the room in horror leaving in his wake an amazed assemblage is comic it also makes the reader aware of the inner struggle he must endure with tragic fortitude.

The "pious business of the evening" (p 64) leaves Claud's wife and other children bewildered, and Charles is equally perplexed when, in another tragicomic scene, his father offers him advice won from hard experience. Claud advises Charles "to mak na odds" among his children, "but remember that they are a' alike thine, and that t'ou canna prefer ane aboon anither without sin" (p 112). His son fails to recognise Claud's oblique confession for what it is and so asks none of the questions the answers to which might have spared both men further suffering. Claud's advice is wise but in his own life he has conspicuously failed to heed it and, in any case, it is advice the affectionate and trusting Charles doesn't need. A failure of communication of this sort, in scenes in which characters speak at cross-purposes, is often at the core of comedy, but in *The Entail* Claud's failures to communicate, comic though they often are, underscore his lonely, sorrowful plight and arouse the kind of pathos we associate with tragedy.

Such pathos is strengthened when Charles's illness and death force Claud to renounce the main purpose of his life and attempt to pull down the legal edifice he has been so much at pains to build. The ludicrous aspect of this situation requires no elaboration, especially when it is remembered that Claud's attempts to atone come too late and are largely ineffectual. But there is also a tragic aspect to Claud's belated renunciation of "the actuating principle of his life" (p 12). It is one Claud himself recognises when he takes a Faustian view of his futile career. He tells Mr Keelevin that

> . . . the curse of God has fallen upon me, my hands are tied, a dreadfu' chain has fastened about me; I hae cheated myself, and there's nae bail—no, not in the Heavens—for the man that has wilfully raffled away his own soul in the guilty game o' pride (p 137).

He is now willing to confess to his lawyer that idolatry has been his cardinal sin:

> Frae the very dawn o' life I hae done nothing but big and build an idolatrous image; and when it was finished, ye saw how I laid my first-born on its burning and brazen altar (p 146).

To Dr Denholm, his minister, he proclaims, "I had ever the right before me, when I deliberately preferred the wrang," and he admits that, foolishly, he hoped to escape punishment by a last-minute trick. But, he confesses, "a' the time there was a voice within me that would na be pacified wi' the vain promises I made to become another man, as soon as ever my conquest was complete" (p 150).

If Claud is ultimately unable to fool himself concerning the true nature of the ends he sought to gain he is equally unable to deceive himself about the means he employed. He has been avaricious in his acquisition of wealth, at first in order to amass enough money to buy back the Walkinshaw estate, and then to provide a fortune for its upkeep and to add lustre to the family name. But his sufferings cause him to acknowledge that "the inner man alone knows, whether in the gifts o' fortune, he has gotten gude, or but only gowd" (p 144). His doleful experience has taught him that material prosperity is not as "the doited and heedless world" thinks of it—analogous to "the green boughs o' a sound and flourishing tree"—but, as life has shown him, like "the smothering growth of the ivy, on a doddered stem" (p 144).

Claud realises that he has, indeed, spent his life fruitlessly pursuing a "phantom" owing to the Faustian folly (against his better knowledge) of acting as if God can be cheated and fate manipulated. For such an absurdity he is punished by the tragic recognition that his life has been meaningless, and he dies in circumstances that are both tragic and comic.

Claud is fated to die as he has lived, tragically isolated and suffering in spirit, because those whom he has injured fear an ulterior motive behind his sudden, incomprehensible transformation from sinner to penitent. The actual scene of his death is comic to the point of farce. Mr Keelevin arrives with a document that will render Claud insolvent and thus break the entail on Walter so that it may be made out in favour of Charles's family. The dying Claud is eager to sign the document but his wife "came rushing half dressed, into the room" to deny the lawyer what she calls "the cheatrie instruments o' pen and ink." She is concerned about the material arrangements for her future and tells the lawyer "Ye's get neither pen nor ink here, Mr Keelevin, till my rights are cognost in a record o' sederunt and session" (p 162). As this comic wrangle over pen, ink and property becomes shrill and heated Claud breathes his last, unable in spite of his efforts to undo the wrong he has done. His tragic stature is not, however, diminished, for the comic circumstances attending his death in this scene intensify the tragic pathos of his fate. They demonstrate, finally, man's inability to control the course of things.

As this scene suggests, Claud's relationships with other characters, as well as his voluntary and involuntary self-revelation, validate the narrator's analysis of him as a tragicomic figure. The narrator so characterises the world of *The Entail* as to indicate to the reader that the plans of one who does not accept that world's reality must inevitably fail. Similarly, a group of monitorial characters within the novel points out to Claud himself that his disinheritance scheme will bring only suffering with it because it is "against nature." These characters are comic in the Christian sense; they are benevolent, humble men who understand human limitation and live harmoniously by not attempting to challenge or transgress the moral "laws" of their world. Gilbert Omit, a lawyer, tells Claud "it would be an unco like thing" (p 31) to proceed with the disinheritance; another lawyer, Mr Keelevin, admonishes Claud that "sic an entail as ye speak o' would be rank injustice to poor Charlie" (p 57); and Mr Kilfuddy, a pastor, warns Claud not to search the Bible for precedents that will justify Charles's disinheritance when he says " ye may hae nae apology drawn from scriptural acts for the unnatural inclination to disinherit your first-born, out o' the prideful phantasy of leaving a large estate" (p 36). Claud, ironically, accepts the truth of these cautionary words, for they underscore what his own conscience tells him, but, absurdly, he sins anyway and suffers tragically for not heeding what he already knows.

Characters who might be described as comic analogues of the protagonist also validate the narrator's assessment of him as tragicomic. Claud's father-in-law, Malachi Hypel, a "hard-favoured fresh-coloured carl" (p 18) of legendary litigiousness, is one such character. Malachi conducts himself in court as his ancestors might have done on a battlefield. His feudal "animosity" of spirit is a comic variation of Claud's passion for the "conquest" of the lost estate of the Walkinshaws. His obsession with the law comically matches Claud's obsession with his entail, and the entail Malachi leaves comically foreshadows Claud's and its outcome. Malachi's entail at his death is found to be "imperfect" so that Claud's second son Walter, who inherits Malachi's lands, is "found under no legal obligation to assume his grandfather's name,—the very obligation which the old gentleman had been most solicitous to impose upon him" (p 30). Malachi is as comically unable to control the future by means of the law as, more tragically, Claud is also unable to do.

The relationship of a central character of tragic stature to comic analogues makes for the double perspective on life that tragicomedy conveys. The analogues reveal the comic face of values and actions more tragically depicted and worked out in the life of the main character, and the reader observes both at once. This effect is also achieved when the author creates comic parodies of the protagonist.

Karl Guthke observes that obsession can be "exaggerated to such a degree that it makes a person comic and tragic at the same time."[44] This is certainly true of Claud Walkinshaw, but the comic element in his obsession is especially emphasised in his encounters with others similarly obsessed. The laird of Kilmarkeckle, Claud's neighbour, is "proud of his lineage" (p 78) but, unlike Claud, he belongs to the comic world for he is a "harmless easy-tempered man, of a nature so kind and indulgent, that he allowed all about him to grow to rankness" (p 79). Like Claud, however, he has an *idée fixe,* but his is comically portrayed. He is monomaniacally pre-occupied with the "art of delineating hieroglyphical resemblances of birds and beasts on the wall of his parlour with snuff," each bird or beast having been suggested by "some peculiarity in the tobacco of which the snuff that they severally represented had been made" (p 78). The spectacle of Claud Walkinshaw bargaining for this man's daughter as a wife for Walter, in furtherance of his obsessive scheme to preserve the name and social position of the Walkinshaws, while constantly being interrupted by the snuff-obsessed laird eager to discuss *his* "hobby," is a comic spectacle. It suggests the folly of all obsession, a point the laird of Kilmarkeckle unwittingly under-scores when he remarks to Claud, "Surely there is a likeness somewhere in every thing that brings another thing to mind" (p 81). When snuff brings to mind family pride the comic aspect of a resolute purpose like Claud's, which has its tragic disposition, cannot be ignored.

Claud is implicitly parodied not only by his neighbour but also by his son Walter, the "natural" to whom he plans to leave his estate. Claud's relationship to Walter is one of aversion—an aversion that at times expresses itself in physical violence. Claud often refers to Walter as a "gouk" or a "creature" only to have his wife bluntly remind him "is na that gouk your ain bairn? . . . surely the man's fey about his entails and his properties to speak o' the illess laddie as if it were not better than a stirk or a stot" (p 25). Walter is indeed Claud's "ain bairn"; the irrationality that makes him a "haverel" parodies the more sinister and more destructive irrationality in Claud himself, which makes him "fey about his entails." Walter's foolishness is the comically depicted counterpart of his father's more tragic folly in entrusting the future of the family name and property to the one member of the family least able to add distinction to the one or effectively manage the other.

If placing a figure who belongs to a tragic world in a comic one leads to tragicomedy then this is particularly the case when that person, like Claud, is married to a woman like the Leddy Grippy, who plays the part of clown in this drama. The Leddy's incomprehension of Claud's inner self and of his compulsions causes him continually to be frustrated, even on his death-bed. She lives largely on the surface of life but for that reason, whatever her other limitations, she has a firmer grip on mundane reality than her more idealistic but deluded husband. She exercises a fool's licence in criticising Claud for his dream of family glory, charging him with ludicrously destroying his family in order to exalt it. She attacks him for his stupidity in trying to "keep faith" with the past at the expense of the present when she tells him "ye would mak stepbairns o' your ain blithesome childer on account o' a wheen auld dead patriarchs that hae been rotten, for ought I ken to the contrary, since before Abraham begat Isaac" (p 26) —a reference with some resonance in view of the eventual "sacrifice" of Charles. The Leddy berates Claud for reducing his family to an abstraction, declaring "a's for the family, and nothing for the dividual bairns" (p 26). She is always at Claud's elbow chattering, goading, protesting in her inimitably comic language. Claud must endure "the speat of her clatter" (p 120) even when she congratulates him, as when he announces that he has decided to arrange a marriage between George, his third son, and a wealthy heiress. The Leddy proclaims "an ye were to set your mind on a purpose o' marriage between a goose and a grumphie, I dinna think but ye would mak it a' come to pass" (p 120). Claud's incongruous marriage to the Leddy is emblematic of his tragicomic status. It is the yoking (ironically, by Claud's own choice) of a man capable of moral grandeur despite his injustices to a woman so firmly of the everyday world which he tries, however perversely, to transcend, that his "union" with the former Miss Girzy Hypel, with all its attendant comic circumstances, increases rather than diminishes Claud's tragic isolation.

V

Events and their sequence, in addition to narrative commentary and analysis, self-revelation, and the relationships of the main character to others in his world, help to make *The Entail* a tragicomic novel. "The emotion characteristic of tragedy," J. L. Styan has pointed out, is induced by "a sense of 'the remorseless' in the drive of the plot towards the dethronement of man in his pride by forces beyond his control."[45] That this sense of "the remorseless" is conveyed by the plot of *The Entail* has been demonstrated by Louis B. Hall. His analysis of the "fable" Galt took such pains to work out shows how it is "organized by the twin principles of Aristotelian peripety and discovery" in order to express "the idea of retributive justice through fate."[46] Such terms suggest the tragic, but the plot of *The Entail,* at least while Claud Walkinshaw is at its centre, is as tragicomic as the other major elements of the novel for, as Cyrus Hoy writes, ". . . the Aristotelian concept of peripety lies at the heart of the incongruities of human experience which are common alike to tragedy and comedy."[47] In *The Entail* the carefully structured sequence of events communicates an unmistakable sense of "the remorseless," but it does so by means of a "causal chain"[48] of peripeties that are comic as well as tragic. They demonstrate the "irony of the course of events" occasioned by the clash of the individual with "the inevitable course of the whole," which Guthke identifies as a central feature of tragicomedy.[49] The plot of *The Entail* substantiates the claim made by the narrator in his analysis of Claud that "human power was set at nought by the natural course of things" (p 115).

Malachi Hypel's entail on Walter, which gives his grandson the estate of Plealands but proves useless for the old man's principal purpose, is the first instance of peripety in the novel. It establishes a pattern which Claud's actions unfold—one that might be described as a pattern of futility according to which everything Claud does that runs counter to "nature" in order to aggrandise the name of Walkinshaw proves to have results the reverse of what he intended or expected. The pattern is basically comic but it has tragic implications as well.

Claud disinherits Charles because he is determined to unite Walter's estate of Plealands with his own estate of Grippy in order to create a sizeable property that will magnify the name of Walkinshaw. In order to carry out this plan he is obliged to make Walter his heir, but his thinking is based upon a comically fallible assumption. In the first instance the law of entail requires a male heir and Claud is confident that when he has married Walter to Betty Bodle, daughter of the laird of Kilmarkeckle, such an heir will appear: ". . . a female heir was a contingency he had not contemplated" (p 115). Yet this is what Walter's marriage produces, in the way of a sickly daughter. The daughter's birth and the mother's death in childbirth ". . . shattered some of the firmest intents and purposes of his [Claud's] mind" (p 114).

But Claud is not to be dissuaded as yet by death or by common sense from pursuing his elusive dream of landed splendour for future generations of Walkinshaws so he persuades George to make a loveless marriage for the sake of the necessary male heirs. He now plans to marry George's eagerly anticipated eldest son to Walter's daughter, at some indeterminate date. This plan will ensure that the estate remains a unit for were Walter's daughter to remain single or to marry outside her own family she would inherit her portion of the estate independently. Contingency puts this scheme to flight also for Walter's daughter dies and George's wife presents him with twin girls and has no more children.

Claud's faulty asumptions concerning male heirs are matched by a very human mistake he makes at the beginning which eventually undoes all his schemes. In order to soothe Mr Keelevin, who believes the new entail an injustice to Charles, Claud stipulates that the succession shall run from Walter to George but then, he adds, "ye may gang back, to please yoursel, to the heirs-male o' Charlie" (p 57). This stipulation gives George, Claud's most avaricious son, a motive to wrest the estate from the mentally feeble, and thus legally vulnerable Walter, thereby frustrating at least Claud's original intent in having the entail drawn up. After his father's death Walter is obliged to suffer the indignity of a court enquiry into his mental competence, a possibility Claud recognised but chose to ignore in his desire to unite the two estates. When Walter is declared a "fatuus" he feels his degradation keenly and loses the will to live. His suffering certainly arouses "pathetic sympathy" even if not quite to a "tragical degree." But George ultimately gains little by his mistreatment of Walter for he dies an accidental, untimely death, without male heirs, and Claud's stipulation to Mr Keelevin brings about the final peripety. The estate Claud took from Charles and his family is restored to its rightful possessors since Charles's family is the only one in the immediate line of succession to produce a male heir.

Unforeseeable events and Claud's casual concession in the making out of the entail on Walter restore Charles's family to its rightful inheritance but before Charles's death—the worst unforeseen consequence of Claud's actions— his father had, tragically and comically, realised that his son's disinheritance was unnecessary. Before the death of Walter's wife, without consulting his "daft" son Claud had exchanged his estate of Plealands for another, the Divethill, which the father covets since it formed part of the ancient Kittlestonheugh estate and is, indeed, the last piece of it to be recovered. While Walter grieves for his dead wife Claud bitterly reflects that ". . . by his parsimony he . . . would have been able, from his own funds, to have redeemed the Divethill" so that "the whole of the Kittlestonheugh might thus have been his own conquest and, as such, without violating any of the usages of society, he might have commenced the entail with Charles" (p 115).

In spite of Claud's realisation of the needlessness of his entail he does not try to undo it for this would mean making himself insolvent. He suffers tragically for this omission when Charles dies after accidentally discovering the nature of his circumstances. Only then does Claud try to undo the entail and, as we have seen, finds himself thwarted once more—and finally—by matters beyond his control. Claud's plans and their inevitable reversal underscore the tragic folly of his actions at every step of the way. His actions and their consequences arouse laughter and tragic pathos together.

VI

Many critics have found fault with *The Entail* after the death of Claud, which occurs somewhat less than half-way through the novel. Explanations of what went wrong are various. A contemporary reviewer who appreciated the comic element in the novel and thought the Leddy Grippy "the soul of the book" reprobates the author for dwelling on the "moral ugliness" of the Walkinshaws, ". . . a most unamiable and sordid race."[50] On the other hand, Ian Jack finds that by focusing attention upon Leddy Grippy after Claud's death "Galt is departing from the true theme of his book, a sombre satire on greed and 'interest' which ought to have a tragic conclusion."[51] Recently, Francis Russell Hart has defended *The Entail* against such criticisms by insisting that "the book is about a tragic fall and a comic redemption."[52] The latter point, it seems to me, comes closer to the truth than criticisms of readers who see Galt's novel as *either* tragedy or comedy, but since it appears to suggest that in *The Entail* tragedy is a prelude to comedy it, too, is somewhat off the mark. It ignores the fact that the tragic fall itself, in all its force and detail, is intimately linked with comedy.

It has been argued in this essay that the power and unity of *The Entail* depend upon the tragicomic character of the work, established at the beginning. But the work's tragicomic character is not sustained, in consequence of which its unity is damaged and its force diminished. In *The Entail* tragicomedy arises from the author's concentration on a complex personality in whose nature, actions, and fate elements of the tragic and the comic are fused. When, close to the midpoint of the novel, that personality is removed and no-one of remotely comparable stature emerges to take his place the novel slips from one genre into another. The world of *The Entail* no longer harbours the tragic but turns fully comic, presided over by Leddy Grippy, a comic "original" who brings the plot to its comically harmonious conclusion. No matter how humorously lively she may be the Leddy brings the single vision of comedy to displace that double awareness of man's "moral bravery" and lunatic folly which is conveyed by, and is the source of the power of tragicomedy. Whatever the reasons that prompted him to do so, Galt made a strategic mistake in transforming a tragicomic work into a social comedy.

In the second half of the novel the laughter aroused by the antics and speech of the Leddy dispels the despair associated with Claud but it is possible that originally Galt intended George to act as the agent of his tragicomic vision after Claud's death. Introducing George to the reader early in the novel, the narrator comments that ". . . his indefatigable, calculating, and persevering disposition demonstrated how much he had inherited of the heart and mind of his father" (p 38). Later, after Claud's death, the narrator refers to George's scheme to dispossess Walter as "new plans and proceedings worthy of the father's son" (p 165). These lines suggest a continuity of character and action from father to son but in between the narrator inserts a significant passage which stresses the difference between the two men. George, we are told,

> . . . wanted something of the old man's shrewdness; and there was more of avarice in his hopes of wealth than in the sordidness of his father, for they were not elevated by any such ambitious sentiment as that which prompted Claud to strive with such constancy for the recovery of his paternal inheritance (p 110).

This qualification, whatever Galt's original intentions concerning George may have been, prepares the reader for the character who comes to prominence in the second half of the novel. Far from being a tragicomic figure who had "inherited the heart and mind of his father" he is a satirically depicted, grasping Glasgow merchant with "little innate delicacy and only eager to become rich" (p 122).

George distinctly belongs to the world of social comedy. He is no idealist, no defier of destiny. He is as incapable of feeling Claud's despair as of understanding his father's sin for he lacks Claud's religious sensibility and latent faith. He takes the estate from Walter not because he shares his father's

189

almost mystical reverence of family, which requires self-sacrifice as well as the sacrifice of others, but because, like other capitalists of his day, he has a self-regarding desire for social status—a desire that obliges him to sacrifice nothing he holds dear. George's proto-Victorian fear of public opinion and public exposure is petty beside his father's fear of God and of the terrors of a violated conscience. His hypocrisy stands in notable contrast to his father's courage. George is a man of his times, not, like Claud, a man who transcends time, and his downfall provokes more laughter than tears.

The difference between the first half of *The Entail* and the second is also illustrated by Charles's son James. He seems destined to experience a fate as tragic as his father's but, as people in comedy generally do, ". . . lives happily ever afterwards." James had his father's romantic sensibility and his father's appreciation of the pastoral ideal. But George tries to make his nephew "barter" (p 237) his heart by marrying Robina, his daughter whom James dislikes, in order that George's branch of the family may continue to be associated with Kittlestonheugh. When this ploy fails George absurdly decides to steal the girl James loves and produce the male heirs so far denied him. Had this wild plan succeeded James would have been destroyed as effectively as his father was destroyed by his disinheritance, that earlier act of betrayal. But in this part of the novel the designing head is not permitted to enthrall the values of the heart. George's accidental death prevents him from doing further mischief; when his son-in-law, Walkinshaw Milrookit, tries to take possession of Kittlestonheugh in Robina's name he is exposed by the Leddy Grippy as a fraud, and James receives his patrimony. Instead of suffering his father's fate he enjoys its comic opposite for he settles in married bliss on the estate Claud strove so long to regain and has nine sons, " 'all male heirs,' as Dirdumwhamle [Milrookit's father] often says with a sigh, when he thinks of his son and Robina having only added daughters to the increasing population of the kingdom" (p 363).

It has been argued that *The Entail* is unified by its plot with its chain of peripeties that continues unbroken until the final peripety undoes all of Claud's legal injustices. Such a view is superficial. Peripeties can be tragic, comic, or a mixture of both; in the first half of the novel they are both tragic and comic but in the second they are uniformly comic so that the nature of both plot and novel is changed. The Leddy schemes with George to deprive Walter of the estate but suffers a comic reversal. Instead of receiving the rewards she had confidently expected she is sent into exile with Walter to "a flat up a turn-pike stair in Glasgow" (p 205)—a doubly ironic circumstance in that George had once assured his mother "It would be extreme cruelty now, in your declining years, to force you to live in the close air, and up the dirty turnpike stairs o' Glasgow" (p 178). Despite the Leddy's pronouncement that living in Glasgow "would soon be the death o' me" (p 178) unlike Walter she thrives in her new environment and lives comically to turn the tables on George. She permits Robina to marry her other cousin, Walkinshaw Milrookit, in the flat to which she has been banished while George is trying to persuade James to marry Robina. When George returns from his fruitless expedition he is manipulated into presiding over his daughter's wedding-feast without knowing it, and can only shatter his glass in impotent rage when the Leddy tells him of how he has been tricked. The spectacle of one schemer outwitting another for having formerly been outwitted is purely comic, and characteristic of the turns of the plot after Claud's departure. Any hint of the tragicomic after Claud's death depends upon the reader's memory of him.

In a letter written to the firm of Oliver and Boyd on January 31, 1823, Galt observed that

> In general, I think the Entail is not considered as inferior to any of my former things, but people are divided as to whether I should confine myself to humorous subjects or pathetic—I think a mixture of both best.[53]

If Galt refers in this letter to the tragic pathos aroused by Claud Walkinshaw's fate he was right: Claud is his most impressive character as the first half of *The Entail* is Galt's most powerful piece of fiction. In the end, however, Galt seems to have found the three-volume format he elected to use too much for him even to the point, in the second half of the novel, of padding his material to the required breadth.

But if *The Entail,* viewed as a whole, is a masterpiece *manqué* it is nonetheless an impressive early example of a work of fiction based upon the same kind of recognition as a novel like *The Mill on The Floss,* in which George Eliot's narrator remarks that tragedy does not have to sweep the stage "in regal robes" in order to be tragic, for

> The pride and obstinacy of millers, and other insignificant people, whom you pass unnoticingly on the road every day, have their tragedy too; but it is of that unwept, hidden sort, that goes on from generation to generation, and leaves no record.[54]

Notwithstanding his failure to sustain his vision it is Galt's achievement to have been one of the first novelists writing in English to have provided, in *The Entail,* a powerful record of the tragic as well as the comic aspect of the life of a man one would pass "unnoticingly on the road"—a man "carrying his staff in his left hand behind him, a habit which he had acquired with his ellwand when he travelled the Borders as a pedlar" (p 60).

NOTES

1. National Library of Scotland. MS. 4008, ff. 182-183. I should like to thank the Trustees of the National Library of Scotland for permission to quote from Galt's unpublished correspondence in this essay.
2. Nat. Lib. Scot. MS. 4014, f. 232.
3. Nat. Lib. Scot. MS. 4008, f. 179.
4. *The Literary Life and Miscellanies of John Galt,* 3 vols. (Edinburgh and London), I, p 318.
5. Nat. Lib. Scot. MS. 4008, f. 182.
6. Nat. Lib. Scot. MS. 4008, f. 186; MS. 4008, f. 190.
7. *The Letters of Sir Walter Scott,* centenary edition, ed. H. J. C. Grierson, 12 vols. (London, 1936), VI, p 468.
8. *The Works of Lord Byron, Letters and Journals,* ed. Rowland E. Prothero, 6 vols. (London, 1922), II, p 373.
9. *The Life of Lord Byron* (London, 1830), p 268.
10. *Lady Blessington's Conversations of Lord Byron,* ed. Ernest J. Lovell, Jr. (Princeton, 1969), p 146.
11. Reported by A. J. Ashley in a letter to *TLS* (September 1930), p 757.
12. *Contributions To The Edinburgh Review,* 4 vols. (London, 1844), III, p 518.
13. *The Scottish Novel, From Smollet To Spark* (Cambridge, Mass., 1978), p 45.

14. See Herbert J. Muller, *The Spirit of Tragedy* (New York, 1956), p 250.
15. The tragicomic vision was not, of course, "new" in itself in the nineteenth century. Plato, in the *Symposium,* has Socrates say that "the same man ought to understand how to compose both comedy and tragedy, and that he who has skill as a tragic poet has skill for a comic poet." Shakespeare and other sixteenth-century dramatists have been considered in the context of tragicomedy. The Bible presents instances of tragicomedy. There is more than a hint of it, for instance, in Psalm 37:

> The wicked plotteth against the just,
> and gnasheth upon him with his teeth.
> The Lord shall laugh at him: for he
> seeth that his day is coming.

It was not, however, until the early nineteenth century that the tragicomic vision entered into the novel in English.
16. *Modern Tragicomedy: An Investigation into the Nature of the Genre* (New York, 1966), p 233.
17. *Concluding Unscientific Postscript,* trans. David F. Swenson; Introd. Walter Lowrie (Princeton, 1974), p 459. In a footnote to this distinction Kierkegaard adds that "the comical is a relation, the faulty relation of contradiction, but free from pain."
18. Guthke, p 25.
19. Guthke, p 103. It is notable that one of the most significant defences of tragicomedy as a Romantic genre—Victor Hugo's Preface to *Cromwell*—was written in 1827, barely five years after *The Entail* was published.
20. *Literary Life,* I, p 24-25.
21. *Ibid.,* p 24. Of Bürger Galt wrote that he was noted "among his countrymen as Coleridge and Wordsworth are among us, not so much for genius as for rejecting what is called the convential phraseology of regular poetry, in favour of popular forms of expression, gathered from the simple and energetic utterance of the common people." *The Bachelor's Wife: A Selection of Curious and Interesting Extracts, With Cursory Observations* (Edinburgh, 1824), p 366. What Galt says of Bürger would also apply, in large measure, to himself.
22. *The Tragedies of Maddalen, Agamemnon, Lady Macbeth, Antonia and Clytemnestra* (London, 1812).
23. *Literary Life,* I, p 106.
24. *Henry Crabb Robinson On Books And Their Writers,* ed. Edith J. Morley, 3 vols. (London, 1938), I, p 137. "The Witness" was published in *The New British Theatre* (1814-15) which Galt edited for Colburn. Its title altered to "The Appeal," it was the only one of Galt's plays actually to be staged.
25. *Tragedies,* p vi.
26. *Literary Life,* I, pp 106-107.
27. *The Entail* has the Aristotelian plot of a Greek drama, an element of the novel which will be discussed later in the essay. Galt's

language is revealing when he writes to Blackwood, 8 October 1822, to ask that "the Entail [be] made up as far as the matter goes—for I wish the second volume to begin with the announcement of a new act in the story." Nat. Lib. Scot. MS. 4008, f. 188.

28. *Tragedies,* p 46.
29. *The Entail,* ed. Ian A. Gordon, Oxford English Novels (London, 1970), p 154. All further references to the novel will be to this edition and will be given in the text, by page number.
30. For an analysis of *Wuthering Heights* as tragicomedy *see* U. C. Knoepflmacher, "Wuthering Heights: A Tragicomic Romance," in *Laughter and Despair: Readings in Ten Novels of the Victorian Era* (Berkeley, 1971), chapter III.
31. For an account of *The Provost* in this connection see my article "The Prince and The Provost," *Studies in Scottish Literature,* VI, No. 1 (July 1968), p 20-35.
32. Nat. Lib. Scot. MS. 4008, f. 166.
33. *Literary Life,* I, p 24.
34. *Life of Lord Byron,* p 327.
35. *Ibid.,* p 217.
36. *Ibid.,* p 327.
37. *Ibid.,* p 216.
38. *Ibid.,* p 328.
39. *Letters From The Levant* (London, 1813), p 200.
40. Guthke, pp 76-77.
41. Guthke, p 78.
42. Cyrus Hoy, *The Hyacinth Room: An Investigation Into The Nature of Comedy, Tragedy and Tragicomedy* (New York, 1964), p 18.
43. The story of Jacob, Esau and Isaac is frequently referred to in the novel. This story from *Genesis,* of one brother who wrongly supplants another, has both tragic and comic elements in it which underscore the tragicomedy of Galt's narrative and which suggest, by the association with Galt's story, the universal validity of the tragicomic vision which informs his narrative.
44. Guthke, p 86.
45. *The Dark Comedy: The Development of Modern Comic Tragedy* (Cambridge, 1962), p 36.
46. "Peripety in John Galt's *The Entail,*" "*Studies in Scottish Literature,* V, No. 3 (January 1968), pp 176-184.
47. *The Hyacinth Room,* p 308.
48. Hall, p 179.
49. Guthke, p 82.
50. Review of *The Entail* in *The Literary Gazette; and Journal of Belles Lettres, Arts, Sciences, Etc.,* VI (December 21, 1822), pp 802, 800.
51. *English Literature 1815-1832* (Oxford, 1963), p 234.
52. *The Scottish Novel,* p 48.
53. I am indebted to Dr Robert Carnie of the University of Calgary for permission to use his transcript of this letter.
54. *Mill on the Floss,* Book Third, Chapter I.

SCOTS AND ENGLISH IN
ANNALS OF THE PARISH and *THE PROVOST*

J. DERRICK McCLURE

The linguistic history of Lowland Scotland over the last four hundred years is the history of a slow and irregular, but pervasive, increase in the use of English at the expense of Scots. This process began with the introduction of an English Bible into the Scottish Kirk by the Reformers, continued with the decline and temporary eclipse of sophisticated literature in Scots following the departure of James VI to London, was accelerated by the conscious efforts of the social and intellectual élite of eighteenth-century Edinburgh to emulate the language and manners of England, and entered on what until very recently seemed likely to prove its final phase with the 1872 Education Act.

Galt's skill in exploiting the Western Scots dialect for literary effect was acknowledged from the first appearance of his novels. However, his achievement in the field of verbal realism is far greater than simply a fluent, lively and philologically accurate representation of Ayrshire speech; and this has not always been recognised. By the supposed period of *Annals of the Parish* and *The Provost,* the complex and ambivalent linguistic situation which—with considerable reservations—still prevails in Lowland Scotland had been largely established. Scots, in its various local dialects, was the normal vernacular of the less educated classes. They were also literate in English, owing to the custom in the parish schools of using as reading material the King James Bible, the Shorter Catechism, and passages from classical and contemporary English writers; and were fully accustomed to spoken English through hearing it regularly from the pulpit. Lawyers, ministers, bailies, merchants, dominies and other more highly educated people were to a large extent bilingual, using English (or at any rate an Anglicised Scots) in their professional activities and vernacular Scots in their day-to-day dealings with friends and acquaintances. English was the

195

accepted language for writing: even in poetry, the use of Scots by Hamilton and Ramsay, and later Fergusson and Burns, was disapproved of by some readers and critics; and the prose writings of men like Hume and Carlyle (though their normal *speech* was much more Scots) were deliberately made to conform as closely as possible to the canons of contemporary English style. The dichotomy between "personal" and "public" language, which has persisted in Lowland Scotland to the present day, had become established by the later eighteenth century.

A feature of the society which Galt describes, therefore, was the facility of some of its members in dialect-switching: or, more accurately, in modulating with considerable delicacy through various degrees of "Scotsness" from unadulterated Ayrshire dialect to quasi-literary English. It is this sociolinguistic situation, and not the mere fact of Ayrshire Scots, which is reflected in his novels. Whereas Walter Scott (and nearly all later Scottish novelists: Grassic Gibbon and to a lesser extent George Douglas Brown are the only major exceptions) make a rigid distinction between Scots (for dialogue) and English (for narrative), Galt throughout *Annals* and *The Provost* uses a language in which Scots forms appear with continuously varying frequency; and thus demonstrates not only the capacity of his characters for expressing themselves vividly in Scots, but the shifting of registers which was, and still is, an inherent feature of Lowland speech. The notably inconsistent language of his memoir-novels has been adversely criticised: the charge was brought against *The Provost* on its first appearance that its language was "neither one thing nor the other," and James Kinsley in his introduction to the Oxford English Novels edition of *Annals* interprets Galt's practice as the use of a narrative style basically English into which Scots passages are inserted as set-pieces. In reality, Galt's art is of a higher order than this suggests. *Annals* and *The Provost* are dramatic monologues in which the narrators, though obviously very different in personality, have this in common: both are educated men who would be accustomed to using English—an English coloured, for each man, by his professional training and cast of mind, and of course spoken with a Scottish accent—as well as Scots; and in whom a natural and habitual tendency to speak Scots in their everyday lives would coincide, and conflict, with an inculcated belief that English was inherently more refined and dignified, more suitable for reference to serious matters, and the customary medium of literature. A tension, that is, is continuously manifest in the memoirs of Reverend Balwhidder and Provost Pawkie: their use of Scots or of English is a matter of choice, though not necessarily of conscious choice. Why they used one language rather than the other on any given occasion is always a pertinent question; and the answer is often revealing. Indeed, Galt's use of language contributes in large measure to one of the most important features of his books: the self-revelation of the narrators.

Very often, Rev. Balwhidder and Mr Pawkie write in English: the English of professional men in Scotland in the late eighteenth and early nineteenth century. It has several distinguishing characteristics. Scottish idioms frequently appear: idioms which might still be heard in the mouths of professional-class Scotsmen who would not think of themselves as Scots-speakers. *Made to me* (*i.e.* for me), *the lend of, I have my doubts, she got the better of it* (a cough), *he was just a father to him, the rheumatics, playing at the cards, gone to the kirk, they got the length of Kilmarnock, by herself* (beside herself), *a small* (young) *family, married upon, by common, it was a sore thing, there was like to have happened, I had on my wig, yon former times, as sound* (asleep) *as a door-nail, very ill off, as little pleasant, two three, like a knotless thread*: expressions such as those have by no means disappeared from modern Scottish speech. Scottish legal and technical terms, often relating to landholding or Church and burgh government, occur in considerable numbers: *arles* (preliminary payment, or an earnest of some future promise), *assoilzied* (found not guilty), *betheral* (church officer), *cess* (land tax—or, in a derived sense, any burden or imposition), *cotter* (tenant on a farm), *deacon* (president of one of the Incorporated Trades), *feued* (of land, allocated for a fixed annual rent), *glebe* (plot assigned to the minister), *heritors* (landowners), *infeoftment* (investing of a new owner with legal possession of his land), *interlocutor* (order of the Court of Session), *intromit* (to handle funds or property), *land of houses* (block of flats), *lones* (the space on a road between the house fronts and the paved "crown of the causey"), *mailing* (piece of arable land held on lease), *mortification* (land or money bequeathed for charitable purposes), *panel* (prisoner at the bar), *policies* (ornamental grounds surrounding a large country house), *sederunt* (meeting, e.g. of a kirk session), *steading* (building site), *synod* (church court), *tack* (tenancy), and *writer* (lawyer), are some examples. The use of words like those in a particular passage, it must be noted, is not in itself sufficient to classify that passage as being in Scots: such words can and do occur in Scottish English. The same is true of the homely descriptive or aphoristic expressions which occur frequently in *Annals* and rather less frequently in *The Provost: a whawp in our nest, out of the body, our life is but within our lip, in the lea of the hedge and the lown of the hill, there never was a silly Jock but there was as silly a Jenny, dinna try to stretch your arm further than your sleeve will let you, no to be particular about the mouth of a gi'en horse, just between the tyning and the winning, lay your hairs in the water.* Fittingly, Biblical phrases pervade Mr Balwhidder's idiolect, though they are virtually absent from Mr Pawkie's: often these occur in a specifically religious context, but by no means always. *The fowler's snare, as the smoke that mounteth up, I then awoke and behold it was a dream, the watches of the night, the wicked cease from troubling, flourishing like the green bay trees, as a mustard seed that grows into a great tree*: many other instances could be cited. In the final chapter, a touching reference to his failing powers takes the form of a phrase which, though commonplace in itself, coming from Mr Balwhidder immediately recalls a Dominical utterance: "the night is coming on." Not all such allusions are exact verbal quotations from the Authorised Version: the minister modifies his citings according to their immediate relevance; and the naturalness—almost, one feels, unconsciousness—with which he brings them into his discourse is a notable feature of his style. Almost the only conspicuous Biblical allusion in the Provost's narrative, by contrast, is the bitter reference to "such a seven-headed and ten-horned beast as the multitude."

The English of Galt's narrators is distinctively their own. At other times, the language of both books becomes Scots rather than English; and some of their most famous passages owe their effectiveness in large measure to Galt's use of the expressive Ayrshire vocabulary. Examples that spring to mind are, from *Annals,* the tea-drinking episode (Chapter 2), the incident of the recruiting party (17), the trick played on Robin Bicker the exciseman (19), and the pay wedding (48); and from *The Provost,* Bailie McLucre's account of his experiences in London (7), the rioting of the meal mob (13), the wig dinner (22), and the storm (24). However, the question why Galt has his narrators writing sometimes in English and sometimes in Scots remains to be answered. As a rule, there is a ready explanation: it lies in the narrator's attitude to his subject-matter. In *Annals,* with a few notable exceptions, the language tends to Scots or to English in proportion as Mr Balwhidder's personal feelings are involved in what he is describing, or as he is writing solely in the capacity of official chronicler or observer. Reminiscences of events in which he has no particular individual interest, religious meditations inspired by the times and seasons, or passing observations on changing circumstances, are generally in English; and sometimes, as in his recollections of pleasant and prosperous years, English of a striking lyrical beauty. Conversely, to express good humour, irritation, disapproval, or any other sharply-felt emotion, he avails himself of the pungency of Scots. Edwin Muir's much-quoted dictum that Scotland is now a nation which "feels in Scots and thinks in English" is illustrated with surprising clarity by this novel. In *The Provost,* the situation is rather less straightforward, appropriately to the memoirs of a much less straightforward man: the use of Scots or English is still linked to the narrator's frame of mind, but in a more complex way. Like his ecclesiastical contemporary, Pawkie uses Scots when frankly enjoying the humour of a situation or when describing something or someone who arouses his dislike (he shows much greater aptitude than would become a minister at finding sarcastic Scots epithets for other characters); and also like him, he prefers English as a language of moralising and reflection. However, his use of the two languages is often specious: when it suits his purpose to seem friendly and familiar, or to seem formal, righteous and dignified, he uses the appropriate language as a deliberate trick: a trick which he does not (though Galt, of course, does) wish the reader to penetrate. The national characteristic of feeling in Scots and thinking in English, for Mr Balwhidder, is simply an accepted habit; for Mr Pawkie, it is a known fact which he can exploit. "I was constrained to loot a sort a-jee" he once says of himself in reference to just this.

Almost any chapter in *Annals* and *The Provost* would demonstrate this use of language; and as space clearly does not permit an examination of the books in their entirety, a few passages will be selected.

Chapter 1 of *Annals* opens in a language which is clearly English: "my marriage upon my cousin," though of course a Scottish idiom, is not sufficient to qualify this. Slight touches of pedantry appear, in keeping with the character of Mr Balwhidder: "The An. Dom. one thousand seven hundred and sixty," "three heads or portions," "there was obliged to be . . .''; and as always, Biblical echoes such as "their hearts were stirred into strife" form a pervasive feature of the language. Suddenly, at the end of the melancholy description of the disturbance at the minister's placing, comes the famous reference to "poor old Mr Kilfuddy of the Brae-hill" getting a "clash of glar" in the eye: and surely the suggestion is irresistible of a smile appearing on the face of Mr Balwhidder in his study as he recollects this incident! No hint of humour is visible in his account of himself and the congregation entering the Kirk via the window: he quickly turns his attention (and the reader's) away from this undigni-fied detail by vigorously expressing his anger at the behaviour of the crowd, underlining it with the vivid word *yellyhooing* (which appears to be Galt's coinage). From this point to the minister's friendly reception by Thomas Thorl, the language remains English rather than Scots, though giving an impression of informality by virtue of its long and loosely-constructed sentences and by details suggestive of colloquial speech ("Thomas Thorl . . . he got up," "Mr Gavin, that was then the minister," "no often called for"). The proverbial phrase "a steep brae" and the ironic nickname "Mess John" are the only Scots expressions until the end of this section; and in neither case is the expression Mr Balwhidder's own. He does, however, describe Thomas's reception of him as an "almous deed," and remark in a parenthesis "I mind him as if it was but yesterday"; and in the next paragraph, relating his con-versation with his new friend, the language becomes much more conspicuously Scots than hitherto. The direct and indirect speech of both Thomas and Mr Balwhidder contains many Scots forms: *gorbies, no ane, mair, mysel, couldna, expectit, was na, observe* (noun), *poopit, would na, lang, I was mindit.* The presumption clearly is that the original conversation was conducted in Scots, and that the written report of it retains some of its linguistic features; but beside this, the implication that Mr Balwhidder is pleasantly aware of Thomas's friendliness in contrast to the hostility he encountered earlier is clearly conveyed by the use of Scots.

The subtle modulations in the language reflecting Mr Balwhidder's attitude to his subject are continued in the section relating to Mrs Malcolm. The minister announces in literary English "I have now to speak of the coming of Mrs Malcolm," and the factual sentence which follows contains no Scots features except possibly the relative *that.* The phrase with which Mr Balwhidder gives his personal impression of her, however, is Scots: "a genty body." Similarly, "she never changed her widow's weeds," an objective report, is in English; but "and she was aye as if she had just been ta'en out of a bandbox," an admiring personal judgment, contains Scots touches. The same impression of warm regard for Mrs Malcolm and her family is conveyed by the frequent use of Scots expressions in the remainder of this paragraph: *the tear was in her e'e, the bairns, their bit and drap, laddie, greeting*: all of which are much more emotive than their English counterparts would be, and suggest a greater degree of personal interest. By using the same language of himself ("I happened to be daunrin' bye") as he does of the Malcolms, too, Mr Balwhidder further emphasises his sympathy with them.

Mrs Malcolm's speech, when her words are quoted, is a combination of Scots and literary English. The sequence is certainly not entirely realistic: the down-to-earth "I canna take help from the poor's-box" followed by the formal "although it's very true that I am in great need," and then the similar changes of register in "it might hereafter" (literary) "be cast up to my bairns" (colloquial Scots) "whom it may please God to restore to better circumstances" (highly formal) "when I am no to see it" (a characteristic homely euphemism), form a discourse which it is hard to imagine as actually uttered by anybody. However, it must be borne in mind that this speech is reported by Mr Balwhidder. It is not likely that, after a lapse of many years (and with his recollection coloured, naturally, by his personal feelings) he would be able to set down Mrs Malcolm's actual words. Nor is it necessarily his purpose to do so: his memoirs, though basically factual, are of course a literary work. (The idea of writing a book, it will be remembered, occurred to him fairly early in his career.) His aim is to suggest the *character* of Mrs Malcolm's response; and from this point of view the different registers acquire almost a symbolic function: Mrs Malcolm's piety, family affection and courageous independence are rendered more neatly and forcibly than could have been achieved by a more naturalistic speech.

The same interpretation could be offered for Mizy Mirkland's soliloquy in Chapter 18, which Kinsley describes as "contrived and unconvincing." Realistic it is not; but Galt is not asking us to "believe" that this soliloquy was actually uttered, in the way that we are to believe in, say, the building of the new schoolhouse. The soliloquy is part of Mr Balwhidder's narrative; and the minister's intention as chronicler is not to suggest that he heard the widow uttering those precise words to herself, or that he actually heard her soliloquising at all. The monologue which he puts into her mouth, which begins in colloquial Scots and ends in the language of the Authorised Version, is simply an economical literary device employed by the minister to suggest, explain, and arouse the appropriate reactions to, Mizy's sad state of mind. And by causing his fictitious Mr Balwhidder to employ a facile literary trick in order to convey what was for him a very real experience, Galt not only presents the essence of this experience but illuminates two of the inimitable minister's traits of character: his artlessness, and his deep sympathy for the misfortunes of his parishioners.

Similar effects are visible throughout the novel: Chapter 3 provides other ready examples. The opening, in which the chronicler reports the events that befell the Byres family, ending with a reference to the providence of God, is in rather plain English: the minister, one feels, has no strong personal interest in these happenings except as curiosities from which a moral can be drawn. The reference to the Sacrament Sabbath, however, evokes a dramatic recollection of the storm on that day, which he describes with expressive Scots words and phrases: *pith and bir, tirled the thack from the rigging.* From the storm as a mere storm, his thoughts pass to the ominous implications which were seen in it; and in response to this sudden widening of the theme, the language becomes formal and weighty: "all the congregation thought that it betokened a mutation to me." Finally, he recalls the smallpox that affected the parish; and his sorrow at the memory of its effects is conveyed in idiomatic Scots: "the smashing that it made of the poor bits o' bairns."

The paragraph relating to Thomas Thorl is in what might be called Mr Balwhidder's "factual" style: an English showing few consciously literary touches, retaining a conversational flavour by the looseness and informality of the syntax, keeping its Scottish character by an occasional word like *income* or grammatical feature like *could no go about,* and showing the minister's natural inclination to rise ("lapse" would clearly not be the right word) into language with a Biblical cast. This style is retained while he supplies the background information concerning Charlie Malcolm's departure; but when his recollection of the actual scene comes into play, Scots words appear with increasing frequency (*begreeten, all the weans of the clachan were at the kirk-yard yett*), and the density of the Scots becomes quite considerable for the humorous picture of "auld Mizy Spaewell . . . hirpling with her bachle in her hand." The Scots remains consistent in his reminiscence of Mizy (*freats, just an oracle, howdies, feckless*), but fades out somewhat at the end of the sentence when her death, which "made everybody wonder," is referred to: when a lively visual remembrance gives way to a thoughtful and slightly uneasy one.

His rather unpleasant memory of the Gilchrists is expressed with added pungency by the expressions *a narrow ailing man, the scrimpetest wretch;* and his use of *every ane that kent her* at the end of that paragraph suggests, in its context, just a hint of personal dislike which would not have been present had the English equivalent been used instead.

In general, indignation and disapproval on the minister's part is expressed in Scots. The galravitching of his servant lassies after his first wife's death, the playrife Lady Malcolm who acts like a petted bairn, Thomas Wilson's doited tawpy

203

of a wife, the clanjamfry of play-actors (at whom he admits in Scots that he would like to have gotten a keek, but immediately recalls in magisterial English that this was a sinful curiosity), the schismatic hobbleshow at Cayenneville: these are far from the only instances. For his masterly rebuke to Nicol Snipe (Chapter 5) he suddenly changes to Scots from the English which is his preferred medium for preaching: the effect of this, added to the unexpectedness of the words themselves, can well be imagined. Emotions of the opposite kind—pleasure or amusement—are also expressed in Scots. When he moves from the details of Charlie Malcolm's trading expedition to his own happy meeting with the returning sailor, even before the reader has learned the reason for the change of mood in the writing the word *gloaming* has signalled it as clearly as a change of key or contrast of instrumentation in a piece of music; and the minister's pleasure and gratification at receiving Charlie's gift of limes could hardly have been expressed with such immediacy in English as by the Scots "it was so mindful of the laddie." Humorous touches like the skraik from Charlie's parrot that made his whole head dirl, the loup of the horse which couped Lord Eaglesham into a reeking and sappy midden, or the Lady's muckle jock with its crap like the kyte of a Glasgow magistrate, are invariably characterised by an increase in the density of the Scots.

The observation that English is the language of Mr Balwhidder the chronicler and moralist and Scots that of Mr Balwhidder the sympathetic human being appears to fail when we are confronted with the deaths of his first and second wives, which unquestionably moved him profoundly but in speaking of which he uses English throughout. However, no reader familiar with the national trait of emotional reticence will find this unconvincing. By leaving Mr Balwhidder's grief at his personal bereavements to be inferred by the reader, rather than having him express it as forcefully as he expresses pleasure, amusement or indignation, Galt not only maintains the integrity of the minister's characterisation (he would certainly consider an excessive emphasis on his own sorrow to be an impropriety), but renders his grief not less but more moving than it would otherwise be. The formal, learned language is used for its distancing effect. Similarly, in the shocking incident of the suicide of Mr and Mrs Dwining, the minister avoids emotive Scots words: though his discomposure is revealed as it were accidentally by the short, simple and rather jerky sentences which contrast with his usual long-winded periodic constructions.

There can be few more striking contrasts, in the field of naturalistic characterisation, than that between the simple open-heartedness of Micah Balwhidder and the shrewd and devious subtlety of James Pawkie. Their narratives are correspondingly unlike: the minister writes what is, as his title suggests, primarily a yearly chronicle of events in his parish, and only incidentally (as far as he intends) a personal memoir; and the provost, an account of his own life and career in which episodes in the history of the town are related with reference to his part in them or their effect on him. The self-revelation in Mr Pawkie's story is therefore of a more complex kind than that in Mr Balwhidder's: the one is very little concerned with his "image" at all; the other fully intends to display himself to his public, but not always in the light in which he actually appears. The modulations from Scots to English in this book are accordingly less simply motivated than in its predecessor.

Pawkie, both by disposition and by the requirements of his calling, is deeply concerned with the impression he gives. He is, of course, basically an honest man, and at times is obliged to record incidents which show him in an unflattering light and actions which from a strictly moral point of view are somewhat dubious; but the response which he wishes to arouse is always carefully manipulated by his use of language, including his choice of English or Scots. The danger of such a procedure is that the listener will perceive the attempt to direct his reactions, and therefore repudiate all the more strongly the standpoint which the speaker wishes him to adopt. In verbally manoeuvring the characters whom he meets in the course of the book, Pawkie is on the whole brilliantly successful: when (as often) he tries the same thing on the reader, however, he sometimes fails.

In Chapter 4, we see a stunning demonstration of Pawkie's skills as verbal tactician. The initial information is given in English, the only Scots feature to appear in the first few sentences being technical terms: *intromit, infeoftment, tacks.* English is used to describe the insinuation against Mr McLucre

—"no little grist came to his mill"—but shortly afterwards we hear that "it was jealoused that the predecessors of Mr McLucre . . . got their loofs creeshed." Pawkie, the suggestion surely is, is conspicuously refusing to commit himself overtly to the point of view of McLucre's "adversaries," but giving more than a hint, by the informality and intimacy of the expression *got their looks creeshed* and the rather obviously laboured euphemism which follows, that he has some sympathy with those who hold this suspicion of the Dean's predecessors. The "no to say an ill word of him, honest man" is a somewhat disingenuous disclaimer of a type which Pawkie employs frequently. While remaining totally equivocal as far as his actual words are concerned, Pawkie succeeds in leaving the reader in very little doubt of his opinion of Mr McLucre; and it is surely no accident that in the chapter recording the latter's death, he is described by the Provost as "my old friend and *adversary."* On the other hand, the homely language also suggests a sidelong smile and a knowing look: Pawkie wants the Dean of Guild's office, with its attendant advantages, for himself; and is inviting the reader's sympathy, even connivance.

In the dialogue between Pawkie and McLucre which follows, each man's attempts at probing and manoeuvring the other while carefully guarding his own position is reflected in the modulations of the language. Basically, Scots is the mother tongue and English the learned language: on the simplest level, therefore, each man would be inclined to suggest openness by Scots and guardedness by English. Both know this perfectly well, however; and could easily employ the implications of either language for equivocation or deception. In conversational fencing of this kind, Pawkie shows himself a master. His greeting—"Whar awa sae fast, Dean o' Guild?" —is in unusually pure Scots, in order to set up a friendly and confident atmosphere. It has the desired effect, as the other unhesitatingly gives the informative response which Pawkie is seeking. The Scots opening of Pawkie's next speech maintains the rapport; but the introduction into the discussion of a new, hypothetical element with weighty implications is signalled by a sudden change to English. Having thus dropped an intriguing hint, Pawkie returns to earth and Scots: "but I fear . . . that's no to be accomplished"; but ends with a suggestive resumption of the hypothesising tone. During this discourse, a reader familiar with the nuances of Scottish speech can not only hear the inflections of the voice but even visualise the expression on the speaker's face. In response to the direct demand which his inflammatory hints elicit from McLucre, Pawkie replies in formal English, seemingly to erect an impenetrable barrier, but with a final Scots word "will gang no further" as if to resume the earlier confidential tone of the conversation: of course, the precise way to arouse McLucre's curiosity still further and thus weaken his guard. And again the reference to his interlocutor's present position contains Scots touches, suggesting the attitude to a simple fact accepted by both men—now that it no longer is this. The Dean replies in English: he is trying the new gambit of meeting Pawkie's sudden reserve with the same degree of formality: and unexpectedly receives an answer in disarmingly familiar Scots ("dinna spear any quistions") of which the intimacy matches the conspiratorial nature of Pawkie's next action. Pawkie now adopts a polite, almost obsequious, tone, using the respectful English of a pupil to a master; but having thus disposed McLucre to listen approvingly to what he says, he adopts the man-to-man, common-ground implications of a denser Scots. Finally, in a few moments, the two men are openly discussing, in the down-to-earth realism of Scots, the possibility of Pawkie's taking over McLucre's post as Dean of Guild! The skill with which the younger man employs his conversational tactics to manipulate his more experienced colleague cannot but arouse our admiration.

In his account of one of the few really discreditable episodes in his career, the placing of the incompetent Mr Pittle in the parish kirk, Pawkie is rather less successful in covering his tracks. There is a defensive note in the careful English of his hypocritical disclaimer, with its ostentatiously self-righteous conclusion: "Whether it was that, by our being used to Mr Pittle, we had ceased to have a right respect for his parts and talents, or that in reality he was but a weak brother, I cannot in conscience take it on me to say." Scots is his preferred medium for personal and domestic details: his unattractive portrait of Mr Pittle is distinguished by such expressions as *no smeddum, just a perfect hushabaa, sorning, could na abide, just a fasherie,* and by the characteristic "I'll no say on account of the legacy of seven hundred pounds." The added pungency which this imparts to the description has a function deeper than its immediate effect: by thus emphasising his obvious and obviously well-grounded dislike of Pittle, Pawkie inadvertently makes his establishing of him in the Kirk for a purely selfish reason appear all the more distasteful. The next paragraph conspicuously switches to English: Pawkie is no longer simply recording personal impressions but seeking consciously to influence his hearer—the reader. "Had I been a sordid and interested man . . .": this phrasing distracts the reader from the full implications of Pawkie's actions, by causing him momentarily to pause and examine the logic of the sentence. "My bairns"—this intimate touch, highlighted by being the only Scots word in this particular sentence, solicits sympathy in a context in which it is clearly undeserved: "my children" would not have done nearly as well. In describing the rather pathetic Miss Lizy, Pawkie resumes a lively Scots; though a hint of humorous understatement wholly absent from his blunt dismissal of Pittle—"[she] gaed may be, now and then, oftener to the Gardevin than was just necessar"—suggests that some measure of affection is present in his feelings for his wife's cousin. The sudden change back to a pompous English at "on the contrary" is amusing: clearly Pawkie has realised the extent of the irony in his "it was far from our hand to misliken one that was sib to us," and vigorously forestalls any possible comment by a righteous assertion of the interpretation which he desires should be taken of his conduct. Galt's use of language to underline the self-revelation of his characters is handled with unerring skill.

The use of English, often with a somewhat magisterial flavour, is a device employed by Pawkie for erecting a façade: a means of asserting or recovering his dignity after incidents in which he plays a less than distinguished part. Of the riot (Chapter 10), he says "I cannot indeed think of it at this day . . . without feeling the blood boil in my veins"; and it is noteworthy that, except for the few passages of direct speech, virtually no Scots forms appear in this chapter. The exceptions nearly all suggest a momentary breach of Pawkie's self-possession: his angry dismissal of the clanjamphry with their misleart phraseology; the table which is couped and dung down, the qualifier "before we kent where we were," and shortly afterwards the clash in the face which he suffers, in the only moments when he loses control of the situation; and his rather spiteful description of the Major who disperses the mob—which Pawkie could not do—as a "vain bodie." In Chapter 11, similarly, the heavy polysyllabic English of the opening conveys most effectively the impression of a man on his dignity, writing from a "sense of injured merit." The subsequent account of his thoughts and plans (including the basic tenet of his philosophy: "it was a better thing, in the world, to have power and influence, than to show the possession of either") is entirely in English: the appropriate language of a Scotsman who is being careful not to show his hand. Later in the chapter, when the situation begins to turn to Pawkie's advantage and he allows himself to relax his guard somewhat in relating it, Scots touches begin to appear. He chooses a subtle means of expressing his opinion of some of the deacons ("I'll no say any of the bailies") by applying to them a phrase very like one which refers to the most celebrated drunkard in Scottish poetry: "the wine began to fiz in their noddles." A few hints of Scots: *out o' the bodie, wised, minted*: in the account of his "very private and satisfactory conversation" with the earl not only indicate a slight mitigation of his defensive attitude but invite the reader to share in the confidential nature of the exchange. Finally, by using the forcefully denigratory word *stramash* of the unfortunate incident involving Bailie McLucre and Mr Sharpset, he pointedly underlines the contrast between his own position at this juncture and that of his less careful colleagues.

By contrast, Scots is much in evidence when he demonstrates his dry sense of humour. The description of perjink Miss Peggy Dainty falling with a great cloyt, of Jean's behaviour in the meal-mob incident ("tinkler Jean, a randy that had been with the army at the siege of Gibraltar, and for aught I ken, in the Americas, if no in the Indies likewise"), or of Robin Boss "so drunk that he wamblet to and fro over the drum as if there had not been a bane in his body." This, however, is far from the most subtle use to which Scots is put in the novel.

From their first appearance, *Annals of the Parish* and *The Provost* were recognised as being at once accurate social histories and masterful essays in characterisation. They are both of these; but it would be misleading to consider the two aspects separately: Galt's highly individual approach, involving a primary importance assigned to the narrator, has ensured that the personal and the social sides of the novels are totally integrated. Each incident is seen through the eyes of Reverend Balwhidder or Provost Pawkie, and the characters of the protagonists are revealed by their reactions to what they see happening around them. Certainly there are some passages where the external subject-matter forms the main locus of attention, and others where it is the sympathy, respect, amusement or (occasionally) disapproval which the narrator arouses in us that is dominant; but there are no sections where the speaker is forgotten or irrelevant. The Scots-to-English modulations in the books contribute to both aspects of their importance: the fact of linguistic variability is an integral feature of the society which Galt is portraying, and the specific reasons for the variations provide insight into the character of the speakers. There are imperfections: cases where Galt has been carried away by his own verbal skill. Bailie McLucre's long speech in Chapter 7 of *The Provost* is a notorious example: splendidly entertaining though it is, it cannot be thought of as Pawkie's report. It is not the Provost but the author who is telling us this. Such lapses are rare, however; and on the whole, Galt's use of Scots or English to reveal the workings of his characters' minds is handled with the utmost skill. This aspect of Galt's art has been largely overlooked: perhaps because English critics are unfamiliar with the subtleties of Scottish speech and Scottish ones so accustomed to them that their representation with this degree of delicacy and accuracy escapes notice. Yet it is a much more distinctive achievement than the simple exploitation of the expressive power of Scots. The dialogue in *The Entail* is much more spectacular than anything in *Annals* or *The Provost;* but it is in those two novels that Galt's unique linguistic skill receives its clearest demonstration.

BIBLIOGRAPHICAL NOTES

W. R. AITKEN

The bibliography of John Galt in the *New Cambridge Bibliography of English Literature* (vol. 3, 1969) is superseded by the fuller and more detailed bibliography appended to Ian A. Gordon's "investigation," *John Galt: the life of a writer* (Edinburgh: Oliver & Boyd, 1972). This study of Galt's literary career is likely to remain for some considerable time the base from which further work on Galt must proceed; the following notes on recent editions and critical studies must therefore be read in conjunction with Professor Gordon's bibliography.

GALT'S WORKS

Recent editions

Annals of the Parish, or The Chronicle of Dalmailing during the ministry of the Rev. Micah Balwhidder, written by himself. Ed. by James Kinsley. London: Oxford University Press, 1967. *Oxford English Novels.*

The Entail, or The Lairds of Grippy. Ed. by Ian A. Gordon. London: Oxford University Press, 1970. *Oxford English Novels.*

"The Gudewife." In *Scottish Short Stories, 1800-1900.* Ed. by Douglas Gifford. London: Calder & Boyars, 1971. *The Scottish Library.*

The Provost. Ed. by Ian A. Gordon. London: Oxford University Press, 1973. *Oxford English Novels.*

The Member: an autobiography. Ed. by Ian A. Gordon. Edinburgh & London: Scottish Academic Press, 1975. *Association for Scottish Literary Studies, 5.*

The Last of the Lairds, or The Life and Opinions of Malachi Mailings Esq. of Auldbiggings. Ed. from the original manuscript by Ian A. Gordon. Edinburgh & London: Scottish Academic Press, 1976.

Selected Short Stories. Ed. by Ian A. Gordon. Edinburgh: Scottish Academic Press, 1978. *Association for Scottish Literary Studies,* 8.

Ten stories: one, "The Publisher," printed from Galt's MS. and published in book form for the first time; a second, "The Howdie," reprinted in its entirety for the first time; and a third, "The Statesman," making its first appearance since its original printing in *Fraser's Magazine* for December 1836.

CRITICAL ARTICLES

Waterston, E. Galt, Scott and Cooper; frontiers of realism. *Journal of Canadian Fiction,* 1 (1) 1972, pp 60-5.

MacQueen, J. John Galt and the analysis of social history. *Scott Bicentenary Essays,* ed. by A. Bell. Edinburgh & London: Scottish Academic Press, 1973, pp 332-42.

Cozza, A. The betheral of Bleakings. *English Miscellany* 24 (1974), pp 167-97.

The theoretical histories of John Galt. *TLS,* 1 February 1974, p 112. Review of Ian Gordon's edition of *The Provost.*

Swann, C. Past into present: Scott, Galt and the historical novel. *Literature and History,* no. 3 (March 1976), pp 65-82.

Gordon, I. A. Three new chapters by Galt: *The Publisher. Scottish Literary Journal* 3 (1976), pp 23-30.

Costain, K. M. Theoretical history and the novel: the Scottish fiction of John Galt. *ELH* 43 (1976), pp 342-65.

Reid, H. The resurrection of Galt. *The Scotsman,* 11 September 1976.

Campbell, D. Galt revisited. *Q,* no. 17 (3 December 1976), pp 9-10. Review article on *The Member* and *The Last of the Lairds.*

Gordon, I. A. Plastic surgery on a nineteenth-century novel: John Galt, William Blackwood, Dr D. M. Moir and *The Last of the Lairds. Library,* 5th ser. 32 (1977), pp 246-55.

Hart, F. R. *The Scottish Novel: a critical survey.* London: John Murray, 1978.

Galt is discussed in detail in chapter 2 (pp 31-52), but there are references to him throughout the book.